CLASSICAL DRAMA
AND ITS INFLUENCE

CLASSICAL DRAMA
AND ITS INFLUENCE

ESSAYS PRESENTED TO
H. D. F. KITTO, B.A., D.-ès-L., F.B.A., F.R.S.L.
Professor Emeritus of Greek at the University of Bristol

EDITED BY M. J. ANDERSON

METHUEN & CO LTD
11 NEW FETTER LANE LONDON EC4

First published in Great Britain, 1965,
by Methuen & Co. Ltd., London
© *Methuen* 1965

PRINTED IN GREAT BRITAIN
BY R. & R. CLARK, LTD., EDINBURGH

CONTENTS

Classical Drama and its Influence

FOREWORD

THE quality and variety of these essays by his pupils, friends and colleagues will be the best possible tribute to Kitto. That this interesting work on classical drama should in this very special manner be ascribed to Kitto is singularly appropriate. By some kind of perverse logic this introduction falls to be written by someone who has no expert knowledge and whose qualification is merely that he has been a colleague of Kitto's and enjoyed his friendship for a long time. And Kitto himself is the least tractable of subjects. It is those who know him best who are most likely to be surprised by his immense versatility and any analysis of them would be absurd. He has so many gifts that he might equally credibly have chosen several other quite different careers, but whatever accident led to his becoming a Professor of Greek was a most fortunate one for all of us as well as, I believe, for him. His rich and varied personality expresses itself in all he does and gives vitality, pungency, breadth and depth to his writing and teaching and also to his many contributions to affairs.

Good linguist that he is, he would not object to its being said of him that he sees in Greek literature and drama man at his best and worst in thought, action and feeling. In this great literature language and literary form match epic, lyric and dramatic inspiration and provide perfect expression of thought and imagination in prose. For him language and literature were integral or, at the least, like the obverse and reverse of the same coin. Similarly in regard to criticism he believes in the kind of organic and total criticism which tears the mind, heart and guts out of whatever is worthy of critical consideration. His great experience of men and other experiences than the literary give him a rare eye for occlusions of thought when they arise and also for sheer downright malice or ill will.

There is always the danger that drama may be regarded either

vii

as literature or as theatre when in fact it should always be both. Kitto certainly sees great drama as being potentially great theatre and theatre as failing in its purpose if it does not do justice to great literature. He always demands, and quite rightly, a mastery of all that lies behind the words as well as an ability to express them; and he sees production and presentation, sound, gesture, movement and rhythm as all of them all the time contributing to drama and dramatic literature. The contributions in this book are focussed on the drama in which Kitto has shown such interest and delight as scholar, administrator and critic. It is fitting therefore that the writer of this introduction should emphasize some of the other facets of his far-ranging and varied activities.

It is fortunate for him that his gifts in music were virtually on a level with his abilities in language and literature. It adds a dimension to his literary studies as well as enabling him to illuminate the contribution which a rare genius for tone, rhythm and movement built into the dramatic literature and poetry about which it is his great pleasure to write, speak and teach. He can himself compose and arrange and demonstrate by voice and instrumentally what he wishes to convey; and he has a mastery of the special notation, grammar and syntax of music as a language and a form of expression.

It is a curious and perhaps fortunate accident that he has a rare gift of number. He is in fact a mathematician manqué. This gives him ground upon which he meets scientists with humility but without fear. It also assists him to give free rein to a puckish tendency deliberately to misunderstand scientific notions by accurately construing some of the Greek words which scientists use for their own purpose. In general affairs this mathematical gift frequently makes him a valuable contributor to discussions about scientific affairs. In short he is no stranger to 'the other culture', if indeed there is such a thing.

Perhaps Kitto during his active life as a Professor in the University was at his greatest and best in the ordinary rough and tumble of university affairs. To all such discussions he brought a rare understanding of motives and behaviour and his assessments, though rigorous, were always good-natured. He retains vividly many such discussions and images of those who took part in them. What is best remembered by the friends who worked with him is his gift of bringing vague thoughts into sharp and clear perspective and dispersing the mist and clouds which obscured them.

All who know Kitto well admire him for setting example above precept and being willing himself to be judged accordingly. Of course he is fortunate to be able to afford to submit himself to such a judgment. He carries a large weight of learning, reinforced by a monumental memory, as though it was so much light and air. It weighs down neither him nor his pupils and colleagues. In ordinary life, in teaching and in discussion he has a deftness in the use of words which can come only from a belief that language has a dynamic existence in its own right, and that it is not merely a matter of abstract form and shape.

In this contribution, the subject of which is Kitto himself, it is very appropriate to refer to what a great author said of another great teacher. E. M. Forster in writing about Lowes Dickinson says, 'He broke up the illiberal distinction between lessons and leisure. . . .' Kitto behaves as though the activities of work and leisure are equally parts of the same life and he is never quite sure whether he is working or merely enjoying himself. Such a man defies analysis as does air, for '. . . if the air a man is breathing is resolved into its components, the result may be stimulating to experts, but the man himself dies'. Who would dare to take Kitto to pieces and attempt to put him together again? Certainly Kitto would not allow any such thing.

Kitto is still full of activity and in much demand in this country and in other parts of the world. Long may he continue to enjoy himself as it pleases him and thus add more pleasure and delight to the lives of all with whom he comes into contact—as he certainly did for his friends and colleagues in the University of which he was for so long an exceedingly active Professor.

SIR PHILIP MORRIS
University of Bristol

January 1965

PART ONE

CLASSICAL DRAMA

I:

THE POET

AND THE MASK

M
R JOHN JONES HAS EMPHASIZED IN HIS RECENT book *On Aristotle and Greek Tragedy* the importance of the mask in Aristotle's theory and in the practice of tragedy. I propose here to state such evidence as I know from ancient art that the mask was considered an essential part of the poet's act of creation, and to ask the further question whether the chief changes which we know in the history of the mask can be attributed to poets rather than to producers or actors.

Of the early history of the mask we know at least that it went back long before the beginning of drama; the earliest dramatists found already in existence a number of masks, as well as other facial disguises, which were worn by dancers, singing choruses and their leaders, and by priests or priestesses impersonating god or goddess. The mask changes the priest from man to god; in the same way the mask changes the actor from fifth-century Athenian to heroic king or queen. Did the poet regard the mask as a means of conveying his conception of the character to the actor, and did the actor accept this transference?

The second question can be answered by two Latin texts. Quintilian (XI, 3, 73) says that skilled speakers borrow their emotions from the masks; in tragedy Aerope is gloomy, Medea fierce, Ajax dumbfounded, and Herakles savage. Fronto (*De Eloqu.*, I) records that the Republican actor Aesopus conformed his gestures and voice to the face of the mask. (I owe this reference to Professor W. H. Davies.) Aesopus was presumably a Greek and therefore gives the Greek tragic actor's approach to his mask in the late Hellenistic period. I know no Greek text to set beside these, but the value that the Greek actor placed on his mask may be seen from the fact that he sometimes dedicated his mask after a successful performance. We have two Hellenistic inscriptions, one from Delos and one from Teos, which record the dedication of a mask by an actor.[1] Early in the third century

[1] *I.D.* 403; Le Bas, III, No. 92.

B.C. Kallimachos wrote an epigram (49 Pf.) on a mask, dedicated (or in his imagination dedicated) by the Rhodian actor Agoranax after a victory in comedy. (Apart from its testimony to the practice of dedicating masks after a successful performance, the epigram is interesting because, as A. W. Mair showed, it describes a double-sided mask, half pale and love-sick and half like a roasted fig, just the mask for the love-lorn, sunburnt Sostratos in Menander's *Dyskolos*.) Much the same date can be given to the original of the picture of the tragic actor from Herculaneum,[1] perhaps Apelles' portrait of Gorgosthenes. He has put his mask on a shelf after the performance and a young woman is writing a label for it, which may be the text of the inscription if it is to be dedicated.

The actor then seems to have respected the mask as conveying to him the poet's interpretation of the character, and in the rehearsal of a satyr-play on the mosaic in Naples[2] the poet has a box of masks to distribute to the actors. Other representations, however, show us the poet with the mask at an earlier stage, and these take us beyond our first question: certainly the poet used the mask to convey his conception of the character to the actor, but he also used it, if the artists are to be trusted, to fix his own conception of the character in the words that he gives to the character. The first of these representations is the grave-relief of a comic poet found in the Kerameikos at Athens and now in Lyme Park, Stockport.[3] It is dated by style to the first quarter of the fourth century B.C. and may even be the monument of Aristophanes himself. The poet sits in a chair with a papyrus roll in his left hand and a slave mask turned towards him in his right hand. An old man's mask is hung on the wall above him. The sculptor clearly meant to show that the poet wrote the speech with his eyes on the mask; perhaps the poet has written the old man's words and is now considering what the slave shall say.

The next example is less certain. It is a Hadrianic relief with a representation of Euripides.[4] He is seated with a roll in his left

---

[1] Bieber, *History of the Greek and Roman Theater*[2], fig. 302.
[2] Bieber, *History* [2], fig. 36.   [3] Bieber, *History*[2], fig. 201.   [4] Bieber, *History*[2], fig. 109.

6

hand, and the mask of Herakles in his right hand. He is handing it over to Skene, a personification of the stage. At his side he has a basket with the masks of Megara and Lykos. It is generally assumed that the artist of the relief was inspired by a seated statue of Euripides made about 330 B.C.; presumably this statue also held the mask of Herakles, and in the original it may well be that Euripides was contemplating the mask rather than handing it over for production. A Pompeian painting,[1] which may be a copy of a portrait by Protogenes of the Early Hellenistic tragic poet Philikos, shows the tragic poet looking at a mask, which is held by a servant. The poet rests his chin on the fingers of his closed right hand, and this gesture from other examples seems to mean that he sees a vision: the character and the story appear before his mind as he contemplates the mask.

This scheme is nearly repeated on a plaster relief[2] from Begram with a portrait, which has been recognized as Menander. The Begram plasters themselves date from the time of Augustus or even later. They were the stock-in-trade of a silversmith or bronze worker, who produced precious vessels with the aid of plaster reliefs based on very much earlier models. There is no reason why the Menander relief should not be an Early Hellenistic conception. Menander sits under a tree, perhaps an allusion to the garden of the Peripatetics; he has a roll on his lap and a Muse holds the mask of a youth in front of him. Here Muse and mask together inspire him to write the speech. On the well-known relief[3] in the Lateran Museum Menander sits with the mask of a youth in his left hand; on the table in front of him are the mask of a young woman and the mask of an old man, and a roll of papyrus falls over the edge of the table; beyond the table stands a woman, who is either a Muse or a personification of Comedy. The three masks suggest that the artist had in mind the characters of a single scene and showed Menander writing the speech of the young man, again under the combined influence of mask and Muse. Here also, as in the Euripides relief, the later

[1] Bieber, *History*[2], fig. 300a.   [2] L. Ghali-Kahil, *Mon. Piot* 51, 1960, 73.
[3] Bieber, *History*[2], fig. 316–7.

artist has probably elaborated a simpler Early Hellenistic conception of the poet with a single mask, such as we see on the Begram plaster, a conception which possibly goes back to the seated statue of Menander made by the sons of Praxiteles for the theatre at Athens.

Yet another late Hellenistic variant on the theme, poet and mask, may be quoted. It is a relief[1] which exists in many versions and used to be called 'Visit to Ikarios'. Dionysos, supported by two satyrs, bursts in on a poet as he reclines upon his couch; involuntarily one remembers Alcibiades bursting into the party which celebrated Agathon's tragic victory in the *Symposium*. Presumably Dionysos inspires the poet, and the box of comic masks beside the couch shows that he is a comic poet. The masks are the characters awaiting the inspiration of the author.

The story is recorded both of Sophocles and of Menander that shortly before the actual production of a play each of them was asked whether the play was ready, and each replied that the plot was constructed and only the verses needed to be written. The plot includes the characters; once the plot was constructed the poet would know which masks to choose from his box. Then with his eye on the mask, he could write the speeches. It is this final process that the artists portray.

We should not be surprised that the essential act of dramatic creation is represented in this way. Both Aristophanes and Aristotle supply texts to support it, and the earliest dramatic poets acted in their own plays. The question which they put was not what can the actor say when he wears this face but what can I say when I wear this face. Aristophanes and Aristotle do not mention the mask in this connection. But when Aristotle demands in the *Poetics* (1455a 29) that the poet should work out his speeches with the actual gestures, the demand is clearly in complete agreement with the artist's picture of the poet writing with his eye on the mask. As Aristotle was writing at a time when acting had already become highly professional, instances of a similar theory appearing in Aristophanes are more likely to be

[1] Bieber, *Hell. Sc.*, fig. 656.

exaggeration than misrepresentation: in the *Acharnians* (410) Dikaiopolis says that Euripides naturally creates lame characters because he always writes with his feet up, and in the *Thesmophoriazusae* (151) Agathon is wearing women's clothing because he is writing a woman's part. Euripides with his feet up, Agathon in women's clothes, are comic exaggerations of the procedure demanded by Aristotle and assumed by the artists.

Originally the mask gave its wearer a new personality. Further, it had to identify him for the audience. Sex and age are easy to show by colour and hair-style. The names of tragic characters also (rightly or wrongly) suggested to the audience how they would behave. The comic poet could use speaking names to a certain extent; but except when he introduced known contemporaries like Pericles, Socrates or Euripides, he must have relied on the mask to tell the audience what to expect. Once at least Aristophanes did not use a portrait mask even for a great contemporary; he says in the *Knights* (230) that the mask-makers were all afraid to portray Kleon. This is, of course, a joke; Aristophanes wanted to give Kleon the mask of a Paphlagonian slave to show the audience how he was characterizing Kleon and to show the actor how Kleon should be played. Slave masks were, therefore, recognizable as early as 424 B.C., and the monumental evidence shows that comedy achieved a considerable diversity of masks very early.

The mask gave the ancient dramatist an advantage over the modern dramatist. To take a typical modern instance, Mr Ray Lawler, who makes detailed demands for the *Summer of the Seventeenth Doll* when it comes to scenery and clothes, is less exigent about faces: Bubba is a dark, shy girl, Pearl has dyed red hair, Olive is cynical and thirty-seven, Emma is wizened and life-battered, Barney has a wide boyish grin; only Roo is more fully described, 'fair hair tinged with grey, a rather battered face with a well-cut mouth. Recent experiences have etched a faint line of bewilderment between his eyes.' The modern dramatist has to take what faces the management provides, and can only rarely predict what any of them will be. The ancient dramatist could predict what the masks would be, and some scholars speak as if he had special masks made for every part. Yet the representations of dramatists which we have been discussing all show masks which are well known from other monuments and can be plausibly identified with masks listed in the encyclopaedia of Pollux. The assumption of the ancient artists seems to have been that the poets drew their masks from stock, and Pollux gives us some idea of the stock (Pollux himself wrote in the late second century A.D. but his lists seem to be based on lists compiled not later than the third century B.C.).

Against this assumption of a common stock may be set the traditions that various dramatists invented new masks, the supposition that the masks of Old Comedy were portrait masks, and the changes that can be observed by studying theatrical monuments from the time of Aeschylus to the time of Pollux and beyond. This, however, only amounts to saying that the stock was not a fixed stock but a stock which changed with the times. For tragedy the monuments show one major change (which incidentally gives a top date for Pollux' list) the introduction of the *onkos*, the triangular tower of hair above the forehead, which came in probably at the same time as the rebuilding of the theatre by Lycurgus, but Pollux also lists a number of special masks which came into the stock from particular plays; he himself notes Euripides' Euhippe and Sophocles' Tyro.

According to Pollux the masks of Old Comedy were for the most part made like the individuals who were satirized, but famous contemporaries formed a small part of the Old or Middle Comedy repertoire, and the monumental evidence suggests that for the rest of the characters some thirty-eight masks were enough. The introduction of some of these can be dated. Two of the masks of bearded men, which have been plausibly identified in the early fourth and later fifth century material, are called Hermonian by Pollux; Hermon is known as a comic actor of the time of Aristophanes and the mask may have been called after him, although according to the *Etymologicum Magnum* the mask was called after the man who made it. The Maison mask, which can also be identified in the early fourth-century material, was said by Aristophanes of Byzantium to have been invented by a Megarian actor called Maison, but Chrysippus gave quite a different explanation of the name. The other mask with a personal name, the Lykomedian, offers no clue; Lykomedes is a name known in Athens in the classical period and Meineke suggested that he too was an actor. These ascriptions of particular masks to actors are therefore doubtful; if they are true, they may only mean that the actor won a victory when wearing the mask; the names may even be due to the fact that it was the actor who dedicated the mask after his victory. Aristophanes' statement about Kleon's mask in the *Knights* implies that the poet and not the actor was responsible for instructing the maskmaker.

It is therefore very tempting to suppose that the poet Menander played a major part in establishing the stock masks of New Comedy, which we know from the lists of Pollux. New Comedy masks differ from Middle Comedy masks in various ways. One is a change of social status in the leading characters: the fathers of New Comedy are better off than the fathers of Middle Comedy and therefore both they and their wives look more respectable: the scanty beards, bald heads, and snub noses of Middle Comedy are dropped. Secondly, since the time of Alexander shaving has become fashionable, and all the young masks of New Comedy are clean shaven, whereas clean-shaven young men were disreputable in the time of Aristophanes, and clean-shaven masks for respectable characters only begin to come in late in the Middle Comedy period.

These, however, are more general changes than one would wish to attribute to a single poet. More remarkable is the distinction of male masks by their hair styles so that three readily recognizable families can be built up consisting of fathers, sons and slaves. The convenience of such a recognition system from the point of view of the audience is obvious, and it is possible that Menander invented it. Pollux' list, in any case, gives an old man with neat hair, an old man with wavy hair, an old man with curly hair, four young men with neat hair, who decrease in age from the Admirable to the Delicate, an older and a younger youth with wavy hair, a young man with curly hair (possibly here too Pollux' rather muddled description conceals an older and a younger version with curly hair), an old slave (who according to the archaeological evidence sometimes has neat hair and sometimes has wavy hair), a neat-haired slave, a wavy-haired slave, and a curly-haired slave. Pollux himself pairs off the neat-haired old man and slave and the wavy-haired old man and slave, and this makes it more likely that the masks were really systematized to make recognizable families.

But New Comedy masks told the audience considerably more about the character than that he belonged to this or that family. Hair-style gives a main characteristic to the fathers and sons of each family (there is no reason to suppose that it is more than a mark of recognition in the slaves). Neat hair suggests orderliness, wavy hair is leonine and suggests courage and wildness, curly hair suggests energy. Finer characterization is given by colour of hair and complexion, forehead, brows and nose. Some help in interpretation is given by the contemporary pseudo-Aristotelian *Physiognomonika*, but most of the points are obvious and Pollux himself gives a number of leads. The colour scale is white, ruddy, brown, black: the delicate youth has a white complexion, the admirable and curly-haired youths have the ruddy complexion of health and energy, the dark complexion of the soldier and rustic suggests exposure. The wavy-haired soldier's black hair contrasts with the brown hair of the second youth with wavy hair; according to the *Physiognomonika* black hair is a sign of lust and anger and brown hair of courage, but the contrast here may be chiefly a contrast of age. Why the studious youth (No. 11) is 'black' is not clear. The furrowed forehead is a sign of courage in the admirable youth and the curly youth. Raised brows show pride, conceit or high spirits. The neat-haired old man, the admirable youth and the neat-haired slave all have raised brows because they are (or think they are) on top of the world. The wavy-haired old man and the studious

The Poet and the Mask

youth have lowered brows because they allow the world to get them down. The hooked nose of the leading old man is a sign of greatness of soul; the snub nose of the rustic is a sign of sensuality.

When the poet chose his masks, he knew that the audience would attribute such and such characteristics to a character who had this or that physiognomy. When the stock was established, as it was by the beginning of the third century, he would presumably choose the masks which fitted best into the plot as he had conceived it. But Menander, at least, knew that appearance and character sometimes conflict, and it is a mark of his greatness that Polemon in the *Perikeiromene* is not the typical soldier and that Knemon in the *Dyskolos* can justify his misanthropy.

T. B. L. Webster

BIBLIOGRAPHICAL NOTES

See further T. B. L. Webster, *Greek Theatre Production*, London, 1956. M. Bieber, *History of the Greek and Roman Theater*, Princeton, 1961.

II: THE CHORUS

IN THE ACTION

OF GREEK TRAGEDY

GREEK TRAGEDY WAS BORN IN ATTICA IN THE SIXTH century B.C. when some poet of genius, perhaps one called Thespis, set into a choral lyric performance insertions of recited solo speech, in a form of verse descended ultimately from Archilochus. The history of Greek tragedy, so far as we can follow it, is to an important extent made by the adjustment of the relation between these two elements, a fluctuating relation, sometimes close, sometimes looser. The spoken element quickly became dominant, since it was the chief vehicle of the forward movement of the action. The Chorus always impersonated a definite group of people; it was 'in' the story, not an impersonal Voice, but its anonymous collectivity tended to push it away from the centre, where things happened. This was emphasized by its physical separation from the speaking actors, in the orchestra where it had room to dance, and from which it had often to watch in silence long sequences of dramatic, even agonizing intensity. Yet it always remained within speaking and listening contact with the actors. Thus half-in, half-out of the action, the Chorus had some curious and even illogical effects on the mechanics of staging – and incidentally proves itself the greatest stumbling-block in modern productions of these plays. But what I want to do here is to consider some effects of the presence of a Chorus upon the progress of the spoken action itself, as composed by the poet; for in this interaction of individuals and anonymous collective lies something of the distinctive character of Greek drama.

Obviously the degree of such interaction varies widely from one play to another. At one extreme, it might seem, are a few plays in which the fortunes of the Chorus itself are the subject of the play. The notion that this was in the earliest dramas universal or even usual is probably false, one of the sweeping conclusions drawn from our former belief in the early date of the *Supplices* of Aeschylus. We have Aristotle's word for it that

17

Aeschylus cut down the proportion of lyric and made the spoken dialogue the most important thing in the play, but that is a different matter. Twice in Aeschylus, in *Supplices* and *Eumenides*, and again in the *Supplices* of Euripides the Chorus itself is a party to the main conflict. But this is not enough in itself to determine the relation of the Chorus to the action; there is no resemblance in this respect between the Aeschylean plays and the Euripidean. In the latter the Chorus (the mothers of the dead Seven against Thebes) is a passive body of sufferers and leaves its cause to be pleaded by actor-characters, Aethra and Adrastus and later Theseus; its own interventions in the dialogue are as scanty as in any play. In sharp contrast to this both Danaids and Eumenides assert their will and dominate the action. Is this simply because the intervening forty or so years had seen such a diminution of the rôle of the Chorus that a change of this sort was inevitable? That is partly the reason, of course, but there is more to it than that. The *Supplices* of Euripides, for all the edifying morality of its ideas, is dramatically not among the most successful plays, and all its characters are rather pallid and unmemorable. But more important is the growth of the rhetorical element in tragedy. If the bereaved Argive women have a cause to plead to Theseus it is unthinkable that at this date it should not be argued in detail, and opposed, in set speeches; and that is something a Chorus cannot do. For it is an unbroken law, all through the history of Greek tragedy, that though a Chorus may join in the dialogue to a limited extent it must never make a set speech, a 'rhesis', never marshal arguments, try to prove or refute a contention, or speak a descriptive set-piece. The whole province of what Aristotle calls 'dianoia', the art of developing at length all that can appropriately be said on a given subject, is closed to the Chorus. In this union of speech and lyric which is Attic tragedy, while the actor's solo-lyric from the stage came in course of time to encroach upon the sphere of the Chorus, the Chorus never trespass upon the actor's ground; the Chorus-leader may *speak to* the actors but he makes no speeches.

Let us now return to Aeschylus' *Supplices* and *Eumenides*. In the former the Danaids have to *explain* their coming to the King of Argos and *persuade* him to grant them asylum. They do not use their father Danaus as an intermediary but speak for themselves. How are they to convey all this complex information? and what 'persuasion' is possible without a rhetorical speech? Surely Peitho is the essence of rhetoric? Aeschylus' solution is interesting. The King enters (234) and comments wonderingly upon the strangeness of this suppliant-band, and the Chorus ask if he is the person in authority. He replies in a speech of 25 lines and asks them to explain *briefly* who they are, since his city disapproves of long speeches. The Chorus obediently state in 3 lines their claim to be Argives themselves, which provokes him to 14 lines of disbelief. The necessary information, or proof, is conveyed in a long interchange of short questions and answers, often line for line; sometimes the Chorus asks the questions (leading questions, these), sometimes the King, and it is established that their views of past history agree. Now they must *persuade*, and they do so in a pattern of lyric appeal alternating with his spoken expressions of doubt, unwillingness and indecision. He argues, but they do not – argument and lyric utterance are in Greek an uneasy association; they implore, they warn, they passionately reject his alternative suggestions. Finally (438 ff.) he sets out his agonizing dilemma in a longer speech and seems on the point of refusing. Stronger pressure is necessary, and the Chorus force a decision in line-for-line spoken interchange – not the kind of stichomythia which answers point with point, thrusting and parrying in rhetorical debate, but something like this: 'You see these girdles?' – 'Yes.' 'There *is* a way ...' 'What do you mean?' 'If you do not do what I ask —' 'What will you do?' 'Hang myself on the images of your gods.' 'Oh horrible!' 'Now you know.' The Chorus have won their point, but by choral methods, not by the rhetoric of reason.

In the *Eumenides* the same technique is even more striking since the action culminates in a court-trial. Athena, arriving in response to Orestes' appeal, first (415 ff.) takes a deposition from each party, from the Chorus in line-for-line interchange, from Orestes in a set speech. When the trial opens (582) Athena calls upon the prosecution to speak first. The Chorus challenge Orestes to admit the deed in a series of questions and answers designed to elicit the facts. Commentators have so often called attention to the echoes in this scene of actual trials in Athenian public life that the remarkable departure from real life tends to be obscured: neither plaintiff nor defendant makes a set speech. The Furies cannot because they are a Chorus; therefore, lest the scales should be too obviously weighted against them, Orestes also refrains, but calls upon Apollo to bear witness for him. The case for Orestes is then argued by Apollo, with short objections interpolated by the Chorus: the command to slay Clytaemnestra was given by Apollo, who always speaks the will of Zeus; she had murdered her husband, a sceptred king, which was a far worse crime than killing a woman. Than killing a parent? The real parent is the father, not the mother; witness Athena born of Zeus. The description of the murder of Agamemnon heaps odium on the character of Clytaemnestra (there is no corresponding description of the piteous murder of Clytaemnestra), and Apollo adds a *captatio benevolentiae* by a promise, if his side wins, of glory for Athens and a faithful Argive ally. Against this the Furies have succeeded in establishing only the bare fact – the murder of Clytaemnestra by Orestes; they are a Chorus and in forensic oratory cannot do more, without an advocate to speak for them. No wonder they lose the case! In the following scene Athena sets to work to persuade them to give up their designs of vengeance upon the city and to accept a new and honourable office there. Her persuasion naturally takes the form of speeches, and the suddenness of their capitulation has often been noted. So long as they remain obdurate they sing, and twice over the repetition of the same stanza underlines their deafness to the voice of reason. The line-for-line exchange in which they yield (892 ff.) is no reasoned debate, but a mere request for information and for guarantees. There is a similar pattern in the *Septem*, 180 ff., where in the scene between Eteocles and the Chorus of Theban women Eteocles' angry but rational exhortations to self-control and obedience meet with reiterated lyric cries of fear and convulsive clinging to the images of the gods, till at the end of the following line-for-line exchange the Chorus abruptly give way. When later in the play (677 ff.) they endeavour to dissuade Eteocles from fighting his brother the formal pattern is the same, lyric against speech and then line against line, but this time neither party is attempting to reason. The Chorus warn and implore, and Eteocles reiterates that it is too late to draw back, since fate and his father's curse and the gods all will it. Neither side can influence or reach the other.

So far, then, we have seen that even when the Chorus takes a large part in the action, whether in its own cause or as the main interlocutor confronting the chief character, its contribution is lyric or emotional in tone, never rhetorical, and its interventions in the spoken dialogue are kept short. This is naturally easiest to see in Aeschylus where the Chorus is more prominent than it later became. But if we turn to the end of the century, we see that though the Chorus has long become fixed in a subordinate rôle it may still have to use similar devices to avoid a set speech. In the *Oedipus at Colonus* the first confrontation of the blind old man and the Chorus is so charged with emotions, anger, fear, horror and pity, that a Kommos, a lyric interchange, is the only possible medium; but later, at l. 461, we find them in a calmer mood advising him to make a propitiatory sacrifice to the Eumenides. Such a sacrifice is indeed in harmony with the theme of the play, but the *necessity* of it at this particular moment is dramaturgical: all three actors – Oedipus and his two daughters – are on the stage, so one of them (Ismene volunteers) must be got off it in order to reappear as Theseus. A mere perfunctory reference to a sacrifice would risk exposing this motive too nakedly; the ritual must be given a circumstantial solemnity. But since the Chorus must not make a speech the description has to be conveyed in short question and answer, even at the cost of some artificiality. 'Wreaths of what?' asks Oedipus. 'Libations of what?', and (several times) 'And then what?' Only the final description of the prayer is allowed to run on a little

21

longer. 'Ah!' says Oedipus, 'this sounds important', and gets seven lines of instruction.

In contrast to this, when in the *Oedipus Tyrannus* we are to be shown the confidence of the citizens of Thebes in their king, though citizens constitute the Chorus the poet has to introduce a special delegation *in the prologue*, so that one of them may make the stirring speech of description and appeal which is debarred to the Chorus. Since the Chorus already represent the ordinary citizens, the delegation has to be composed of boys and old men.

It is interesting to note that the longest continuous speech ever given to a Chorus in our texts of the tragedians is *Agamemnon*, 489 ff., which runs to 14 lines – and in the MS. tradition is spoken *not* by the Chorus but by Clytaemnestra, except for the last two lines, which as we read them stand in awkward detachment from the rest, and are by the MSS. given to the Chorus. The passage was restored to its right shape by the latest edition of the play, that of Denniston-Page. Apart from the more technical points of interpretation of the text and of staging well argued by the editors, it would be altogether abnormal for a Chorus to speak at such length, or indeed in such highly wrought metaphors. No Chorus ever *said*, though it might have *sung*: 'My witness is mud's sister and next-door neighbour, thirsty dust', whereas Clytaemnestra constantly speaks in that style.

Leaving now plays in which the Chorus is itself a party to the main conflict or at least has much to say to the protagonist, what of the much larger area of tragedy in which its rôle is subordinate and its spoken interventions slight? This is in some aspects a well-worn theme; we need not go into the effect of this collective presence on the unities of time and place, nor do I want to make a list of those passages where the Chorus helps a 'sympathetic' character by keeping watch, or calling for help, or misdirecting his enemies, or where it is embarrassed by its own failure to intervene in the action. My present concern is with the different degrees of penetration of the action by the choral presence; setting aside the choral odes, where has the poet composed a play, or a scene, to achieve an effect which would be impossible in a chorusless form of drama? It is clear, for instance, that the Chorus of Theban Elders make the whole of the *Antigone* after the prologue a *public* action; proclamations, reports, prophecies, defiance, repentance, all concern the community and make an impact on public opinion. This continuous publicity is simply and economically attained by the choice of chorus and by Creon's didactic insistence on the identity of his will and the interests of the state. The Persians, and the citizens of Colonus, have in their very different ways the same kind of effect on the scope and reference of the action in their plays. There is nothing like it in later drama, where any audience effects have to be specially contrived each time – crowd-scenes, courtiers, soldiers and the like, much as the Greek poets do on occasion in their prologues, as in the *Oedipus Tyrannus*, or the *Septem* where Eteocles addresses the citizen-soldiers. Contrast with this a play like the *Trachiniae*, where apart from the lyrics the Chorus simply plays the part of a confidante to Deianeira and thus in the later part of the play, between Heracles and his son, has no particular function at all and is almost silent. The 'agon' again, the set debate between antagonists, is sometimes played to a choral audience involved or passionately interested in the outcome, as in the second half of the *Ajax* or the *Trojan Women* (Hecuba *v.* Helen), as well as to the great surrounding audience; but sometimes, as in the disputes in the *Andromache* or the scene between Admetus and Pheres in the *Alcestis*, the agon seems in this relation little more than a quarrel before the servants. This is not to criticize the dramatic effect of such scenes in themselves, but simply to show how the Chorus as a factor in the action can either keep us aware of its presence or recede so far into the background as to be all but invisible.

It has often been pointed out how the growing elaboration of plots and the development of intrigue and deception as tragic motifs make the Chorus at times something of an encumbrance to the movement of the action. So long as the Chorus is sufficiently devoted to the interests of one of the participants there is no difficulty; in the *Philoctetes* for instance there is an admirably effective contrast between the eager support they give to their young master's deception of the castaway and their troubled incomprehension in face of his later scruples, which they leave him to resolve alone. But the number of Euripidean plays in which the Chorus has to be sworn to secrecy indicates a certain stereotyping and loss of vitality in the choral function. There is, however, a considerable difference between one play and another in the use of this device. Medea sets herself at her first appearance to win the sympathy of the Corinthian women and asks them to keep her secret if she can devise some scheme of revenge. The whole of the action is thus played against this complicity, and at each stage of it Medea takes them into her confidence as fellow women; we are made to feel their approval of her first moves, their acquiescence in the earlier murders and horrified rejection of the later. When she extracts a day's grace from Creon and fools Jason into thinking she has had a change of heart her dissimulations acquire an extra zest from being *played at* this appreciative audience. In the *Hippolytus* there is some superficial similarity, but Phaedra, in extracting the oath of silence just before she leaves the stage, tells the Chorus nothing of her plan except her resolve to die. They wish no ill to either Hippolytus or Theseus, but though they know the message left by Phaedra to be a lie, and beg Theseus to unsay his curse, they show no particular trouble or uneasiness, when left alone, at their failure to act and save an innocent life. Hippolytus ought to be able to call them as witnesses of his innocence, but he appears, now as earlier, unaware of their existence, and only wishes that the walls of the house could acquire a voice and speak for him. The *Hippolytus* is a profounder play than the *Medea*, but in it Euripides has left the Chorus with little more than its lyric function; for most of the spoken dialogue he wishes us to be scarcely conscious of its presence.

The famous 'irony' with which Sophocles achieves such tremendous tragic effect in the *Oedipus Tyrannus* and which Euripides tends to use in plays of lighter calibre, like the *Iphigeneia in Tauris*, and *Helen*, and *Ion*, is in its most characteristic form directed over the heads of actors and Chorus alike at the audience, whose fuller knowledge hears in the words of the ignorant speakers an unconscious significance which is either ominous or piquant, according to the type of play. But irony can take another form, in which only one actor-character is ignorant, while his antagonist deliberately leads him on to collaborate, in deed and in fateful word, in his own undoing. In such a scene the Chorus always shares the knowledge of the superior party, and the irony reaches the audience, as it were, through the medium of the Chorus. In such a scene as the deception of Theoclymenus by Helen the long string of *doubles ententes* make her seem to be continually winking at the Chorus; but the effect can in a different setting be of the grimmest. At the end of the Sophoclean *Electra* when Clytaemnestra has already been killed, the conspirators are waiting to waylay Aegisthus. The Chorus warns them of his arrival, and urges them to speak him fair and falsely, so that he may rush into the trap which justice has set. Every line uttered by the brother and sister and by the wretched victim is pregnant with double meaning. Aegisthus calls triumphantly for a public exhibition of the body (Orestes, as he thinks), and thus ensures his own public discomfiture. The veiled corpse is thrust before him, Orestes standing by. 'Uncover the face; family mourning is a tribute due even from me.' 'Lift the veil yourself; this is a sight for your eyes, your greeting, not mine.' 'I will; call Clytaemnestra if she is at home.' 'She is close by you, no need to look further.' Aegisthus' enemies, actors and Chorus, press around him, savouring every mocking word.

The scene is short, and Aegisthus is not a character to win our sympathy, so we are not too disturbed by it. One reason why the *Bacchae* is such a terrible play is that some degree of mutual understanding of this kind links Dionysus with the Chorus all through. It is not so complete as in the *Electra*; that would impair the dramatic effect. The god appears to them in the guise of his own prophet, endowed with strange powers, and there is in this an additional layer of irony directed over their heads at the audience, who learned the truth in the prologue. But he is in continual rapport with them, and when he begins to assert his power over his victim he demands their admiring attention; all the scene in which Pentheus is robbed of his will and reason and made the unconscious instrument and mouthpiece of his own doom is played against their excited complicity. Even when Dionysus is no longer on the stage his presence and his power are felt, and the Bacchae egging on the demented Agave, brandishing her son's head, to further flights of horrid exultation are still responding to him. When the revulsion comes the Chorus fade from the picture and we are allowed to forget them. The technique gives to the theme a peculiar gloating cruelty which for us further blackens the character of the god himself. Whether it was so intended by Euripides is perhaps not so clear; what is certain is that the problem of keeping the Chorus within its own sphere and yet a vital force in the action of the drama has never been more brilliantly solved.

It is evident even from this scattered treatment of the subject that the significance of the Chorus for the action follows no straight line of chronological development. The *Philoctetes*, the *Oedipus at Colonus* and the *Bacchae*, which exemplify three quite different kinds of significance, are among our latest plays; while the *Iphigeneia at Aulis*, in the same posthumous group as the *Bacchae*, has a Chorus whose function is as nugatory as any; when Agamemnon (542) adds a line commanding them to keep silence about what has happened it seems a perfunctory salute to a worn-out convention. Nor is the excellence or interest of a play to be measured in these terms; the poet sometimes sacrifices this consideration to other aspects which are more important for his immediate purpose. But those plays which make the fullest use of the forms and conventions peculiar to their tradition do attain thereby a kind of characteristic harmony and balance of structure. Let us end by considering for a moment one use of the Chorus in the *Agamemnon*, a small point to set beside the splendour of the lyrics but telling in its own way. At this period in Attic drama no free interchange of dialogue between three speakers is possible: if the Chorus first engages the Herald in conversation,

Clytaemnestra must wait till that exchange is finished. But when she in turn (587) addresses the Herald the whole of her speech is directed *at* the Chorus. '*I* raised the cry of triumph long ago when the fire-messenger came, and there were some who spoke sharply to me for being a woman and credulous. . . . You need not tell me more now, for my husband will be here. Tell him to come quickly, and how we long for him, and how well I have looked after everything and given no cause for gossip to link my name with any other man's.' It is an act of public defiance, repeated even more recklessly on Agamemnon's arrival (855). She confronts king and Chorus, and the air is cold with undeclared distrust and hostility. The manner of her address would be scarcely possible outside the accepted Greek stage convention that the Chorus is a proper recipient of reports. Instead of greeting Agamemnon 'Dear husband, how I have longed for your return', she makes a public proclamation of her love and suffering: 'My lords of Argos, I will so far forget my modesty as to describe to you what a loving wife I have been'. For the first part of the description Agamemnon is 'this man'; then she slides into the second person in explaining, with an insinuation of popular disloyalty, the absence of Orestes; then again in a burst of flaunting hyperbole she declares the joy and relief of 'this man's' arrival; finally comes a direct endearment, with the invitation to walk the purple. The Chorus is held within the action in order to point the relation of one character to another.

A. M. Dale

III:

TRAGEDY AND

GREEK ARCHAIC THOUGHT

W HEN DODDS DESCRIBES SOPHOCLES AS 'THE LAST
great exponent of the archaic world-view',[1] it is a
description which most of us would accept, provided
we are allowed to write glosses upon it. This essay is, in part,
such a gloss.

The Greek archaic world-view was a collection of mental
habits which included thought at different degrees of rationality.
If it cannot be defined with precision, it can be depicted in its
manifold variety; and no one has depicted it more skilfully than
Dodds in the book from which I have quoted. Certain aspects
particularly relevant to tragedy will be brought into relief in the
course of the following discussion. During the second half of the
fifth century there was a change in the general climate of thought
which is often referred to as the Enlightenment; and it was
characterized by the rejection or modification of various modes of
archaic thinking. It had its forerunners in Ionia, men like Xeno-
phanes and Heraclitus; the enigmatic Euripides displays its
influence; the Sophists spread the ferment of ideas; and finally
Plato imposed upon this welter new patterns of thought, the
influence of which is still so powerful as to be often unobserved.
Indeed I sometimes wonder whether Plato is not largely responsible, along with Christian theology, for the differences of opinion
between modern scholars as to the mental competence of such
writers as Aeschylus and Sophocles; and whether the point at
issue is not so much what they actually thought as what a
respectable thinker may be allowed to think.

Aeschylus and Sophocles. But are we right to bracket them
together as representatives of an earlier mental world? Dodds
makes a reservation.[2] 'In his thought Sophocles (save perhaps in
his latest plays) still belongs entirely to the older world. ...
Aeschylus, on the other hand, struggling as he does to interpret

[1] E. R. Dodds, *The Greeks and the Irrational*, 49.   [2] Op. cit. 50, n.1.

and rationalise the legacy of the Archaic Age, is in many ways prophetic of the new time.' To some the very word 'thought' as applied to Sophocles appears inappropriate. They do not of course mean, quite literally, that Sophocles did not think: it would be a remarkable feat to write the *Oedipus Coloneus* without thinking. They mean that, whereas Aeschylus wrestled with fundamental moral and religious problems, Sophocles simply swallowed an existing system of thought and feeling – swallowed it, we might say, steadily and swallowed it whole. They mean that, untroubled morally or intellectually by the old ways, he averted his eyes from the new – and therefore cannot be taken seriously as a thinker. This is not a view that has commended itself to the scholar in whose honour these studies have been collected;[1] and it is not the view which will be maintained in this essay.

2

The *Oedipus Tyrannus* holds a special place in the work of Sophocles. The most powerful of his tragedies, it distils the essence of one aspect of his thought, itself a legacy from the archaic age. I refer to the breach between the divine and human modes of existence, the frailty of man and his dependence upon a god-given destiny. This thought receives its classical statement in the first stanza of the ode which the Chorus sing, when Oedipus leaves the stage having learnt the truth about his life. 'What man wins more of happiness (*eudaimonia*) than just a semblance and, after the semblance, a decline? I call no mortal blessed, for I have the example of your *daimon*, Oedipus, before my eyes.'[2] What do they mean – what did Sophocles mean – by the *daimon* of Oedipus? And by *eudaimonia?* Certainly more by *eudaimonia* than Aristotle meant, when he said that this was the good at which all men aim; and more by *daimon* than we mean,

[1] Cf. H. D. F. Kitto, *Sophocles Dramatist and Philosopher*, passim.

[2] τὸν σὸν τοι παράδειγμ' ἔχων,
τὸν σὸν δαίμονα, τὸν σόν, ὦ
τλᾶμον Οἰδιπόδα, βροτῶν
οὐδὲν μακαρίζω. (1193-6)

32

when we speak vaguely of a man's destiny. To quote Dodds again:[1] 'A third type of daemon, who makes his first appearance in the Archaic Age, is attached to a particular individual, usually from birth, and determines, wholly or in part, his individual destiny. .... He represents the individual *moira* or "portion" of which Homer speaks, but in the personal form which appealed to the imagination of the time.' The fate of Oedipus, then, is ascribed to a malign superhuman power which had attended him from birth. Surely this provides no evidence of independent thought in Sophocles – or of anything but popular fatalism with superstitious overtones?

The idea of malignity does not indeed occur in the stanza. But let us go back a little in the play. To set the fears of Oedipus at rest, Jocasta has told him about the oracle given to Laius that seemed not to have been fulfilled. But the mention of the place where three highways met rouses a dreadful apprehension in the king's mind, and at last he tells her the story of his encounter at just such a place. If there is any connection (so he puts it, euphemistically) between the old stranger he killed and Laius, who could be more wretched, *of a more hostile daimon* (τίς ἐχθροδαίμων μᾶλλον; 816), than he now is; for he is liable to his own ban pronounced upon the killer of Laius, and he is sleeping with the wife of the man he killed. Not only so, but he is in exile (so he thinks) from his native land for fear of wedding his mother and killing his father. 'Would not a man be right to judge of me that these things come from a cruel *daimon*' (ἀπ' ὠμοῦ ... δαίμονος, 828). Oedipus, then, attributes to a cruel and hostile superhuman power the destiny which is so much worse than he yet knows. When it becomes known, when Oedipus, knowing it, has entered the palace, the Chorus argue the nothingness of man from the *daimon* of Oedipus.

Later in the ode they sing (1213 f.): 'All-seeing time has found you out (ἄκοντα); it brings to justice the monstrous marriage in which the begotten has long been the begetter'.

[1] Op. cit. 42. On *daimon* in Sophocles cf. G. M. Kirkwood, *A Study of Sophoclean Drama*, 185 f.

This inadequate translation of the untranslatable omits one word: 'unwilling' or 'unwitting' as the epithet of Oedipus. The conscious criminal seeks to evade detection, which comes upon him against his will. But this does not apply. What, then, was contrary to the will or knowledge of Oedipus? There is perhaps at this point a deliberate ambiguity,[1] which is cleared up, when, a few lines later, a servant comes out of the palace, now polluted (as he says) with new evils which will soon come to light – 'evils wrought consciously and not unwittingly' (ἑκόντα κοὐκ ἄκοντα, 1230). A distinction could not more clearly and emphatically be made between the unwilled and the willed deeds of Oedipus; and it is reinforced by the Messenger's general comment, that 'those griefs sting most that are seen to be self-chosen' (αὐθαί-ρετοι, 1231). The distinction is clearly made, and we expect it to be clearly maintained. When he killed his father and wedded his mother, Oedipus was a victim of the gods, but, when he blinded himself, he was a free agent. How attractive to look at matters in this way, and how limited the truth of it may be!

The messenger tells his story of the suicide of Jocasta and the self-blinding of Oedipus. The doors open again, and the blinded Oedipus comes out. The reactions of the Chorus are governed, as those of any audience must be, by this sight, the most dreadful they have ever seen. 'What madness came upon you? Who was the *daimon* that leapt, with a bound exceeding the extreme, upon . . . ?'[2] Upon what? The whole expression is, once more, essentially untranslatable, but Jebb's translation here seems to miss the point and, above all, the relationship of these lines to the preceding choral ode. I can only conclude with a free expansion: '. . . upon that *moira* of yours that was already a *daimon*'s evil work.' The evil destiny of Oedipus had seemed to have

---

[1] 'He had not foreseen the disclosure which was to result from his inquiry into the murder of Laius' (Jebb); he had not known that his actions were crimes. Cf. also *O.C.* 977, 987.

[2]
τίς σ', ὦ τλᾶμον,
προσέβη μανία; τίς ὁ πηδήσας
μείζονα δαίμων τῶν μακίστων
πρὸς σᾷ δυσδαίμονι μοίρᾳ; (1299–1302)

reached an extreme point and to have provided the perfect paradigm of ill-starred humanity, but there was still a further point of misery to be reached, and that too is ascribed to the assault of a *daimon*. A few lines later, groping in his sightlessness, hearing his voice 'borne from him on the air in a direction over which he has no control',[1] Oedipus exclaims: 'Oh *Daimon*, that you should have sprung so far!' (ἰὼ δαῖμον, ἵν' ἐξήλου, 1311). It is clear from his preceding words and from the response of the Chorus that he is thinking of his blindness. Later again, the Chorus ask: 'How could you bring yourself so to destroy your sight? What *daimon* moved you to it?' (τίς σ' ἐπῆρε δαιμόνων; 1328). Oedipus might have said – and critics sometimes write as though he had said: 'As to my other sufferings[2] they were the work of Apollo, but, when I struck my eyes, the responsibility was mine alone (and you are wrong to ask what *daimon* moved me)'. Actually he replies: 'It was Apollo, my friends, it was Apollo that was bringing these sufferings of mine to completion. But it was none other's hand that struck the blow: it was I.'[3] The reiterated name of Apollo must answer the question: 'What *daimon*?' The expression 'these sufferings of mine' cannot exclude and may primarily denote the visible suffering which dominates the scene. It would be tidy to suppose that, while Apollo was responsible, through his oracle, for the earlier sufferings of Oedipus, the self-blinding was an act of independent will unmotivated by divine power. But that is not how it is seen by either Oedipus or the Chorus.

What then, we may well ask, has now become of the clear distinction between involuntary and voluntary acts with which Sophocles introduced the scene? What, for that matter, has become of the unconsidering Sophocles? Surely here is a mind at work upon a train of thought – working with the formality

---

[1] Jebb, on 1310.
[2] As though it were τὰ μὲν ἄλλα . . .

[3] 'Απόλλων τάδ' ἦν, 'Απόλλων, φίλοι,
ὁ κακὰ κακὰ τελῶν ἐμὰ τάδ' ἐμὰ πάθεα.
ἔπαισε δ' αὐτόχειρ νιν οὔ-
τις, ἀλλ' ἐγὼ τλάμων. (1329-32)

traditional in Greek literary art in a verbal technique reminiscent of Aeschylus. (Might it not be suggested that, if thought imposes form, equally a poet who works with certain formal methods is almost forced to think?) It was a mind, surely, not unaware of what contemporary minds were thinking. The thought has links with Homer and Aeschylus, but also with Socrates and Euripides. If the play was written in the early 420's (which is as good a guess as any), Socrates may already have been preaching that 'no man errs wittingly'; and, since the self-blinding of Oedipus was the error of a mind clouded by passion, Socrates might have argued that it was not properly a witting or willing act.[1] Euripides, according to Snell,[2] controverted this Socratic doctrine in the *Hippolytus* of 428. This may or may not be true. Euripides, who about this time was writing tragedies of passion, may have been a purely humanistic psychologist or may have believed that irrational passions were external forces of a daemonic character.[3] It is at least clear that the nature and origin of passion was a living issue about the time when the *Oedipus Tyrannus* was written.

When I ask what has become of the clear distinction between involuntary and voluntary acts, I do not wish to imply that it has disappeared, but merely that it has been made to appear in a new light. The distinction has not disappeared, but both kinds of acts have been drawn within the ambit of the operation of *daimones*. What, then, did Sophocles mean, when he represented the 'evils wrought wittingly', the 'self-chosen grief', as the work of a *daimon*, as the work of Apollo? We can perhaps find the answer in two directions. The self-blinding of Oedipus was, as Socrates might have called it, a mistake. The Chorus think that it was the result of an onset of madness. They ask what *daimon*

---

[1] The relationship between action (δράσας, 1327; αὐτόχειρ, 1331) and passion (πάθεα) is a subtle one – and τλήμων can carry both suggestions. In the *Coloneus* Oedipus, looking back, can say (266 f.): τά γ᾽ ἔργα μου | πεπονθότ᾽ ἐστὶ μᾶλλον ἢ δεδρακότα.

[2] B. Snell, *Philologus*, 97 (1948), 125 ff.

[3] This question bulked large in the discussions at the Fondation Hardt in 1958. Cf. *Entretiens*, VI, esp. 73 ff. – the discussion of A. Rivier's paper. I would suggest that Euripides was a poet caught uneasily between two worlds and only at his greatest when he comes closest to the archaic world-view.

brought him to it; and the word they use (ἐπαίρειν) is appropriate to a transport of emotion. It is true that Oedipus, like a Greek,[1] gives a reason: 'What needed I to see?' But we cannot suppose that he struck his eyes on a purely rational consideration. And the argument progressively breaks down, as it becomes clear that all he has done is to lock himself in a dark prison with the memories of the past.[2] Now, to see in an emotional impulse the work of a *daimon* or god is Homeric; it is Aeschylean; it is a view which may even have left traces in Euripides. But this ascription of the self-blinding to a *daimon* is also part of the whole fabric of the play. By identifying the *daimon* with Apollo, Oedipus links his witting and unwitting acts, so that the self-blinding appears as the culmination of the evil destiny that has attended him since birth. It has often been pointed out – by no one more cogently than by Kitto[3] – that the divinely-appointed destiny of Oedipus comes about largely through actions on his part which spring directly from his character: it was *like* Oedipus that he must leave Corinth to discover the truth about his birth; it was *like* Oedipus to pursue his judicial enquiries with such energy; and so on. ἦθος ἀνθρώπῳ δαίμων : character is destiny. Looked at from this angle, the play might seem to be a commentary on the saying of Heraclitus. Yet, when, still acting characteristically, Oedipus blinds himself, the action is attributed to the influence of a *daimon* – and Heraclitus is turned inside out. There is a kind of symmetry. It needed the unwitting characteristic actions of Oedipus to bring about his fated destiny; it needed the influence of a *daimon* to explain his deliberate act. The divine

---

[1] And a character in a Greek tragedy. R. W. Livingstone, in *Greek Poetry and Life*, 160 f., and B. M. W. Knox, *Oedipus at Thebes*, 185 ff., seem to exaggerate the rationality of his action. 1271 ff. express an instinctive revulsion (upon which he acts with characteristic impetuosity); 1369 ff. are a rationalization, which is then shown to be illusory (see n. 2 below). This criticism does not of course affect the value of Knox's remarks about 'the recovery of Oedipus' (op. cit. 185).

[2] The illusion of 1389–90 (τὸ γὰρ τὴν φροντίδ᾽ ἔξω τῶν κακῶν οἰκεῖν γλυκύ) is immediately dispelled, as Oedipus reviews his life, and above all by the vivid picture of 1398 f. Cf. 1401 (ἆρά μου μέμνησθ᾽ ἔτι ...;), but it is Oedipus who must live with this memory (cf. 1318).

[3] *Greek Tragedy*[3], 136 f.

and human worlds inter-penetrate; and this inter-penetration is Homeric and archaic. It is also Aeschylean.[1]

3

It is clearly beyond the scope of a brief essay to deal adequately with the relationship between the tragic, which means the religious, thought of Aeschylus and Sophocles. There is a similarity and a difference. I shall end by stressing the similarity, which arises out of a similar use of the categories of archaic thought. But, since Sophocles seems to present archaic thought in a purer form than Aeschylus, something should perhaps be said about their differences, though it must necessarily be brief and summary.

Aeschylus dealt with the Theban story in a trilogy of which only the *Septem* remains – a trilogy which Sophocles must have known as well as he clearly knew the *Oresteia*. If we are not in a position to compare the one Oedipus with the other, we can, in one respect, compare Oedipus with Eteocles. Eteocles, in the *Septem*, is confronted with the decision to fight or not to fight his brother in single combat. The human motives and impulses are clearly displayed – his sense of honour, his hatred of his brother. But, along with them, we see – and he sees – divine powers determining the event – the Erinys of his father's curse, a god hastening on the destruction of the hated family of Laius. A *daimon* and a god; and when Eteocles speaks of a family hated by Phoebus and greatly loathed by the gods,[2] we may well compare the ἐχθροδαίμων of the Sophoclean Oedipus, along with all the other passages of the *Tyrannus* which we have been considering. In both plays, divine and human causes run in parallel. The Aeschylean and the Sophoclean character can alike see himself as hated by heaven. Hated by heaven on what grounds?

[1] The best discussions of the relation between divine and human causation in Homer and Aeschylus are among the most recent: for Homer, A. Lesky, *Göttliche und menschliche Motivation im homerischen Epos*, Heidelburg 1961; for Aeschylus, E. R. Dodds, 'Morals and Politics in the Oresteia', *Proceedings of the Cambridge Philological Society*, 186 (1960), 19–31, esp. 25 ff.   [2] *Septem*, 691, 653.

Believe that events – unpleasant events – are caused by divine powers, and sooner or later you will speculate about the motives by which the divine powers are actuated. And here the tradition which Aeschylus and Sophocles had inherited from the Archaic Age was two-fold: the Inherited Conglomerate (to use a term of Gilbert Murray's) included both the jealousy and the justice of heaven. In the concept of the jealousy of the gods (φθόνος τῶν θεῶν) there was a strong element of sheer malignancy. But the longing to find justice in the ordering of the universe – and the fact that justice sometimes seems to be done – had led to another line of thought. Disaster is seen as a punishment, Zeus as the upholder of a moral order, Justice (Dike) as the daughter of Zeus. This conception is explicitly developed by Hesiod and Solon, through whom the line runs to Aeschylus. In a famous chorus of the *Agamemnon* the old idea is rejected that excessive prosperity alone is sufficient to account for disaster: it is rather the impious deed that produces a disastrous progeny. There must be some likelihood, though of course no certainty, that in the Theban trilogy the disastrous history of the house of Laius was interpreted in terms of justice at every stage and, in particular, that Oedipus was culpable.

We must of course be cautious about inferring the views of a dramatist from views expressed by his characters. Eteocles may not have been gifted with the insight of his creator. By what right do we attribute to Sophocles the interpretations placed upon events by Oedipus and the Chorus? In one circumstance at least we may sometimes be entitled to read the mind of the dramatist; and that is where the words of his characters (or of his chorus) carry, by dramatic irony, implications of which they are unaware. Let us return again to the *Tyrannus*.

Oedipus has been led for the first time to suspect that he may be the killer of Laius; and that to the threat of pollution hanging over him has been added a pollution actually incurred. On either score – and he does not know they are one and the same – he sees himself as the victim of a cruel *daimon*. In the ode which follows (863 ff.), the Chorus reacts to the preceding scene. Few odes of Sophocles have led to more perplexed discussion. For, after a first stanza in which they pray for a destiny – a portion (*moira*) – of purity and piety in accordance with the eternal laws, they appear to shoot off at a tangent. 'It is *hubris* that breeds the tyrant.' Did they think – did Sophocles mean us to think – that Oedipus was, or was becoming, a tyrant? There was indeed enough in his bearing towards Teiresias and Creon to make them uneasy. But could it be said that he was guilty of the conventional catalogue of sins contained in the third stanza? If not, why are they listed? I must limit myself to four observations.[1]

(i) The notions of *daimon* and *moira* are closely linked. When, therefore, the Chorus prays (863 ff.) for a *moira* of purity, we are to think of the destiny of Oedipus which he already feels to be impure as the result of a hostile *daimon*.[2] (ii) The next stanza tells of *hubris* falling headlong from the heights; and once it has begun to fall, the process is inevitable – as inevitable as the force of gravity.[3] So Oedipus falls; and no move he makes can save him. (iii) For such a catastrophe, arrogance – along with the whole catalogue of its manifestations – would provide a possible, a likely, and a religious explanation. Against the arrogant man the Chorus prays: 'May an evil *moira* seize him!' But Oedipus was not guilty of these offences. Nor was he a tyrant, but a ruler that strove for the good of the city. Such an ambition the Chorus prayed the gods to preserve (879 ff.). Yet Oedipus has an evil *moira* from the gods. (iv) The explanation was perhaps not only plausible and religious, but Aeschylean. I suspect, though of course I cannot prove, that the content of the third stanza was prompted by the *Oedipus* of Aeschylus. I cannot prove it, though there are strong hints in the *Septem* that wealth and luxury may have been significant themes in the earlier plays of the tri-

---

[1] I owe much to Sir John Sheppard's discussion in the Introduction to his edition of the play: cf. esp. xxxv f.

[2] 816 (with 821 f.); 828 f. (with 823). For μοῖρα cf. also 713, 1302, 1458.

[3] ἀκρότατα γεῖσ' ἀναβᾶσ'
ἀπότομον ὤρουσεν εἰς ἀνάγκαν
ἔνθ' οὐ ποδὶ χρησίμῳ
χρῆται. (876–9)

logy.[1] The explanation may or may not be Aeschylean. If it does not fit, what explanation does? Oedipus may be near the truth.

4

If Sophocles in the *Tyrannus* rejects by implication the idea that the disasters of Oedipus are due to his crimes, in the *Coloneus* Oedipus is made to reject it explicitly.[2] There is no reason to suppose that Sophocles had changed his mind between the one play and the other, though it may well be that he had given further thought to the problem of Oedipus in the light, not perhaps of Aeschylus' Theban trilogy, but of the *Oresteia*. It is through the *Oresteia* alone that we at least are able to grasp how Aeschylus, in the last phase of his thought, envisaged the operations of divinity in the world of men.

It was not the existence, but the character, of the divine justice that created a problem for Aeschylus. 'It was', writes Dodds[3] of the Archaic Age, 'a misfortune that the functions assigned to the moralised Supernatural were predominantly, if not exclusively, penal.' But it is characteristic of Aeschylean tragedy that the penalties are inflicted by human-beings on one another. When Zeus strikes down Capaneus with the thunderbolt, that is a clean end to the affair. But, in the *Oresteia*, Agamemnon is punished by Clytemnestra and Aegisthus, and they by Orestes. The justice of heaven is penal, is retributive, is a matter of *talio* (δράσαντι παθεῖν); and it is carried out by human-beings pursuing their own revenges, actuated by a motive basic to the Greek scheme of values, the desire to retaliate. The exception proves the rule. Orestes is pursued by Furies (Erinyes), but human avengers have already been represented in that rôle. The Furies tell us nothing strictly new about the divine justice: they merely bring home in the most vivid and dramatic way its

---

[1] Cf. *Septem*, 733, 771, 950. I will risk the speculation that, when our Oedipus accuses Jocasta, wrongly, of family pride, a trait has been borrowed from the Aeschylean Jocasta.
[2] Three times; 266 ff., 510 ff., 969 ff.
[3] *The Greeks and the Irrational*, 35.

retaliatory penal character. Once again, then, we find that inter-penetration of the divine and human worlds, so characteristic of archaic thought, but this time through the inter-locking of divine and human *talio*. The process is as frightful as the Furies look and sound. Evil is perpetuated through its own punishment; and out of the evil past come intolerable constraints which seem to make a mockery of human freedom. This divine penal justice, coercive and violent, horrified Aeschylus, as it horrifies us.

'Aeschylus, struggling as he does to interpret and rationalise the legacy of the Archaic Age, is in many ways prophetic of the new time.' That he interprets and rationalizes is true, but he does not deny the responsibility of the gods for evil or proclaim the autonomy of the human will. If he was able to end the *Oresteia* upon a note of joy, it was not by subtracting anything from the grim vision of divinity that he had inherited, but by adding something to it which was itself rooted in Greek ideas. Persuasion (*peitho*) was the natural antithesis of force (*bia*). So, in the *Eumenides*, the problem cannot be solved by Apollo, who can only abuse and threaten the Furies, but only by Athena, through whose persuasions the Erinyes take on a new – and by all the old ideas paradoxical – character as Eumenides or spirits of good-will. In short, Athena – and behind Athena is her father Zeus (ἐκράτησε Ζεὺς 'Αγοραῖος)[1] – shows the 'moralised Supernatural' acting, not as a coercive, but as a persuasive agency; and this may have been the great contribution of Aeschylus to Greek religious thought.

Sophocles knew and had pondered the *Oresteia*. If I say that he had perhaps re-thought the Oedipus story in terms of this trilogy, my justification is this: that it is unthinkable that he could have placed the end of Oedipus against a background of Eumenides without regard to the poet who had virtually created the tragic significance of Furies.[2] We know how the *Oresteia* ends: it ends with the conversion of Erinyes and with joy. How

---

[1] *Eum.* 973.

[2] I have discussed the relationship of the *O.C.* to the *Oresteia* at greater length in *J.H.S.* 74 (1954), 16–24.

does the *Oedipus Coloneus* end? We might be tempted to say that it ends with a mysterious solemnity and with a kind of reconciliation between Oedipus and the gods. But this is not quite true, for actually the play ends with Antigone asking Theseus to send her to Thebes: 'to prevent, if we can, the bloodshed that is coming upon our brothers'.[1] The play ends with a window opened upon fresh tragedy directly resulting from the action. By ending with Antigone and her brothers, it takes us back behind the scene of the passing of Oedipus to that in which the father cursed the son he hated and, in doing so, condemned to death the daughter he loved.

That curse has led to some uneasy apologias: such anger, such concentrated malevolence, in the man whom the gods are about to take to themselves! No apologia is needed, no watering-down admissible, if we understand what Oedipus is, what has made him, where he is, and what he is to become. He is a man of wrath (*thumos*), which rises in a crescendo through the play to the cursing of Polynices. His wrath is the product of ancient as well as of recent wrongs – of the sufferings to which he was bred as the son of his father, to which as a father he adds, and of which his blindness is the visible symbol. He now stands close to a grove of the Eumenides, but it was not spirits of good-will that had presided over his own destiny and that he will evoke by his curse. Past this grove he will shortly go to become himself a *heros*, a chthonian power; and it is by his curse that he has well established his claim to be one. By accepting and honouring him, the divine world is, it would seem, ratifying the kind of justice he has administered, which is a vindictive justice, provoked by suffering and issuing in retaliation. He had spoken of the 'ancient Justice that sits with Zeus according to primaeval laws' (1381 f.); and the event bears this out against the rival claim of Polynices (1267 f.) that it is Mercy (Aidos) that shares Zeus' throne. It is justice not mercy that prevails; the violence of Oedipus, not the persuasions of Antigone. At every point Antigone seeks to persuade, and at every point she fails. Her ultimate failure is outside

[1] *O.C.* 1769 ff.

the play, but foreshadowed at the end of the play, and relevant to the play. For the justice of Oedipus destroys the innocent with the guilty.

5

Sophocles shares with Aeschylus a belief that human destiny is influenced by divine powers in a way which involves the very psychological processes of the human-beings themselves. The horror of punitive divine justice is common ground. What Sophocles seems to reject – or to neglect – is the mitigation which we find in Aeschylus, certainly at the end of the *Oresteia* and probably in other trilogies.[1] The gods of Sophocles are pitiless; and against their pitilessness human pity, so pervasive a theme in his tragedies, stands out in a clear, and often an ironical, light.

It is perhaps presumptuous to ask what caused this difference between the two poets, though answers of a kind can be given. One answer might be in terms of technique. It was the trilogy that enabled Aeschylus to range within sight of ultimate solutions. Abandon the trilogy, and you are forced to concentrate upon an irremediable disaster; focus your single tragedy upon a figure of vivid personality, and you must concentrate upon his disastrous destiny. The Aeschylean Orestes passes from Argos to Delphi, from Delphi to Athens, and then leaves the stage to the gods; the Sophoclean Electra remains at the end of the play – and therefore to the end of time – the warped person that tragic events have made of her.[2] This argument, however, is hardly conclusive. Did the form influence the content, or did the tragic concept dictate the form?[3] The horizons of the *Oedipus Coloneus* are wide enough; and yet, when Sophocles does look beyond the confines of his play, he looks out on new tragedy. Certain answers may be rejected: that Sophocles could not or would not think; that Sophocles was pious. Doubtless Sophocles was emotionally

[1] Cf. *J.H.S.*, 81 (1961), 151 f.

[2] Cf. *Proceedings of the Cambridge Philological Society*, 183 (1954–55), 20–26.

[3] Cf. C. H. Whitman, *Sophocles, a study in heroic humanism*, 39.

attached to the ancient pieties and cults. But there is nothing to prevent a ritualist from making distinguished contributions to theology – nor a believer in miracles or oracles[1] or a plurality of personal gods. We should not fuss too much about these things: the beliefs of twentieth-century man – of all twentieth-century men – will seem one day a very curious Conglomerate.[2] Nor is it clear why conventional piety, as such, should have led Sophocles along these gloomy paths of thought. More, surely, is to be attributed to his trade and to the age in which he lived. His trade he shared with Aeschylus: tragic poets are forced to become connoisseurs of evil and, if they have keen minds capable of general thought, to consider the metaphysics of evil. His age was later. Aeschylus lived through the terrible, but inspiring days of the Persian invasions; he knew the hopes, if also the dangers, of the new Athenian democracy. His optimism (if such a word may be used) was not easy, but it was possible: he could believe in Zeus Agoraios. Sophocles, the urbane friend of Pericles, lived also in the world depicted for us by Thucydides – a world in which the democracy had become an imperialism,[3] arrogant, feared and fearing, based on force and evoking retaliation. He lived to write the majority of his extant plays during the Peloponnesian War. It was not only Thucydides, not only Euripides, that observed that war with an understanding mind. How strange that Sophocles, who had the luck to live to see the Peloponnesian War, should have turned his back, not only on the Enlightenment, but even on the strivings of Aeschylus towards the light!

6

My attempts to define some of the differences between the tragic thought of Aeschylus and Sophocles have, I trust, only emphasized the common legacy that they share from the Archaic Age.

[1] Cf. Kitto, *Sophocles*, 24, 54.

[2] I therefore hesitate to attach much importance to the Holy Snake that lodged temporarily in the house of Sophocles.

[3] Cf. B. M. W. Knox, *Oedipus at Thebes*, 101 ff. (though I cannot agree that the reference to Athens is necessary to explain the relevance of *O.T.* 863 ff.).

Is it to their discredit as thinkers that they thought in archaic terms? The archaic is now fashionable in art, but in the realm of thought the word is still used as a term of disparagement. I would suggest that, under the pervasive influence of centuries of Platonic and Christian thinking, there is a tendency to under-value the categories of archaic thought as a means of expressing important truths about the universe. There is an implicit criticism which I will put in so extreme and indeed absurd a form that it could not possibly be ascribed to any living scholar. Why, if Aeschylus and Sophocles were thinkers worthy of attention, did they not abandon the Urdummheit of the Archaic Age and become good Platonists before their time? It is true that, if they had enrolled proleptically under Plato's banner, they would not have been allowed to write tragedy, but this would have been no hardship, since, having once given their adherence to Plato, they would have lost both the will and the power to do so.

It is a sad – perhaps even a tragic – fact that advances in human thought tend to be bought at a price, which is the exchange of one set of difficulties for another. We have been concerned in particular with two related features of Greek archaic thought, which may or may not be its most salient characteristics, but are certainly those most relevant to tragedy. One of them might be called the involvement of the mind, the other the responsibility of the gods for evil.

The discovery of the mind (to use Snell's phrase), the disen-tanglement of the individual human personality, was vital to the development of morals and of civilization. Until the personality has been isolated, it cannot be valued; and it was not for nothing that Whitehead devoted an early chapter of *Adventures of Ideas* to the civilizing influence of the Platonic and Christian con-ceptions of the soul. Behind Plato is Socrates and the 'tendance of the soul' (θεραπεία ψυχῆς). But the soul cannot be tended, until it has been recognized; you cannot appeal to conscience except on the basis of the freedom of the will. This would seem pure gain. But then the danger appears. The autonomous will becomes an abstraction; the soul cuts loose from its connections

46

with a body (becoming the ghost in the machine), from its connections with other souls and other bodies and with the totality of the universe. It is characteristic of much modern thought that it stresses the involvement of the human personality in its environment and the consequent limitations upon human freedom. The saying of Heraclitus, already quoted ($\check{\eta}\theta o s$ $\dot{\alpha}\nu\theta\rho\dot{\omega}\pi\omega$ $\delta\alpha\acute{\iota}\mu\omega\nu$), was, one supposes, a protest against superstition – and a fine one. But one problem it does not solve: it does not tell us where the *ethos* comes from. Syntactically reversible,[1] it yields as good a sense the other way round. It is doubtless a great advantage to be rid of superstitious fears and ideas of mechanical pollution and to get a clear juridical distinction between deliberate and unwitting actions. It may not be so good to forget that our deliberate acts are themselves in large measure the product of innumerable causes in the past over which we have no control. That is something that archaic thought was not tempted to forget – and that tragedy must never forget.

What the Greek poets expressed in terms of a mythology, we may express in psychological terms so little precise and so little understood that they have almost the status of a modern mythology.[2] We argue about free-will and determinism within a philosophical framework unknown to the Greek poets, but the debate is not exclusively a modern one. The Greeks loved liberty above all things and knew what it meant to be deprived of liberty. A slave-owning agricultural society presented obvious paradigms – metaphors which occur again and again in Greek tragedy. The free man follows his own choices; the slave and the yoked animal obey the bidding of a master; they are subject to compulsion (*ananke*). Feeling their liberty confined not only by external circumstances but even in the realm of their own minds, it was not surprising that the Greeks should ask themselves how far the free man was still free, in what degree he was constrained by the forces they conceived as gods. The question of psychological

---

[1] As this most oracular philosopher may conceivably have realized.

[2] J. de Romilly (*Crainte et angoisse dans le théâtre d'Eschyle*, 104 f.) has some interesting remarks on the relationship between Aeschylus and modern psychological ideas.

47

determination merges into the wider question of the responsibility of the gods for evil, which was such a rock of offence to Plato.

It was an offence that the tragedians – and he cites Aeschylus in particular – made the gods responsible for evil.[1] How far he really understood Aeschylus we cannot tell, but the better he understood him, the more the Plato of the *Republic* was bound to disapprove of him. The gods responsible for evil! But, if the gods are inside nature, as the Greeks' gods so obviously and so firmly were,[2] how can they not be responsible for evil? It was Plato's problem, not the tragedians'. It was Plato's problem how the gods could be made not to be so responsible. To put it rather crudely, the solution involved taking the gods out of nature and then trying to bring them back into it. If we look for the divine in Plato's thought, we find it, primarily, in a perfect world of Forms – and above all in the Form of the Good – to which the soul of man, itself divine, has access. It is, however, the rational soul that is divine and has such access; and we are left with the problem of irrational impulses and desires and the havoc they cause. In the *Timaeus* a divine demiurge is represented as making the world upon the model of the Forms; and, whether he is an external creator god or, as is more probable,[3] a mythical symbol of the Divine Reason working for good ends, we have to account for the manifold imperfections in the world he made. Plato, who on the whole speaks with such confidence and clarity in the *Republic*, was exercised – and, it would appear, increasingly exercised – by these problems. In the *Timaeus* he ascribes the imperfections of the craftsman's work to the imperfect tractability of the material (the metaphysical status of which remains rather obscure): he says[4] – and it is one of the most remarkable sayings in Plato – that 'the generation of this universe was a mixed result of the combination of Necessity (*ananke*) and Reason'.

---

[1] Plato, *Rep.* 379c–380c.

[2] 'The Greek gods ... were subordinate metaphysical entities, well within nature.' A. N. Whitehead, *Science and the Modern World*, 202 (Pelican Books edition).

[3] Cf. F. M. Cornford, *Plato's Cosmology*, 34 ff.

[4] 47e–48a (translated by Cornford).

And he goes on: 'Reason overruled Necessity by persuading her to guide the greatest part of the things that become towards what is best; in that way and on that principle this universe was fashioned in the beginning by the victory of reasonable persuasion over Necessity'. Cornford, in an Epilogue to *Plato's Cosmology*, associated this passage with the closing scene of the *Eumenides*; and one would indeed like to think that Plato had taken Aeschylus to heart and that in this his most profound – perhaps his only profound – contribution to the problem of evil he links hands with Aeschylus and Sophocles – with Aeschylus who was pre-occupied with the successes, with Sophocles who was pre-occupied with the failures, of persuasion in the moral field.

But the *Timaeus* lies between the *Republic* and the *Laws*. It is not the hard sayings of the *Timaeus*, born of metaphysical perplexity, that have influenced subsequent thought and feeling so much as the ardent religious conviction and sheer literary power of the *Republic* and, particularly, the Myth of Er with which it closes. In this eschatological myth, souls are seen to choose their own destinies, but first they are addressed by a Prophetes, or Spokesman of the divine powers. His words are virtually a manifesto against the archaic – and the tragic – world-view. Though he speaks in the name of the Allotting Goddess (Lachesis), daughter of Necessity (Ananke), we find that lot affects only the order in which they choose and necessity only ratifies inflexibly their choice. 'It is not', he says,[1] 'that a *daimon* will get you by lot, but that you will choose a *daimon*. . . . Virtue owns no master. . . . The responsibility is the chooser's; God is not responsible.' But in the *Laws* a disillusioned Plato has swung to the opposite extreme. Twice[2] he makes the Athenian speak contemptuously of men as puppets, playthings (perhaps) of the gods, jerked this way and that by their hopes and fears and passions, dancing on a string.

Such disillusionment is perhaps the nemesis that attends upon

---

[1] 617d–e. οὐχ ὑμᾶς δαίμων λήξεται, ἀλλ' ὑμεῖς δαίμονα αἱρήσεσθε . . . ἀρετὴ δὲ ἀδέσποτον . . . αἰτία ἑλομένου· θεὸς ἀναίτιος.   [2] 644d–e; cf. 803c–804b.

49

a too confident idealism. It is, however, no part of my purpose to deny such truth and value as may reside in the words of the Prophetes, but merely to suggest that neither puppets nor human-beings who are in complete control of their destinies can be the subjects of tragedy. The categories of archaic thought, primitive and obstructive though they might be in primitive minds, allowed Aeschylus and Sophocles to write tragedy, because – ascribe it to inferior logic or superior insight – they were able simultaneously to see man as free and as subject to determining powers, and so to produce that tension between freedom and necessity which seems essential to the tragic paradox. At least it can be said that, because of their archaic notions, and the presuppositions on which they were based, they were not tempted, as so many thinkers have been, to fudge the evidence in the interests of the autonomy of the will and the innocence of heaven.

R. P. Winnington-Ingram

IV:

HOMER AND SOPHOCLES'

'AJAX'

IT WOULD BE HARD TO NAME A PROMINENT ANCIENT Greek author who is not in some way Homeric. Epic story and Homeric language were a thesaurus for all writers after Homer, a recognized basis on which they built, assuming in their audience a knowledge that automatically produced a special significance when they markedly followed or altered an epic incident or a Homeric phrase. Greek poetry is full of examples of Homeric words so turned as to yield, by implicit comparison, a striking new meaning; to give one example of one type, out of several types and many examples, Pindar's phrase 'fleet-footed day' (*Olympians*, 13. 38) is memorable because of its transference to a new context of a familiar and fixed Homeric epithet.[1]

But some writers are especially notable as Homeric. Archilochus, though he consciously represents a different outlook from Homer in many ways, is such a poet because his lines resound with Homeric phrases and imitations; Stesichorus is another, both because he uses material that Homer used and because his poetry had something of the narrative amplitude of Homeric poetry. Prose writers are not excluded from the tradition, for Herodotus and Plato, in different ways, are clearly Homeric. Sophocles' presence in the ranks of the Homerists is not altogether secure, though ancient critics usually grant him some standing. The Suda and Diogenes Laertius both quote the philosopher Polemo's assertion that 'Homer was an epic Sophocles, Sophocles a tragic Homer'. Dionysius of Halicarnassus names Sophocles with Homer as a representative of μεσότης in style, an admirable blend of the austere and the smooth;[2] but this is a broad stylistic category and not an exclusive or intimate pairing. The *Life* that has come to us in the oldest MSS. of Sophocles' text and thus is

[1] A. E. Harvey, 'Homeric Epithets in Greek Lyric Poetry', *C.Q.* 51 (1957) 206–23, gives a brief but most illuminating study of Homeric epithets in archaic monody.

[2] *De compositione verborum*, Chapter 24.

53

probably a direct report of ancient scholarship cites, rather incoherently, a number of opinions attesting Sophocles' affinity to Homer, including the declaration of 'a certain Ionian' or perhaps 'a man named Ionikos' that Sophocles was Homer's only pupil. But not all critics of the ancient world were of this opinion. The author of *On the Sublime* finds no place for Sophocles in his group of *Homerikôtatoi*. Zoïlus, a speaker in Athenaeus' *Deipnosophistae* (277e), accurately says that 'Sophocles took delight in the epic cycle, and even wrote whole plays [or 'many plays', ὅλα or πολλά; the text is uncertain] following its story line'; this does not necessarily imply a specific *Homeric* proclivity.

Sporadic notice has been taken by modern scholarship (by which I mean scholarship of roughly the past century) of the Homeric characteristics of Sophocles.[1] Critics have seen what must be seen, that there are a number of Homeric passages and reminiscences in the extant plays; sometimes the presence of a more generally diffused Homeric colour has been asserted. Thus Pearson, in the introduction to his edition of the fragments, makes the interesting generalization that Sophocles 'laboured ... to present under new conditions the majesty of life which Homer had first portrayed'.[2]

Sophocles' portrayal of life, while significantly different from Homer's, shows in my opinion such strong Homeric influence, wherever a direct comparison can be made, as to render Pearson's view largely acceptable. But I cannot regard the apparent grounds of Pearson's opinion as cogent. He appears to draw his conclusion

---

[1] There are a few – only a few – pertinent comments in Jebb's Introductions to the plays, especially to *Ajax* and *Electra*; Gennaro Perrotta has a valuable comparison of the family scene in *Ajax* with the farewell scene in *Iliad* 6, in *Sofocle* (Messina–Milano, 1935), 144–7; W. K. C. Guthrie, 'Odysseus in the *Ajax*', *Greece and Rome*, 16 (1947), 115–19, compares Sophocles' Odysseus with the Homeric figure, especially in his relationship with Athena; Chapter 8 of W. B. Stanford's *The Ulysses Theme* (Oxford, 1954) is an excellent study of Odysseus in Attic drama. Stanford's edition of *Ajax* (London, 1963), with introductory material on the pre-Sophoclean tradition, came to hand after this study had gone to the printer. There are several nineteenth-century essays on the general topic of Sophocles' relationship to Homer, none of them of great value.

[2] *The Fragments of Sophocles*, I (Cambridge, 1917), xxxi.

from Sophocles' proclivity to *epic* matter, and to make no distinction between Homeric and epic. But for Homeric influence we must, it would be reasonable to suppose, restrict our range to Sophocles' connection with the *Iliad* and the *Odyssey*. The degree of Sophocles' dependence on epic stories for his plots is a point of interest in Greek literary history and has its bearing on the comprehension of Sophoclean tragedy, but it gives no evidence about the playwright's dependence on the poetry of Homer in his portrayal of the majesty of life. Of the seven extant plays two, *Ajax* and *Philoctetes*, are on Trojan themes and include characters who occupy a prominent place in Homer; in *Ajax* there is a scene that imitates a famous Homeric incident. That is the extent of the direct dependence of Sophocles on Homer for material, and the present paper will work within the limits set by this specific material.

I believe that an examination of the specific passages and characteristics in these plays (principally in *Ajax*) that are unquestionably and profoundly Homeric will help to provide a basis for a broad view of Sophocles' relationship to Homer, and of Sophoclean imitation in general and its significance for Sophocles' work. Surely one of the best ways to learn what Virgil means in the *Aeneid* is to take careful note of his imitation of Homer and his differences from Homer; Shakespeare's plays on classical subjects can be illuminated by a reading of North's Plutarch; and I am confident that an examination of Homeric passages and qualities in *Ajax* will reveal with special clarity what Sophocles means. On this belief rests the justification of my study.

Forty-three of Sophocles' one hundred and twenty-three plays were on Trojan themes, a far higher proportion than in Aeschylus or Euripides. We can say with Zoïlus in the *Deipnosophistae* that 'he delighted in the epic cycle'. But neither Trojan themes nor even the use of Homeric characters need mean Homeric imitation or reminiscence, as can be seen readily from the depiction of Menelaus and Agamemnon in *Ajax*. Beyond the trifling fact that Menelaus is very much the dependent younger brother in the play as in the *Iliad*, there is not the slightest trace of Homeric quality in either one of the Atridae. Agamemnon, with his arrogance, bluster and tendency to bully, and his confession to Odysseus that 'it is not easy for a *tyrannos* to be pious' (1350), is an Athenian, not a Homeric, conception; he is cousin to the Creon of *Antigone* and *Oedipus at Colonus*. There is, of course, in the portrayal of these characters, as everywhere in Greek literature, some general Homeric background, but nothing that need concern us here. There are just a few major areas or aspects of the play in which Homeric influence is clear and dominant: the family scene of Ajax, Tecmessa, and their child Eurysaces, based on Hector's farewell to Andromache and Astyanax in *Iliad* 6; the depiction of Ajax himself, throughout the play; the depiction of Odysseus; and the presentation of the relationship between deity and men, in particular the reminiscence of the relationship between Athena and Odysseus in the *Iliad* and the *Odyssey*, which appears both in the relationship between Athena and Odysseus and in that between Athena and Ajax. Though not numerous, the Homeric characteristics of the play are pervasive; analysis of them can hardly fail to involve our understanding of the play as a whole.

I begin with the one conspicuous and extensive reproduction by Sophocles of a specific Homeric passage, the family scene, *Ajax*, 430–595, recalling the farewell scene in *Iliad*, 6, 390–502. Merely to list points of obvious similarity gives a strong impression of Sophocles' dependence on Homer. The groups are numerically equal; in each case the woman begs the man not to desert her, leaving her a widow and the child an orphan; both women point out how wholly dependent they are on the man. Just as in Hector's speech there is a direct quotation of what will be said in Greece when Andromache, her husband dead, has been taken there as a slave, so in Tecmessa's speech there is a like direct quotation of what her captors will say; the imitation is underlined by the close imitation of the Homeric ὥς ποτέ τις ἐρέει (462) with which the quotation is followed, in the Sophoclean words, τοιαῦτ' ἐρεῖ τις (504). To appreciate how strong and deliberate the imitation is at this point one must notice that Sophocles is actually using Homeric 'ring composition': the quotation is also preceded, in Sophocles (500) as in Homer (459), by words to the effect that 'some will say'. This construction is a familiar feature of Homeric diction; with its naïveté and amplitude it could hardly be less Attic, less Sophoclean. As in Homer Hector reaches for his son (466), so Sophocles' Ajax calls for his son (530). Hector's son shrinks from his father's waving plume (467–70), Ajax's son has been hidden away from the danger of his father's madness (531–3). Hector prays that his son may delight his mother's heart (461), Ajax bids Euryaces bring joy to his mother (559). Finally, even as Hector at the end bids Andromache to go home to her work (490), so Ajax ends by bidding Tecmessa take the child and go into the hut (578–9).

We are dealing, then, not with only a rather close general likeness to the Homeric incident, but with a scene that borrows numerous precise details and locutions, and this fact puts it beyond doubt that the playwright wants to call attention to the borrowing, intends his audience to have the Homeric scene sharply in mind as a basis for the meaning of his own scene. If one were to stop at this surface examination, the conclusion might well be that Sophocles depended very much on the spirit and content of the Homeric scene.

But there are features of the Sophoclean scene that are not just different from Homer's picture, but in striking contrast with aspects of that picture that are brought to mind by the playwright's imitation. The contrasts are, in fact, more extensive and more conspicuous than the specific likenesses. There is one general difference, of profound importance for meaning: the shadow lying behind Tecmessa in her pathetic helplessness is as strong as that behind Andromache and far more terrible: it is Achilles who has destroyed Andromache's home and will destroy her remaining security; it is Ajax himself who has brought Tecmessa to her present lowly state, and it is Ajax who will by his suicide complete her desolation. The pathos of the Homeric scene has darkened, in the play, into desolate bitterness. That Tecmessa is a concubine, not a wife, heightens the contrast; Andromache's captors will say, 'This was Hector's wife' (460); Tecmessa's will say, 'Behold the bedfellow of Ajax' (501).

But the contrast between Hector and Ajax, heightened by the imitation, is more extensive and more vital to the play than that between the two women. Both are great warriors and proud men. But while Hector can speak of himself as 'gaining great glory for my father and myself' (446), the unhappy Ajax must contrast himself, about to die 'dishonoured', with his father, who won glory in his time at Troy (434–40). There is nothing in the words of Ajax that is like Hector's sympathetic and compassionate speech. Ajax says little, and that abrupt, before calling for his son, as Hector calls for his. The contrast continues: Hector gently removes his helmet to calm the baby's fears (472); Ajax dourly insists that a real son of his will not be afraid to look at bloodshed, and must learn to adapt himself to his father's rough ways (545–9). In the play there is no laughter shared by the parents as they join in love of their child. Hector, with winning modesty and fatherly ambition for his child, hopes that Astyanax will be called a greater warrior than he (479). Ajax bids his son be better off in luck than he, and otherwise as good (550–1). Finally, the words and tone of Ajax's dismissal of Tecmessa are peremptory (578–95), recalling and contrasting with Hector's gentle bidding to Andromache (486–93).

Comparison of the scenes with attention fixed on the differences introduced by Sophocles brings us to a very different idea from the initial impression based on the likenesses. The impression of close dependence changes to a recognition that the playwright puts emphasis on what in his scene is unlike the Homeric incident; and we may begin to think that the point of the imitation must be to set up a contrast rather than to reproduce anything Homeric. There are other aspects of the scene that lead to the same impression. If we compare the style of the two passages, especially the language in the speeches of the two women, we cannot fail to be struck by the immeasurably greater tension, rhetorical emphasis, compression, and urgency of

Tecmessa's speech. The difference is especially clear in the two passages in which the hero is appealed to as the sole protector and refuge of his woman, 6. 413–30 and *Ajax*, 514–19. The Sophoclean passage is much shorter; it is without the naïve narrative character that marks Andromache's description of how her whole family was destroyed; the Sophoclean passage is brief and harsh; in place of Homer's narrative there are a few terse words (515), 'For you destroyed with the spear my country'. Nothing in the Homeric passage remotely resembles in tone the strongly rhetorical opening words of Tecmessa (485–6):

> *Lord Ajax, of all the ills of man*
> *There is none greater than inevitable chance.*

The weight and urgency of these lines are totally un-Homeric. This is only partly a difference between trimeter and hexameter; it is also that the Attic leanness, the compression felt in each word, is altogether Sophoclean and foreign to Homer.

The second, revised impression that I have been trying to convey might be summed up thus: Sophocles asks his audience to call to mind the famous family scene in *Iliad*, 6, and to notice that here too is a family; but this is a concubine, not a wife; the shadow over the scene is not a heroic enemy but the ruthlessness of Ajax himself; in place of gentleness, soft tears and laughter, parental warmth, chivalrous considerateness, there is harshness, peremptory disregard of feelings, fierce stubbornness, and bitter despair.

The differences in the imitation are more vital to the playwright's meaning than the likenesses. It is nevertheless a superficial view of the scene that does not recognize the importance of the general likeness, and in the area of likeness to Homer the figure of Ajax has a central place, as it has in the play as a whole. In his behaviour in this scene he is almost entirely in contrast with the figure of Hector in the corresponding scene in the *Iliad*. But all through the play, not excluding this scene, the picture of Ajax has deep Homeric roots. Indeed, I hope to show that while the final product and the effect of Ajax in the play are very different from anything in the *Iliad*, there is no way in which Sophocles' Ajax is other than a true development from Homer's Ajax.

Homer's Ajax is above all the brave and stubborn holder of the line of battle. He is not lacking in intelligence (the famous simile of the ass in the field, in Book 11, means stubbornness, not stupidity) but he is a fighter, not a speaker. He is a curiously unsung hero in the *Iliad*. In spite of the fact that he is, beyond doubt and as everybody agrees, the greatest warrior after Achilles, he never has much of a place in the lists of leaders. In the Catalogue he gets a scant two lines (2. 557-8); in the Teichoscopia Helen gives him one line (3. 229) and hurries on to talk about Idomeneus of Crete. Alone among leading warriors he has no identifiable *aristeia*; incidents wherein he is the main figure are always matters of retreat, or defence, or draw.

There are six principal passages in the *Iliad* where Ajax is featured: the duel with Hector (Book 7), the Embassy (Book 9), Ajax in stubborn resistance and slow retreat (Book 11), the defence of the ships (Book 15), the defence of Patroclus' corpse (Book 17), and Ajax's part in the games (Book 23). Later on I shall call attention to which of these scenes Sophocles uses, and consider why he selects as he does. But first let us look at the picture of Ajax created by these passages. The duel with Hector is a draw, though Ajax has had much the better of it, and both his contests in the games of Book 23 end as draws; two of the four remaining passages are defences (Book 15, Book 17), and a third, the retreat in Book 11, is much the same in spirit, since Ajax is the last to go on fighting, when all the rest of the great warriors are wounded, and his retreat is in no sense a flight. Thus Ajax is always the maintainer rather than the winner; no one can outdo him in strength or bravery, but he is not permitted to outdo anyone else altogether and finally. In the one remaining passage, the Embassy, Ajax is the silent envoy; in contrast to the skilful rhetoric of Odysseus and the emotional appeal of Phoenix, Ajax contributes his presence as a warrior to Achilles' liking (645), and, in his brief speech (623-42), a bluntness and frankness of disapproval of Achilles' conduct in contrast to what has preceded, especially to the tact and caution of Odysseus. It is the speech of a soldier, not an orator.

Thus in his relations with his fellow warriors Ajax is characterized distinctly: the stubborn and dependable defender, blunt and sparing of speech, no counsellor, but forthright and no fool.

His relations with the gods are not dissimilar, and again they are unusual. Unlike other great heroes, Ajax seems never to have divine support. Achilles has his mother and Zeus; Diomedes and Odysseus have Athena; Agamemnon has Zeus, Hector Apollo; for Ajax there is never any special favour or notice. It is not that he is disliked by the Olympians; he simply does not figure, in a personal way, in their plans or affections. Conversely, Ajax does not have much to say to the gods. In Book 7, before his duel with Hector, he utters no prayer of his own, but briefly bids the Achaeans pray to Zeus (191–9); in Book 15, Ajax alone of the Greeks fights on when divinity has ordered the defeat of the Greeks, until finally (at 119–22) Ajax at last recognizes the opposition of divinity and retires. But it has taken him a long time to recognize it. There is no suggestion of impiety or disobedience toward heaven; but there is a quality of isolation, a lack of connection unique among the heroes.

The little that is revealed about Ajax's outlook accords with these qualities of independence, simplicity and stubbornness. The best statement is in Book 15, where, opposing Hector when the rest of the Greeks are in flight, he declares (511–13): 'It is better to die or live, once for all, than to be thus worn out vainly in the toil of battle beside our ships at the hands of inferior men'. Once more, complete and independent bravery and forthrightness.

Sophocles has taken this Homeric figure in its entirety for the depiction of his tragic Ajax. He has imported nothing whatsoever that is not in accord with it. Ajax is called, by implication at least,[1] *anoêtos* in the play, but this clearly means 'rash' rather than 'stupid', and elsewhere (by Athena, 119–20) he is said to be

---

[1] Calchas generalizes about the dangers incurred by περισσὰ κἀνόητα σώματα (758); application to Ajax, though only implicit, is certain.

second to none in prudence or in action. (It would be wrong, however, to take these words as evidence of special skill as a counsellor. What Athena's words suggest is that Ajax has in the past shown himself to be no fool, in contrast with his present mad folly.) Teucer, in defending his brother, emphasizes the independence of Ajax in battle (1276, 1283); in the report of Calchas's words about Ajax we are told how he preferred to stand alone without divine support; his bluntness, apparent everywhere, we have already witnessed in the scene with Tecmessa and their child, for example in his refusal to spare his son the sight of gore and in the peremptory dismissal of Tecmessa. His outlook is characterized in the last lines of his speech to Tecmessa (479–80), and its statement is characteristically terse in utterance:

> *To live well or die well befits*
> *The noble man.*

The attitude comes almost directly from the statement of Homer's Ajax in *Iliad*, 15.

Sophocles has drawn his Ajax straight from the *Iliad*, merely emphasizing and developing those characteristics of the Homeric Ajax that contribute to the tragic picture he wishes to create. Thus the Homeric Ajax's comparative separation from deity is transformed into a refusal to accept the aid and guidance of deity; the stubbornness of behaviour in battle becomes a refusal to accept the authority of the leaders; isolation becomes a refusal to accept life on the terms that he sees that most men must abide by.

In the scene of farewell a further dimension is added to this general expansion and variation of Homeric material. What Sophocles has done here is to transfer the incident from Homer's Hector to an Ajax who is both the playwright's own creation and a faithful development of the Ajax of the *Iliad*. It would have been just as impossible for Homer's Ajax to behave, in such circumstances, as Hector does, as it is for Sophocles' Ajax. The continuous reminiscence of the Homeric Ajax is here sharpened and deepened by the contrast with Hector.

While the Sophoclean picture of Ajax is drawn from the

Homeric picture as a whole, not all the Homeric incidents are used. To observe which scenes are specifically recalled and which omitted is instructive, and it is easy to be precise about the matter in the case of the Homeric Ajax, since he is either at the centre of things or simply not in the picture at all. Sophocles has not directly used either of the places in the *Iliad* wherein Ajax and Odysseus are directly linked: the Embassy and the wrestling match. To make a specific reference to any intimacy of relationship between the two men apart from the one (post-Homeric) incident of their rivalry for the arms of Achilles would perhaps have reduced the effect of sharp antagonism that is necessary for the play, especially since both incidents are essentially friendly, and in one the two men are even in a sense comrades in an undertaking. Similarly, the playwright has seen fit to pass by the famous scene in Book 17 in which Ajax and Menelaus are comrades in arms in defence of Patroclus' body. Sophocles' Menelaus is not Homeric; and it would have merely confused matters to have recalled an occasion on which the Homeric Menelaus proved himself a brave fighter. Of the other three Ajax-passages in the *Iliad*, all of them descriptions of Ajax in action, two are used and one omitted. Used (in Teucer's speech on the greatness of Ajax, 1266–1315) are the duel with Hector and the defence of the ships. Equally conspicuous in the *Iliad* and equally complimentary to Ajax is the scene in Book 11, where Ajax holds the field alone, with great gallantry, when all the rest have retired. But in this scene Ajax is at length forced to retreat. The general effect and intent of the scene are the same, so far as the picture of Ajax is concerned, as in the incidents used by Sophocles; but its connotations are not altogether what Sophocles wants. By a judicious selection of incidents he can, perhaps, control his audience's recollection of the specific acts of Ajax in the *Iliad*, though he neither can nor wants to alter the general impression of the Homeric Ajax.

It is Ajax, the central figure of the play, who shows the strongest and most consistent Homeric qualities and is derived most completely from the *Iliad*. The next most Homeric figure, and the next most important character of the drama, is Odysseus. Here again there is nothing in the Homeric picture that is altogether missing in Sophocles (though of course the portrait is much slighter) and nothing in Sophocles that does not have its roots in Homer. Yet once more the meaning and impression created by the character are unlike anything in Homer.

In Homer, though Odysseus is a brave and effective fighter, he is most conspicuous in two other realms: as the counsellor, the member of the expedition who never loses sight of the aims and the general good of the expedition; and as the undertaker of difficult, unpleasant, dangerous missions that call for skill and tact. He is the returner of Chryseis in Book 1, the recoverer of the army in the near runaway of Book 2, the leading figure in the embassy to Achilles; he shares with Diomedes the spying expedition in Book 10 and is conspicuous in the reconciliation in Book 19. The enlarged portrait of the *Odyssey* expands but does not much change these characteristics, except that there is a greater emphasis, especially in the second half of the poem, on the wiliness of Odysseus. In the *Iliad* his daring and skill in undertakings, along with his greatness as an orator and counsellor, are emphasized; in the *Odyssey* none of these qualities vanishes, but Odysseus becomes increasingly the guileful plotter: the *polymetis* must become above all the *dolometis*, to gain his ends. It was from this development of Odysseus' personality in the Odyssey that there sprang the picture of the unscrupulous trickster, the son of Sisyphus, that may have begun in the Epic Cycle and was prevalent in drama.[1] In the *Odyssey* there is a delight in deception for its own sake that would readily lead to both censure and humour; already in the *Odyssey* Athena finds her protégé's skill and delight in falsehood a matter of amusement as well as admiration.

In the Odysseus of *Ajax* there is hardly a trace of the guileful adventurer of the *Odyssey*. The picture is drawn almost entirely from the *Iliad*, though one detail, to be mentioned below, recalls a memorable passage in the *Odyssey*. In the play as in the *Iliad*

[1] Cf. Chapters 6–8 of Stanford's *The Ulysses Theme*.

we find Odysseus undertaking a dangerous mission, this time tracking down the truth about Ajax's madness; we find him the key figure in working for the advantage of the army, both in the opening incident of discovery about Ajax, and later in preventing the vindictiveness of the Atridae from refusing to recognize the great merits of Ajax. No doubt Odysseus in some way represents the Athenian spirit of democracy, but this contemporary influence should not blind us to the extent to which Sophocles draws upon Homer for the spirit as well as the material of his portrayal. The one passage of the *Odyssey* that Sophocles seems to have had specifically in mind is the encounter of Odysseus and Ajax in the underworld, where the gentleness, reflectiveness of tone, and genuine admiration expressed by Odysseus for Ajax are like the most attractive aspects of Sophocles' Odysseus in *Ajax*. In *Odyssey*, 11, 553–60, Odysseus says:

> Ajax, son of noble Telamon, would you not even in death forget your anger against me because of that ruinous armour? The gods laid sorrow upon the Argives when you, who were their tower, were destroyed; and we grieved for the loss of you as much as we did for the mighty son of Peleus, Achilles. Zeus alone, none other, was responsible; he hated the army of the Danaids exceedingly and imposed your fate upon you.

These words breathe the same spirit of reflective calm and sympathy as some of the lines that Odysseus speaks in the play:

> *I pity him*
> *In his unhappy state, even though he is my foe;*
> *When I see him yoked to evil ruin*
> *I see his fate no more than mine.*
> *And I perceive that all we men who live*
> *Are no more than phantoms or empty shadow.* (121–6)

> *Injury to a good man when he dies*
> *Is unjust, even though it chances that you hate him.* (1344–5)

> *I am more moved by a man's worth than by hatred.* (1357)

The Odysseus of *Philoctetes* owes something to the later tradition. Homer's Odysseus would never have subscribed to the cynical opportunism expressed in *Philoctetes*, 81–2:

> *Since achievement of victory is sweet, endure;*
> *We shall show ourselves honest another time.*

Homer's Odysseus is a man of action as much as a man of words; the Odysseus of *Philoctetes* is no longer the man of action, and he has no scruples about the way he uses words. Apart from his amoral cynicism and a marked lack of disposition to engage in fighting, the Odysseus of *Philoctetes* is essentially the same figure as the hero of the *Odyssey*. He is still, as in Homer, a tireless worker for the group; he is again the undertaker of a difficult and dangerous mission; he is still the servant of deity. If we dislike the way in which he is serving deity in *Philoctetes* we should remember that some of the exploits of the *Odyssey*, for which he has Athena's firm backing, are not of an Achilles-like or Ajax-like moral forthrightness. Even in the *Odyssey* Odysseus was content to work by guile when guile was most effective. And we must never forget that Odysseus in *Philoctetes* is on the side of divine will; Philoctetes must go to Troy, and Heracles is no less emphatic in declaring that this is the will of Zeus than Odysseus is.

The two portrayals of Odysseus are two different developments of Homeric material. In both, Odysseus is the worker for the community and the worker under divine will; in both he is the undertaker of difficult enterprises. But in the one play the enterprising counsellor is also a philosopher with a broad, humane sympathy and a regard for moral values; in the other he is cynical, shifty and callous. Both are legitimate developments of the Homeric figure, however much each may owe to post-Homeric and contemporary influences.

Something must be said about the relationship between deity and man, especially with regard to the divine attitude toward Ajax. For once more the Homeric background is of primary importance in the Sophoclean picture. But the place and depiction of deity in Homer and in Sophocles are notoriously complex and difficult topics, and here only such aspects of them as are immediately and narrowly relevant can be discussed.

'This I bid you: be always at my side, such an ally as now', says the hapless Ajax, in his madness, to Athena (116–17). The words are ironical and pathetic; the relationship between Athena and Ajax is a travesty of the Homeric intimacy between god and hero. In *Ajax* the goddess has ensured that the hero will wreak havoc among sheep and cattle and bring ruin on himself. But the words reach a more tragic and broader meaning when we learn that Ajax, when sane, repeatedly rejected the help of Athena with high-spirited bravery, and with a touch of arrogance too (774–5):

> *Mistress, stand by other Argive warriors;*
> *The line of battle never will break here.*

The meaning of this ill-starred relationship between goddess and hero is deepened by the accompanying spectacle of a proper relationship between deity and man, that between Athena and Odysseus. Once again a Homeric theme is being used both by imitation and by contrast.

A closer look is needed at the imitative use of the theme, the relationship between Athena and Odysseus. Here there is a real rapport, in contrast to the travesty of intimacy between Athena and Ajax. There is all the difference in the world between the offhand and hearty familiarity of Ajax's manner toward Athena (especially the casual rebuff in 112–13 when Athena has urged him not to mistreat Odysseus: 'I bid you please yourself in other things, Athena; but Odysseus will pay no slighter penalty than this' [i.e. whipping and death]) and the extreme reverence of Odysseus' attitude. The contrast has of course an immediate point in emphasizing the dangerous irreverence of Ajax's behaviour. But it is just as important that the casual manner of Ajax is a good deal closer to the manner of Odysseus in the *Odyssey* than is the docile caution of Odysseus in the play. In other words, there is in the play a very different concept from the Homeric of the kind of relationship that is possible between deity and man. Gone is the smiling indulgence toward a favourite's guile, as in

Odyssey, 13 (287 ff.), gone the humanization of deity that is a feature of Homer (as when Athena compares herself among gods to Odysseus among men, *Odyssey*, 13. 298–300; how utterly un-Sophoclean this is), gone the mother and son intimacy of the *Odyssey* (as when in 13. 288 Athena uses the same formula of address to Odysseus as Thetis uses to Achilles in *Iliad*, 1. 361), gone is the freedom to scold deity as Odysseus scolds Athena for not helping him enough (13. 318–19). In Sophocles this breeziness is arrogance and madness; the sane human being maintains distance and reverence.

Deity in Sophocles is quite unlike deity in Homer in another respect that is immediately relevant. Though Athena appears in the play, as it is mythologically appropriate for her to do, since her traditional protégé Odysseus is engaged in an exploit, the divine background of the action is really quite impersonal. Ajax, in his suicide speech, does not so much as mention Athena; only Zeus among the gods of the upper world is mentioned. And when Teucer and Menelaus argue, Menelaus says that he was saved 'by *theos*', and Teucer in reply bids him, if he has been saved by 'gods', not to be impious toward 'gods'. There is no mention of Athena as the divine worker of these events. Sophocles is far from Homeric anthropomorphism. His gods are remote and impersonal beings; divine action and will are not separated into conflicting or even distinguishable personal wills and decisions. The presence of Athena in *Ajax* is only outwardly Homeric.

The outward Homeric shell is, in general, a good deal more closely reproduced in this play than are the spirit and meaning of the Homeric original. Athena is present to help Odysseus, just as in Homer; but the alliance and *camaraderie* of the Homeric picture are in Sophocles transformed into the madness of Ajax's supposed intimacy with Athena. The warmth and pathos of the Homeric family scene become instead sorrow and harshness. The sturdy independence of Homer's Ajax becomes embittered isolation. The general form is kept and many details are reproduced exactly, but a deeply changed presentation of the conditions of life leads to a new meaning that transforms the imitation.

But this transformation of spirit, profoundly significant though it is for Sophoclean tragedy, is not the only important aspect of Sophocles' response to the Homeric model. I am not even sure that it is more important than the other kind of imitation, in which Sophocles reproduces and uses for his meaning authentic Homeric substance. The depiction of Ajax gains much of its force from the fact that the Sophoclean Ajax is recognizably and fundamentally the Ajax of the *Iliad*, embittered and defeated by the post-Iliadic incident of the contest for Achilles' armour. The character of Odysseus in *Ajax* is drawn almost entirely from the *Iliad*, only made more mature and philosophical (as in *Philoctetes* he is made more mature and cynical) and deprived of his intimacy with Athena. In all this, the very heart and substance of Sophoclean drama are deeply indebted to the Homeric spirit, not alone to the Homeric incidents.

The Homeric character of *Ajax* has one further dimension that needs to be noticed, one that is much involved with the meaning of the play. The contrast between the blunt man of action and the philosopher is an important element of the play; the recognition by Odysseus of Ajax's greatness both brings a solution to the immediate problem of the dramatic action, by ensuring honourable burial for Ajax's body, and contributes much to the meaning of the play, since it shows in a dignified and impressive way that, for whoever has the grace and insight to see it, there is in the warrior virtue of Ajax a measure of human worth of the highest order, in spite of the limitations of his outlook and the violence of his actions.[1] This basic contrast is a very sensitive development of an implicit contrast in Homer, and is not just an exploitation of the explicit tradition of conflict in the contest for the armour. The Homeric hero who is most intimate with deity is paired with the one whose divine connection is the least among major figures; the Homeric *polytropos* with the unmoving and almost immovable defender of the battle line;

---

[1] This is in essential agreement with the interpretation of the play in Kitto, *Greek Tragedy*[3] (London, 1961), 118–23.

the orator with the man of few words. In *Iliad*, 3, we are told that Ajax is a head taller than anyone else, Odysseus a head shorter; in Book 9 Odysseus speaks first and at length, Ajax last and briefly; in Book 23 the two physically contrasting figures are matched in wrestling and wrestle to a draw. Out of these contrasts, implicit but not featured in the *Iliad*, Sophocles has fashioned the very nucleus of his play.

The degree and kind of Homeric influence present in *Ajax* justify assent, in the case of this play, to Pearson's declaration that Sophocles was concerned to 'present under new conditions the majesty of life which Homer first portrayed'. The phrase 'under new conditions' is, if the foregoing analysis is correct, an extremely important limitation to keep in mind in defining Sophocles' affiliation with Homer; but the affiliation is undeniable, and is to be reckoned with in interpretation of the play.

'Others imitate one of their predecessors or contemporaries, only Sophocles plucks the brightness from each one', writes the enthusiastic biographer to whom we owe the ancient *Life*. His metaphor is mixed, but his enthusiasm is well-placed, if Sophocles' use of Homeric material is a fair sample. Presumably it is, and can help, by analogy, in the interpretation of other plays as well. Observation of what Sophocles does with Homeric matter in *Ajax*, and, to a slighter extent, in *Philoctetes*, ought, I think, to induce us to hesitate to suppose that *Electra* simply gives us 'modified for drama, the story that Homer tells', as Jebb rather uneasily suggested was the case.[1] In view of what we see in *Ajax*, we shall not expect any such *tour de force* of archaism, and can more readily accept *Electra* as a subtle and original reworking of material used by Aeschylus. A great artist's meaning must be first of all his own; when he imitates, the result will be a fusion of inheritance and originality such that we are conscious of both and yet need an effort of analysis to separate one from the other.

G. M. Kirkwood

[1] In his introduction to *Electra*, p. xli.

V: ARISTOPHANES:

ORIGINALITY

AND CONVENTION

THE COMEDIES OF ARISTOPHANES HAVE IN MODERN times been widely acclaimed (to many of the ancient critics their bawdiness made them reprehensible). They are mines from which scholars have quarried information about the events, men and manners of the fifth century B.C. Their structure has been revealed, their vocabulary examined. This study has not only been invaluable to all who care about the great age of Athens and its decline but has also increased immeasurably our understanding of the plays and our delight in reading them. Yet, whereas the greatest Greek tragedies have been evaluated as drama, as poetry, and as philosophy, and are still stimulating writers and composers to re-create them in modern terms, Old Comedy has had to rest content under a general blanket of praise. Or, perhaps worse, it has been dismissed as satire, inaccessible to the modern reader, or as mere fantasy.[1]

There are some signs that this situation may be changing. Satire is fashionable again, probably too fashionable for its own good. The 'theatre of the absurd' is becoming accepted. Since this is so, it is both easier and more urgent to reconsider the earliest manifestation of satire and fantasy blended into one, sweetened and spiced, moreover, by the addition of wit and humour of many kinds, lyric poetry, music and dance. They are to be studied not for the light they shed on Aristophanes' political, ethical and social opinions, but to reveal him as dramatist and poet, and to illuminate the nature of comedy.

The main stumbling-block in the way of appreciating Aristophanic drama *qua* drama is not, as is sometimes thought, the references to unknown Athenians and other incomprehensible allusions. These are irritating to students, who have to try to remember all the accepted or tentative elucidations, and, what is worse, they sometimes obscure the point of a joke, but they are too few, and too trifling, to be more than minor blemishes on our

---

[1] But see now C. H. Whitman, *Aristophanes and the Comic Hero.*

pleasure. It is the conventions of Old Comedy which get in our way, and we too easily assume that Aristophanes like us had to climb over or round them.

Aristotle in his terse way tells us that Sophocles invented the third actor and scene-painting; that is, changes were possible in the conventions governing tragedy, and indeed we can see for ourselves as we read the plays that Euripides' aims and methods were not those of Aeschylus. We can trace no such development in Old Comedy, for the multitude of non-Aristophanic fragments that have survived are a rag-bag from which to extract assorted scraps of culinary lore, accidence, gossip and metrical theory. They do not, with two possible exceptions, disclose story, structure or theme. Nor does Aristotle himself give us un-ambiguous guidance. Changes may have occurred: we assume that they did. Can we then say that Aristophanes worked within a framework that he gladly accepted?

I should like to consider two points: the nature and extent of the conventions of Old Comedy and the use Aristophanes made of his opportunities for artistic freedom. By this sort of study I believe it can be shown that Aristophanes is truly original, original not in spite of dramatic conventions, but because of them. Separate consideration of these two problems would involve much repetition and I shall therefore attempt to describe different aspects of convention as they affect the plays.

Aristophanes claimed that in his plays, as Rogers paraphrases,[1]

'Always fresh ideas sparkle, always novel jests delight,'

and ancient critics could find no harsher condemnation of a poet than to accuse him of plagiarism. It was probably Euripides who was charged with 'licking Sophocles' honeyed lip'[2] and many similar gibes could be cited. For the modern spectator of comedy too originality is a *sine qua non*. It may be revealed in plot, character, theme, scene or language. A typical notice might run: 'Mr A's play, while presenting stock characters in stock situations, was redeemed by its witty dialogue and original *mise en*

---

[1] *Clouds*, 547. [2] Aristophanes, fr. 581 K.

scène (it took place in a laundry)'. At one time in the history of
comedy originality of plot has been the first demand, at another
freshness of wit. In recent years it has been possible to discern
differences in this respect between types of theatregoer: some seek
above all comedy of situation, in which one awkward confrontation is succeeded by another, and the plot has no purpose but to
introduce the mother-in-law, the policeman, the boss, just when
he or she is least welcome, and leave them to say exactly what all
but the least sophisticated of the audience is expecting to hear;
others derive the greatest pleasure from unpredictable words and
the normal situation which conceals oddities: the small town
apparently calm on Sunday morning – except that outside in the
street the gallop of a rhinoceros is heard; the verbal inconsequence
of the trial scene in *One Way Pendulum*.

The atoms of comedy are its jokes: they resist dissection.
Nevertheless it may be possible to generalize about them. Some
jokes owe their nature to the wider demands of plot or individual
scene; a play set in Hades has a source of comic subject-matter
denied to one set in a stately home, while within the plays a
torture competition or pistols for two in the long gallery each
requires appropriate treatment. By no means all Aristophanic
wit is thus prescribed; we think of comic lists, absurd word-
fabrications, distorted quotations and proverbs, vulgar subject-
matter dressed in high-flown language, obscene punning and
innuendo. If there is a dramatic reason for their use in any
particular place it is rather some basic demand in the play's
emotional rhythm than a response to subject-matter. (This is a
field of enquiry strangely neglected.) We might then make the
generalization that most of the jokes in Aristophanes are independent of convention; he employs each where he chooses.
We might go on to say that common to all of them is the element
of surprise or incongruity, the delighted shock with which we
hear a tragic lament end in the vegetable plot, or an ignorant
porter succeeding in verbal disputation. We might even be
tempted to add that surprise, incongruity and originality are
akin. Then we remember that jokes are often repeated. Does this

mean merely that their endings may have been forgotten and so
may still surprise (as when we re-read a 'thriller'), or shall we
infer that a measure of familiarity improves some jests? (The
elderly anecdotes with formulaic beginnings – As I was on my
way to the theatre tonight, and the like – suggest that there is
some appeal in the well-known.)

We cannot escape this paradox when we consider the next
ingredient of Aristophanic comedy, its scenes and characters.
Under this heading I place minor characters (the protagonist, at
least, is best discussed in connection with the play's theme and
story) and those short scenes which illustrate, more than they
advance, the argument of the play. They would be hard to separate. We can deny the existence of the paradox by saying that the
plays end with a series of unconnected scenes in which stock
characters appear, imagining Aristophanes consulting a file in
which he had noted the content of earlier plays. This is to assume
the supremacy of convention, an extraordinary complacency in
his audience, and a surprising lack of artistry, to say nothing of
genius, in the dramatist. As Professor Dover pointed out,[1] radio
programmes like *The Goon Show* are useful to the student of Old
Comedy. Week by week we meet the same characters whose
diction and mannerisms please because they are old acquaintances.
(It is worth pointing out that such programmes have a structure
more rigid than anything in Aristophanes.) Or consider the strip-
cartoon: Feiffer's young American intellectuals with their self-
analysis and neuroses are variations on a given type of character.
Visual humour too gives parallels for the use of stock scenes as
well as characters; the pages of *Punch* show again and again the
married couple at breakfast, the desert island, the psychiatrist's
consulting room. Some of these are apparently timeless, others
reflect modern preoccupations. Similarly some of Aristophanes'
minor characters, the gluttonous Heracles, foreigners, inn-
keepers, officials, stupid or lazy slaves, form a different category
from the demagogues, informers, oracle-mongers and sophistic
intellectuals who were the particular butt of Aristophanes' own

[1] *Fifty Years of Classical Scholarship*, p. 98.

day. A not uncommon type of scene consists of interruptions. In the *Acharnians*[1] and the *Birds*[2] the hero is seen preparing for a feast: in the first play interlopers come to ask favours, in the second, to meddle. One further type of comic scene deserves mention. At the end of the *Acharnians*,[3] Dicaeopolis, the hero, and his adversary Lamachus are both making preparations, the one for a feast and the other for battle. Dicaeopolis mocks Lamachus' preparations, so producing a most amusing symmetry of words and actions, and emphasizing the difference in their fortunes. There is a similar dramatic device in the *Knights*[4] in which demagogue vies with demagogue in blinding Demus with oracles.

The artist, then, knows he is working for people who take pleasure in recognizing the familiar. In consequence he need not waste time in exposition (the newspaper propped against the marmalade jar at once establishes the situation), but may concentrate his verbal wit. He does not tell us that oracle-mongers are frauds and poets conceited poseurs, but plunges at once into detailed parody of their effusions. Moreover, since we know that women are given to drinking and adultery, we take greater delight in their protestations of sobriety and chastity, and appreciate the skill with which Aristophanes occasionally portrays the exception to the comic rule. Thus convention frees Aristophanes for greater inventiveness.

So far we have seen Aristophanes using traditional material, together with what he invents, to fulfil his artistic purpose. When we turn to conventional structure the problem is rather different, but its difficulties have perhaps been overestimated by critics who forget that the artist has always to marry form and content: in opera, for example, a notably hard task. However, Old Comedy is a field in which the demands of structure are particularly compelling. It is well enough known that Aristophanes inherited and continued to use a formal structure consisting of prologue, parodos, agon, parabasis and exodos, two of which had their own regular internal form. Three of these elements belong to the

---

[1] *Acharnians*, 1018–68.   [2] *Birds*, 851–1055.
[3] *Acharnians*, 1085–1142.   [4] *Knights*, 997–1110.

chorus, the parodos and exodos being respectively their entrance and exit songs, and the parabasis their address to the spectators in the middle of the play. The agon requires two mutually hostile characters (or where the term is loosely used a single character in conflict with the chorus). Not only, then, does the inherited structure affect the working-out of the story, but it dictates that there should be a conflict, and that the plot should allow the intervention of a chorus. An exhaustive analysis of the form of the plays would be out of place here,[1] but it should be noted that Aristophanes obviously felt himself free to interchange the order of agon and parabasis, and to adjust their internal form. Although we may begin to understand how form and story can work together in general, for many the parabasis remains a cause of offence. They complain that it breaks the dramatic illusion and that its tone is inappropriate to a festive occasion. This may well be so (though I doubt whether the comedies were intended to create 'dramatic illusion' as we use the term), but it is at any rate clear from the content of, and intensity of feeling in, parabases that their authors did not regard their composition as unavoidable drudgery. And audiences too valued the chorus's address to them, since, we are told, it was the parabasis of the *Frogs* that caused its unprecedented success.

Within these formal limits it might seem that the story could be freely invented, but in fact we find that stories have so much in common that we begin to discern tradition at work again. Antiphanes envies tragic poets since they have no need to make up their plots:[2] he might rather envy them their freedom, so much greater than that of the comic poet. The tragic poet has the power to decide the importance of his chorus, the nature of his hero, and within limits the mood of his play, and since *Helen*, *Agamemnon* and *Bacchae* are all tragedies, these limits enclose a vast area of feeling. Contrast the needs of Comedy. Tragedy usually reaches its emotional climax about two-thirds of the way through: the comic poet has the harder task of producing a *crescendo* to the

---

[1] See Pickard-Cambridge, *Dithyramb, Tragedy and Comedy* (Second Edition, revised by Prof. T. B. L. Webster), pp. 213–29.   [2] Antiphanes, fr. 191K.

very last line. There may be levelling off for a time, but no renewed *piano*, except, I think, in *The Clouds*, where Strepsiades solves one difficulty to find that a worse befalls him.

The plots of Old Comedy are simple and can be briefly summarized. A man is in difficulties; he hits on an absurd solution, carries it out, and triumphs. Intrigue and counter-plot, necessary alike to New Comedy and modern farce, have no place, since plays depending on them will not admit the absurd and fantastic. Ionesco's *Rhinoceros* demonstrates the validity of this rule today.

A plot of this sort imposes its own conditions. Its hero must gain our sympathies at the outset so that we can finally enjoy his triumph. He must therefore have much in common with the ordinary man, even if he bears the name of a god. He is neither heroic in stature nor morally an example to us. He is nearer the 'little man' of Charlie Chaplin than the tragic hero of the Greeks. Strepsiades is a bit of a rogue and Dionysus a coward, but we want them to succeed. The dramatist must make us feel for his hero; and he must make us laugh at him.

The exposition of the play is therefore vital. Aristophanes' prologues show two ways of handling it. The more successful, but harder to achieve, is the monologue, and when Aristophanes wrote the *Acharnians* and *The Clouds*, the only two plays to begin in this way, he must surely have had a superb actor at his disposal. The hero is alone, or virtually so, on the stage, and his dramatic isolation is established. In one play he is the only Athenian to want peace; in the other he is the only one of his family to lie sleepless, tormented by debts. While we feel for him we laugh at him as he belches and fidgets or tries to kill bugs. The other plays begin with a dialogue between the hero and a companion, or between two characters about the hero. The first alternative gives scope for jokes, particularly if one of the characters is a slave; the second builds up to an imposing entrance for the hero.

The hero's problem may be a private one, for instance his debts or, as in the *Frogs*, his desire that the dead Euripides should return from Hades to Athens, but the working out of the story must not only touch the sympathies of the human beings in the audience, but appeal to them as citizens. We want Strepsiades to evade his creditors, but we doubt whether the ability to make the worse cause appear the better is for the good of the Polis. We want Dionysus to be happy, but would Euripides' return benefit the state?

Granted that the stories must demonstrate the progress of the individual from adversity to triumph in such a way as to be amenable to the demands of established structure, it would surely seem that the dramatist has scope for considerable originality of plot. Is this so in fact?

So far little has been said either of satire or of fantasy, but now an attempt must be made to understand the way in which they are woven into the story, and the extent to which each of them is susceptible to the pressures of tradition. It would be rash to be dogmatic about comedy's origins, but a tentative account of them does help us to try to answer our questions. Comedy is generally believed to have developed from a religious rite performed by a kômos, or band of revellers, sometimes in disguise. If so, it is likely enough that they set out looking for adventure, perhaps with a definite object, like the drunken youths who seized one of Aspasia's courtesans,[1] and that they met with adversaries to be fought or jeered into surrender, or less likely, fell out among themselves. If there were rites of this sort they were certainly not drama. We know neither the name nor the date of the genius who transformed ritual into drama by substituting the individual for the mob. The continuance of the custom of naming comedies by their choruses suggests that the Greeks themselves were not entirely aware of the significance of this step.

These beginnings are ritual. That is of the greatest importance because it demonstrates that these apparently disparate elements formed a unity in the worship of the god, a unity still felt to exist when ritual had become drama. The germ of satire is there in the mocking of bystanders, itself still an element in Aristophanic

[1] *Acharnians*, 526 f.

comedy, and this broadens into criticism of policies and classes as well as individuals. Fantasy is there in the chorus' assumption of animal dress.

To return to the story. As its importance grew it could develop, and stress, one or other of its inherent possibilities. The quarrelling could produce a plot based on conflict, or the spirit of adventurousness could turn into an account of a quest. In fact all Aristophanes' comedies have something of each element, to however small a degree, but conflict is more obvious and more dramatic.

Let us look in more detail at the stories. Dicaeopolis has to struggle against the Acharnians, Cleon against the Sausage-seller, Strepsiades against Pheidippides, Bdelycleon against Philocleon, Peisthetairus against the Birds, Lysistrata against men. Even when the hero is not involved in a major struggle there is still conflict, at the end of the *Peace* for example, where there are minor arguments with interlopers, or in the agon of the *Frogs* between Aeschylus and Euripides. In the 'conflict' plays the quest takes a minor rôle, the treaty mission in the *Acharnians* or the theft of oracles in the *Knights*, but in some plays it is the mainspring of the action. The *Peace* is, literally, a quest for peace; the *Birds* for a better Polis. The object may be an abstraction, or a person, like the dead Euripides, or the acquisition of some power, as in Strepsiades' desire for skill in argument so that he can evade his debts. The quest is a simple theme which has inspired much in mythology and art, and in comedy it allows for chance encounters on the way, the difficulties of the journey, and the shift of scene to some strange setting, a thinking-shop or the kingdom of the Birds.

It is not, then, in creating the main outlines of the story that the dramatist aims at novelty, but in the marriage of fantasy and theme. By theme I mean that public issue which the play presents, peace versus war, or new education versus old, for example. It must not be thought that the reason why discussion of theme has been postponed till now is because it is the corner-stone of Aristophanic comedy. In modern jargon, while Aristophanes may be a 'committed' poet, he is far from having a 'message for humanity'. (If one were clearly discernible there would have been fewer arguments about his personal beliefs.) Contrast the case of Shaw. We have Shaw's word for it that those of his plays which discuss contemporary problems have a message made acceptable and memorable by being expressed wittily in dramatic form.[1] It is hard to believe that Aristophanes began with a message and that story, fantasy, song and dance were merely so many spoonsful of jam to get the pill down the patients' throats. Plays with no public theme could have existed, and probably did, and political issues would not have been raised unless they had power to touch the hearts of the audience and their imaginations. To 'regard the play as primarily a vehicle for ... philosophy, is an outrage to the thing the poet has made for us'.[2]

Nevertheless, there are plays where dramatic expression of the theme is simple and we can be sure of Aristophanes' views. The *Acharnians* and *Lysistrata*, the two 'peace' plays with stories based on conflict, are of this sort. Dicaeopolis wants peace and converts the Acharnians who want the war to continue. Then he overcomes those who are jealous of his prosperity. The two views are argued by characters face to face, and the individual defeats the crowd. Conflict in these plays is something that happens to the hero; it is not of his own seeking. In the *Knights*, the most violent of the plays, there is no hero but there is a struggle between Cleon and the Sausage-seller, though even here the latter has conflict forced upon him. In plays of this type, the political or moral theme is not demonstrated in obvious terms on the stage. Two points of view are put and two speeches of self-justification are made by characters mutually hostile. There is no simple issue between good and bad, and the dramatist's aim is not self-revelation.

If we dare to picture Aristophanes at work, we shall visualize a man whose first inspiration is an eccentric idea, completely

[1] Epistle Dedicatory to *Man and Superman*, *passim* and cf. A. W. Gomme, *More Essays in Greek History and Literature* (ed. D. A. Campbell), p. 83 f.
[2] C. S. Lewis, *An Experiment in Criticism*, p. 82.

novel, or with a novel twist. If, as all those Euripidean choruses were always wishing, we were birds, we could create a happier city than Athens, in the air. The idea has a political context; it comes to a citizen who has endured almost two decades of war. From the idea stems the plot, and the detailed working-out of character and incident. Even when the fantasy is not completely original, as in the *Frogs* (there had previously been other quests to Hades), there is a freshness of inspiration not only in the serio-comic conflicts first between Dionysus and various adversaries, including the frog-chorus, and secondly between Aeschylus and Euripides for the throne of poetry, but also in the use of literary criticism to poke fun at literary criticism.

Aristophanes then is not an innovator: tradition or contemporary events furnished him with form and content. His achievement is the rarer one of true originality, like that of Mozart, whose acceptance of the restrictions of classical opera brought forth *Don Giovanni*. Fantasy rules the progress of the play. The fantastic, which is the impossible or highly improbable, is blended with reality in such a way that the whole is imaginatively true, and we share for a while that 'sort of passionate sanity' which is comedy's gift to us. When Old Comedy died, fantasy lost its freedom and, for many centuries, its place in drama, while comedy itself submitted to new chains. Fantasy was pressed into service by the system-builders, to be used in Plato's *Republic*, Butler's *Erewhon*, or Orwell's *Animal Farm*. We are so accustomed to this secondary function that it is hard for us to appreciate the effect that fantasy had in Old Comedy, and its power when allied with laughter and guided by tradition to lead us into a world of play in which failure and disappointment will be unthinkable. Comedy was 'a time when all went well', a transformation of ordinary life in terms of a logical fantasy, dissolving tensions in joy, triumph, and laughter. 'God alone is worthy of supreme seriousness, but man is made God's plaything, and that is the best part of him. Therefore every man and woman should live life accordingly, and play the noblest games and be of another mind from what they are at present. ... What, then, is the right way of living? Life must be lived as play, playing certain games, making sacrifices, singing and dancing, and then a man will be able to propitiate the gods, and defend himself against his enemies, and win in the contest.'[1]

Rosemary Harriott

[1] Plato, *Laws* VII, 803 c, d, e.

VI:

THE

VULGARITY

OF TRAGEDY

AT THE END OF THE 'SYMPOSIUM', WHILE MOST OF THE guests sprawled over the tables in drunken slumber, Socrates remained awake, forcing the sleepy Aristophanes and Agathon to admit that the man who could write tragedy could also write comedy, and vice versa. I wish to maintain Socrates' thesis, but by maintaining it I do not intend an identification of myself with the great philosopher, still sober while all the other distinguished contributors to this symposium lie in stupor. Far from it; my thesis must be maintained from the point of view of Aristophanes, convinced by the master. My thoughts on Greek tragedy have certainly been stimulated at every turn by Professor Kitto. But that is not the only reason why I identify him with Socrates. One of his last actions as Professor of Greek at Bristol was to take the part of Socrates in a production of *The Clouds*, which I mounted in the Studio Theatre. Having seen to it that he should dress himself in a great false paunch, and rush round a stage making vulgar noises, and having been pleased at the reception of this spectacle by audiences, first in the theatre and then for a brief moment on West Region Television, I should like to acknowledge my debt to Professor Kitto by claiming him as an argument for my thesis. I suspect that he has been able to make a unique contribution to the study of Greek tragedy precisely because he is the sort of man who in the year of his retirement can still enjoy performing the slapstick and bawdy of Greek comedy.

I am taking Socrates' thesis to mean roughly that tragedy involves a certain attitude to life, and comedy involves an opposite one. Both are slightly distorted attitudes, implying exaggeration of some kind. As a result either is inadequate as a total attitude to life, and so by itself will not produce the greatest drama, which needs the contrast and combination of the two. Now of course it is obvious that this is where the greatness of Shakespeare lies. I am maintaining that Greek drama shows a similar combination. I shall not discuss Aristophanes here. But no one can seriously argue that Aristophanes could have written plays anything like the ones he did if there had been no tragic festivals. I shall confine my remarks to the tragedians, and especially Aeschylus, but I am claiming that they have wider application.

I put this thesis in another way: many people have an idea of Tragedy, something exalted, solemn, noble and rather statuesque, involving a tragic hero, someone larger than life. This idea fits the drama of Corneille and Racine, or that of Wagner. It does not fit the drama of Shakespeare. Many people have thought that it fitted that of the Greeks. I am sure that this is totally wrong. But to argue against it requires detailed examination of all extant Greek tragedies, requires a book rather than an article. I have tried to do this, and can but refer to the result.[1] Here I wish only to draw a crude distinction between two attitudes of mind which have been responsible for Western European tragic drama: on the one hand that of Racine, or Wagner, or those who have the idea of Tragedy to which I have referred; on the other that of Shakespeare and the Greek tragic poets. On the one hand a noble outlook, on the other a vulgar outlook.

Here are three examples of what I mean by this vulgar outlook, taken from climactic moments of three great plays, and presenting clear images of this outlook with reference to the three 'eternal commonplaces' of poetry: death, erotic love and God. Hamlet touches earth twice. Once is over the body of Ophelia, in a moment of the highest tension, a clash between Christian belief, sexual desire, revenge and common sympathy. The other time is when he holds a skull during the scene of macabre comedy with the gravedigger, which scene immediately precedes the burial of Ophelia.[2] In *Danton's Death*[3] Marion tells of the one time she really loved anyone, in a moving lyrical speech. Immediately

[1] *Greek Tragedy and the Modern World*. Methuen.
[2] *Hamlet*, V. i.
[3] *Danton's Death*, translated by Stephen Spender and Goronwy Rees. Act I. pp. 16–18.

The Vulgarity of Tragedy

afterwards Lacroix comes in and describes how he has just seen a mastiff and a poodle copulating in the street. In the *Wakefield Second Shepherds' Play* the shepherds kneel twice over a cradle. Once they kneel to the Christ-Child, but just before they have bent over the cradle in which lies the sheep Mac has stolen.[1] And both inmates are referred to as 'little day starn'. A skull is a quaint and funny object, and something to make us weep when we remember that living eyes looked out of it once. The act of love is one of the most sacred and beautiful things in which man and woman can join, but it involves a ridiculous physical position. A man kneeling in simple worship may be someone who has found God, or someone totally deluded by a false image. Both aspects are true, and so drama that only presents one aspect is less than completely adequate.

By saying that the Greek tragic poets had a vulgar outlook, I refer first to the fact that they were judged at the festival on four plays. The first three were tragedies, and the fourth was a bawdy farce. We shall make nonsense of the tragedies unless we assume that the religious images which bulk so large in them are indeed as central as they appear. But we shall also fail to understand the attitude of the tragic poets and their audience if we forget the way in which they made fun of their religious and moral conventions in the fourth play. The Greek tragedies were popular plays in a way in which no other drama except the Mediaeval Cycles has been. Like the Mediaeval plays they were presented before an audience of virtually the whole population, at a festival. Like the Mediaeval plays the aim was didactic, and the poet was judged according to the advice he gave the state.[2] All this means that the outlook and function of the Greek tragedies is very different from the drama of Racine or Wagner. Furthermore, we are not asked to view Greek tragedies from the point of view of a 'hero', but from that of the chorus, the ordinary citizen body. Indeed no extant Greek tragedy has a

[1] Printed e.g. in *Everyman and Other Old Religious Plays*, edited by Ernest Rhys. Everyman edition, pp. 72 and 77.
[2] Cf. Aristophanes, *Frogs*, 1054.

'hero' in the sense usually understood. The *Oedipus Tyrannus* is the only play which it is possible to take as having a hero, and even then this means ignoring the chorus. No one has succeeded in applying the concept of *hamartia* even to Oedipus. It is clearly ludicrous to ask who is the 'hero' of the *Persae, Medea, Trachiniae* or any of the trilogies. Questions about tragic heroes are bound up with the question as to whether tragedies can have happy endings. And this kind of question seems totally irrelevant when we are beginning to understand Greek tragedies. It is obviously irrelevant to the *Oresteia*; and this has led to the ridiculous result that some people have called this, the crowning glory of Greek drama, not quite a tragedy.

There has been a tendency to treat Greek tragedy as a noble, statuesque art form. As a result there is a tendency to minimize the sensational elements in it. The extant tragedies are full of sensational, and even grotesque, moments. The natural reaction of a producer reading the end of the *Prometheus Vinctus* is to devise a sensational cataclysm on stage to match the cataclysm of the poetry. What else could have been done? The play was performed in broad daylight. There is a description involving the main actor, the chorus and a rock disappearing into a chasm. The text demands a sensational ending, not merely to create a theatrical scene of horror for its own sake, but because the message of the play is sensational. Two occasions when we see actors on all fours provide two more examples of the way the tragic poets grasped the opportunity of crude, even grotesque sensationalism, when it suited their message. In the *Hecuba* we see how the cruelties of war turn Hecuba and her women more or less into beasts. The climax is when they lynch Polymestor, and he crawls out of the tent with blood dripping from his eye sockets, where the pins of brooches have torn out his eyeballs.[1] Bestial and ugly; a deliberately sensational scene, and precisely what Euripides wanted to convey about the nature of war. We think of Goya's etching making the same point, *Y son fieras*,[2] where a young woman with a baby under one arm drives a pike

[1] *Hecuba*, 1056 ff.   [2] *The Disasters of the War*, 5.

into a soldier's stomach with the other. We may compare the sudden reappearance of the prophetess of Apollo when she sees the Eumenides.[1] We felt an atmosphere of peace at her gentle words with which the play opened. Peace is a long way away yet. We are jerked awake by the ugliness of panic. It is a sensational moment, but Aeschylus had more to come, if we believe the story that the actual appearance of the Eumenides made women have miscarriages. It is a sensational play, and meant to be; the Eumenides are meant to cause horror and havoc. One of the most magical scenes in all drama is when Pentheus comes out of the palace as though drunk,[2] seeing two suns, and has his woman's hair put straight by the gentle hands of Dionysus, who is about to see that Pentheus shall be torn into small pieces by the hands of his own mother. Heroic, noble or elevated are not adjectives we would most readily apply to that scene, or indeed to the whole of that play, with its abandoned dancing chorus. And the climax of all Greek tragedy is immediately preceded with a description of Orestes, son of the eagle, minister of the vengeance of Zeus, as a baby wetting his nappies.[3] With Aeschylus' outlook it gives an added dimension to our relations with Orestes to hear his old nurse. Shakespeare is full of similar examples. But it would spoil our appreciation of *The Ring* if we were asked to visualize Siegfried wetting his nappies.

This is what I mean by my contrast of the noble mind and the vulgar mind. There is an attitude of mind which thinks that the dignity of love is lessened if we are reminded of the ridiculous physical position necessary for sexual intercourse, or the dignity of a king is lessened if we are reminded that he must excrete as much as a peasant does; and there is an attitude of mind which glories in the contradiction. In terms of drama this latter will manifest itself in violent contrasts, the contrast between a dancing, singing chorus and relatively static actors, between the mood of Apollo's prophetess and the mood of the Eumenides, between the atmosphere of worship created by the three tragedies, and

[1] *Eumenides*, 36 ff.   [2] *Bacchae*, 917 ff.

[3] *Choephori*, 734 ff.

the buffoonery of the satyr play with which each day of the festival ended.

The best way of understanding the relation of the satyr play to the other three is with reference to the tetralogies of Aeschylus. Aeschylus was famous for his satyr plays, and he very probably invented the tetralogy, four plays on one theme, three of them serious, the fourth farce. Aeschylus did not have to submit tetralogies; he did not do so for example in 472, the year when the *Persae* was produced. He used this form for a purpose; and Aeschylus' writing shows a clearer sense of the way all things fit together in a pattern perhaps than any writer in any language. To our great loss we have of course no complete tetralogy surviving. But I think we can make out the form of the *Supplices* tetralogy, and I shall devote the rest of this article to the *Supplices*, because this work seems to contain all the characteristics of what I have called the vulgar mind.

The extant first play has never fitted well with the theories of those who say that Greek tragedy is noble and statuesque. But until recently it was put on one side as primitive drama, written many years before any other play which has survived. This is no longer a possible attitude. It is very likely that it was written in 463, only five years before the *Oresteia*, and almost certainly it belongs to the 460s.[1] It must be accepted as a play of Aeschylus' maturity.

It is certainly not a statuesque play. The climax is a rape scene,[2] an excited dance in which the assailants are likened to spiders[3] and serpents.[4] These images give us some idea of the choreography. The rape is then prevented by the arrival of Pelasgus with an escort, presumably of about the same numbers as the assailants. There are supposed to be fifty Danaids. Aristotle says that Aeschylus' chorus was only twelve, but I just do not think that an audience would tolerate fifty people being represented by twelve. Perhaps Aeschylus' chorus was twelve on all other occasions, and this exceptional work was the one exception

---

[1] The evidence is summarized in H. D. F. Kitto, *Greek Tragedy* (3rd ed.), pp. 1–2.
[2] *Supplices* 825 ff.   [3] ib. 887.   [4] ib. 895.

to the rule. The end of the play is a dance of the Danaids and their attendants. Presumably there must have been one attendant to each Danaid, especially since they would have been played by the same people as did the Egyptians. It is therefore likely that twice in this play alone the orchestra is to be filled with an elaborate dance involving a hundred participants. We should notice too the exclamations of Pelasgus at the strangeness of the Danaids' costume, which are very emphatic, and which the Danaids admit are reasonable.[1] We cannot avoid the fact that this play involved enormous numbers on stage, exotic costume and violent dancing.

Although we only possess three lines from the *Aiguptioi*, the second play, and ten lines from the *Danaides*, the third, we can make out the outline of the action of the trilogy. We possess the synopsis of the *Amymone*, the satyr play,[2] and I shall try to show how exactly the action of this counterpoints that of the trilogy.

The main action of the trilogy is the wrong-headed flight of the Danaids from marriage with their cousins and its disastrous consequences. I shall return to the wrong-headedness in a moment. The *Supplices* starts with the arrival of the Danaids in Argos which they claim as home, for it was the home of Io from whom they are descended. They invoke Zeus and Epaphus, the son of Zeus and Io; but it is the mystery and the power of Zeus which are emphasized in this song. We are partly prepared for the realization that Zeus' view of the matter is very different from the Danaids'. Pelasgus the king of Argos now arrives, and asks the Danaids to prove their lineage, whereupon they tell the story of Io, and then invoke the wrath of Zeus as protector of suppliants while they threaten to hang themselves on the altars. Pelasgus agrees to accept them if the city agrees, and they tell the story of Io in song and dance, ending their song with the hope that Zeus may order all things well. Danaus their father returns at this point with the news that the city has accepted them, but then the Egyptian herald, followed by the chorus of Egyptians, arrives. Tension mounts till the rape scene; in the nick of time

[1] ib. 234 ff. & 246.   [2] Apollodorus, *Biblia*, ii. 13.

the rape is prevented by the return of Pelasgus with a band of Argives; the Egyptians retire discomfited. The Danaids are now to be received into the city. After a strange and significant speech in which Danaus tells them to guard their virginity, they are escorted off by the chorus of servant girls singing that Aphrodite must also be honoured as well as Artemis whom alone the Danaids will praise.

The three lines from the second play,[1] the *Aiguptioi*, do not help us with the story. But we know roughly what must have happened. Somehow or other the Egyptians did succeed in forcing their cousins into marriage. But all the Danaids except one, Hypermnestra, murdered their husbands on the wedding night; she loved him too much. From the title it is reasonable to guess that the principal chorus this time comprised the Egyptian bridegrooms, and that the play contained the marriage, the murder and Hypermnestra's refusal to kill her lover.

Two fragments survive from the third play,[2] the *Danaides*. One refers to a bridal chamber, and the other describes the marriage of heaven and earth, and the resulting birth of corn and pasture. Some critics think that Hypermnestra was tried, and that this was the substance of the third play, the second fragment being part of a speech spoken in her defence by Aphrodite. Alternatively Aeschylus may have used the version of the story to which Pindar refers.[3] Forty-eight Danaids were won in marriage by suitors who competed for them in a race. I incline to this latter theory for a reason I shall return to. But at any rate we can say that whether through marriage or through the direct intervention of Aphrodite the Danaids are made to realize the importance of sex.

I called the Danaids' flight wrong-headed. I think that in this tetralogy Aeschylus takes the virgin's fear of sex as an image of man's fear of the power that governs the world. While we flee, it is terrible; when we submit it is wonderful. It is the equivalent in terms of Aeschylus' religion of *The Hound of Heaven*. Io is the perfect image of this. She fled from the lust of Zeus, and as a

[1] Frs. 373 & 78.   [2] Frs. 43 & 44.   [3] Pindar, Pythian IX. 111 ff.

result she suffered great hardship. But eventually she gave up. Instead of the terror she expected, Zeus touched her, not even violating her maidenhead, and with that touch begot Epaphus. The Danaids clearly regard themselves as in the same situation as Io; their strange appearance is paralleled by the strange appearance of Io;[1] and there is little point in the long chorus describing Io's wanderings, unless Io in some sense stands for the Danaids. They pray that Zeus will help them as he helped Io,[2] but they do not realize that Zeus did not help Io until she let herself be caught, and that he had first pursued her and caused her to suffer. The implication is that the pursuit by the Egyptians is of the same nature as the pursuit of Io by Zeus.

Three points in the play show quite conclusively that we are meant to see the Danaids as mistaken. First is the strange scene in which Pelasgus persuades them to leave their position of clinging to the altar, and come down on to unsanctified ground.[3] This is an action of the same kind as that of Agamemnon walking on the purple carpet: one that typifies a general wrong-headedness; with Agamemnon, the wrong-headedness of the arbitrary despot, the man who killed his daughter Iphigeneia; with the Danaids, the wrong-headedness of those who trust in men now, not in the powers of heaven. Secondly there is the speech of Danaus[4] in which he advises them to value chastity more than life, and to guard against their fruit being picked.[5] He is not speaking to Christian nuns, but to girls whose natural end is marriage. In a country as poor as Greece the image of the fruit is perhaps stronger than it is here. Fruit is meant to be picked, and indeed to prevent it from being picked permanently is a crime when there are hungry people all round. Never in the play, except by the Danaids and their father, is it ever suggested that there is anything wrong with the marriage. Thirdly, right at the end of the play, the Danaids pray to Zeus for *kratos*.[6] Weir Smyth, in the Loeb translation, renders this incorrectly in a way which is illuminating, as 'victory'. The meaning is 'mastery';

[1] *Supp.* 565 ff.   [2] ib. 1 ff. & elsewhere.   [3] ib. 506–24.
[4] ib. 980–1013.   [5] ib. 996–9.   [6] ib. 1068.

for women to pray to have mastery over their men is much more obviously to pray for something unnatural, and even more obviously so in fifth-century Athens.

The main image which recurs throughout the play is that of the pursuit of one animal by another. Mostly the Danaids are referred to by bird imagery;[1] probably this was also brought out in the choreography. They are also heifers chased by wolves,[2] and the prey of spiders.[3] The most detailed images are the first and second; in the second they are doves chased by hawks.[4] The first is more complicated.[5] If my interpretation is thought elaborate, it must be remembered that the audience was used to the allusiveness of early choral lyrics, and knew the stories referred to very well. The Danaids in their song wonder if they may be mistaken for Metis, the nightingale wife of Tereus, pursued by Tereus, now a hawk. There is no other mention of Metis in literature. Tereus' wife is normally Procne, and he is normally made to turn into a hoopoe, not a bird of prey. The nightingale is Philomela, his wife's sister. Aeschylus has changed the story, and must have done so for a definite point. The usual version of the story is that Tereus seduced Philomela, and Procne, in revenge, made Tereus eat a meal of their son Itys. In other words there is wrong on both sides. In Aeschylus' version the only action that is mentioned is the unnatural, wrong act of the mother killing her own child. Tereus is represented first as guiltless, and secondly as a hawk not a hoopoe. Very subtly Aeschylus is indicating that the Danaids think they are being pursued wrongfully, but the pursuit is both justified, and natural. The pursuit of the nightingale by the hawk is proverbial. It is told by Hesiod.[6] The nightingale is told that it is foolish to complain of being gripped by the hawk; the hawk will eat her or let her go as he chooses. I am saying then that the point Aeschylus is making with the trilogy can be summed up in three images: first, the generalized image of nature, animal hunting

---

[1] *Supp.* 60 ff., 223 ff., 329, 510, 779–82.   [2] ib. 351.
[3] ib. 887.   [4] ib. 223 ff.   [5] ib. 60 ff.
[6] Hesiod, *Works and Days*, 202 ff.

animal for food; secondly, the story of the Danaids who flee a natural marriage with their cousins, thus rousing them to such an extent that they attempt force, with the result that force is used against them and they are murdered; chaos reigns, until finally the Danaids have to capitulate; and thirdly, it is the story of Io, a human being who shrinks to face up to the power behind the world, and suffers until she capitulates. The trilogy presents a world view which is very stern, but eminently reasonable; the world is a harsh place. It is no good running away from the world; the world is at it is, and will not be otherwise.

The best way of seeing how the various strands of the action of the *Oresteia* are woven together is to trace the two main images, the net and light, in their developing course from the first metaphor of light by the watchman to the final torchlight procession. I suspect that the *Supplices* also would show the same sort of development of linked images. This is why I believe that Aeschylus used the version of the story that Pindar used. Men racing for the Danaids would be an effective climax for the *Danaides* and it would fit with the image of animal pursuing animal. I wonder also whether the opening of fragment 44 is not an allusion to the same image:

> *The holy heaven desires to* wound *the land,*
> *Desire to be thus wedded takes the earth.*

'Wound' is a literal translation. It is an odd word; there is some deliberate point in it. Perhaps the image of the hunting animals is finally connected with the rain hunting the earth, with all the fruitful results that we know.

This theme is perfectly presented in the story of the *Amymone*. Being in a waterless region Danaus sends his daughters for water. One of them, Amymone, aimed a dart at a deer, and hit a sleeping satyr, who woke up and tried to rape her. She was saved by the appearance of Poseidon who, however, slept with her instead, and afterwards showed her the spring of Lerna. The pattern is exactly the pattern of the trilogy. Only here it is broad farce. We notice the hunt image turned upside down. Now it is the weak

Danaid who goes hunting, and a pretty poor job she makes of it. Clearly too there must have been a climactic chase scene with Amymone trying to escape the satyr as the Danaids try to escape the Egyptians in the first tragedy, and Poseidon appearing as Pelasgus does with his Argives. Presumably Aeschylus took delight in parodying his own choreography. We cannot tell the importance of the water, but it has a clear relevance to the idea of fertility. Apart from the image of the rain in the *Danaides* that I have quoted, there is an odd allusion to water right at the beginning of the tetralogy.[1] The Danaids invoke 'City, land and fair water'. In the *Supplices* this is never taken up; but presumably it acquired significance in the course of the trilogy.

If this is a right interpretation, what then does the tetralogy 'mean'? Let us start by visualizing rain wounding earth. Heavy rain after a long drought. It does seem to be doing violence to the dust, stabbing it all over, bringing it out in pustules, tearing down its protective covering of plants and leaves. And yet the earth needs the rain. And yet flood water can cut a great gash through the earth, can destroy part of it. I have talked of the 'wrong-headedness' of the Danaids' flight. But I do not wish to suggest that we should not sympathize with their fear. We sympathize with the dove pursued by the hawk. We sympathize with a girl who is frightened of a man. We still sympathize with her even if her fear is partly or largely her own fault. We still sympathize with the fox even if we are hunting it. It is frightening how much damage an innocent girl can do if she panics. A virgin's defence of her virginity is a mysterious and wonderful thing. But it is also very curious that a woman should take so much trouble in keeping herself from that activity which is of all activities most likely to give her pleasure. All these things are true, and none of them on its own is the complete truth, even if all of them together seem to contradict each other. The truth is the combination of the contradictions.

I have tried to suggest an interpretation of one aspect of this great and complex work. I have not dealt with Pelasgus and the

[1] *Supp.* 23.

political aspect because this has no relevance to my present purpose. Although parts of my interpretation are conjectural I am making two firm claims about the tetralogy. The main action is the wrong-headed, though understandable, flight of the Danaids and its disastrous consequences. This action is given depth by being seen against a background of predatory nature on the one hand, and the story of Io on the other, in which sexual submission and the submission of prey to predator is used as an image of the submission of man to the powers that order the world. Secondly, the same story is presented first in the trilogy as an aid to our religious understanding, as a kind of worship, and then in the satyr play as hilarious parody when the action is turned upside down and inside out.

I am also claiming that this work should not be pushed aside, and treated as an exception to the normal pattern of Greek tragedy, but used as a unique instance in what is left to us of certain features which are central to Greek tragedy. I am claiming in short that if we are to make the foolish attempt to understand Greek tragedy on the basis of one play, the *Supplices* is a more useful play to examine than the *Oedipus Tyrannus* on which so many accounts of Greek tragedy are exclusively based. If one ignores the chorus, it is almost possible to treat it as a play about Oedipus, and therefore a play with a hero who is a king, and larger than life. If one concentrates on the fact that he blinds himself off stage, and ignores the horrific moment of his appearance with blood dripping from his eyes, it is almost possible to say that this is not a sensational play. I think it can be shown that all extant Greek tragedies are popular, not noble, written from the point of view of the community as a whole, not from that of a hero, always stimulating the audience to think about the relationships of men with the community and with the powers that order human life, and written by men who used every resource of the theatre – song, dance, spectacle, ritual, farce and sensationalism – where it suited their purpose to do so. I hope I have shown that all this applied very obviously to the *Supplices* tetralogy. I think it is important to realize this about Greek tragedy, because there is much talk at the present time about the possibility of modern tragedy. I am very doubtful whether tragedy as it is conceived by noble minds is suitable to the present day. Its lofty sentiments belong to a civilized age, and Western Europe is no longer a civilized place. But it should be an encouragement to our vulgar, sensational age that the drama of Aeschylus was also vulgar, sensational . . . and a series of masterpieces.

Leo Aylen

VII: PLAUTUS,

TERENCE AND SENECA:

A COMPARISON

OF AIMS AND METHODS

EVERYONE ADMITS THAT PLAUTUS WAS A MAN OF the theatre. Everyone admits that Terence, though a practising dramatist, had something more in his mind than the mere entertainment of the multitude. Everyone admits that the Senecan tragedies are pieces of rhetorical character intended to startle and dazzle the listener. The three dramatists differ markedly from each other in style. I will venture to say that scarcely a line of any one of them could be supposed to have been written by either of the others.

A handsome tribute has recently been paid to Plautus by Peter Arnott, whose puppet-show productions of classical plays have been seen in Bristol University as well as in many other centres of classical study. 'Plautus', he says, 'was a man of the people. He was also more wholly a man of the theatre than any of the Greek writers, in that he wrote plays for his living, thus depending on satisfying the public taste....' 'Plautus is no great literary figure, and for this reason is often underestimated. Of all the dramatists we have considered, he loses most through being read rather than seen.'[1]

Is it true that Plautus is so dull to read? St Jerome after a night of weeping over his sins, used to console himself by reading Plautus – but God forbid that St Jerome should be suspected of wanting to see the plays performed. The best performance of Plautus I have seen was, I think, that given of the *Mostellaria* by an Italian company – at the Delphiad in Bristol, in Italian. Careful rehearsal, graceful, studied movement, almost developed into a dance, split-second timing, all gave the performance a sophisticated quality.

I suppose one could claim that Plautus was one hundred per cent a theatre man. Perhaps one would go on to maintain that Terence, who undoubtedly wrote for public performance but undoubtedly had more in mind than mere stage success, was,

---

[1] *An Introduction to the Greek Theatre,* 161 f.

shall we say, only fifty per cent a man of the theatre. And as for Seneca, it is not certain, indeed it is very much disputed, whether he wrote for the theatre at all; so that on the same line of reasoning he might come out with a theatre sense approximating to zero.

I partly believe all this. But I do not think that it is the whole of the truth. I think that Plautus was a considerable poet, who had a mastery of the Latin language and of rhythm. I think that Terence longed for popular success, that he had very definite theories as to how to achieve popular success, and that, in spite of what we are told by modern writers, to a large extent he *did* succeed on the public stage not only of his own day but even of centuries later. As for Seneca, I will maintain that, whatever his aim in writing his plays, there are scenes in them which are really dramatic, that there is dialogue which would make a powerful impression on an audience, and that in certain ways he comes nearer than the Greeks to our notion of the theatrical.

Plautus, the successful dramatist, I picture as a working dramatist wholly engaged in preparing Greek plays for the Roman stage. He knew women, and he knew men. He knew the Roman streets, the forum, the shops; he knew the rich quarters and the poor, the temples, the taverns, the Tiber and its island and bridge, the roads leading out of Rome. He probably did his own shopping; he had a wide command of language, when it came to consumer goods; he had a great variety of meats in his mind – I think he was specially fond of bacon; and it stands to reason that he was not a teetotaller. He knew all the terms of fashion; he had an astonishing vocabulary for women's dresses. He kept his eyes and ears open as he walked along the streets or listened to the orators in the Forum. He took stock of the Greek philosophers stalking along as grave as a Scot on Sunday, not above slaking their thirst at a thermopolium, then going their way solemn-faced and half-seas-over, *tristes ebriolique incedunt.* He could deal with cheeky slaves, swaggering soldiers, street bullies, street-walkers. If you asked him his politics, he might reply with a wink that he supported the *boni uiri.* A man with few illusions but with wide interests, he loved to note the racy dialogue of the streets, the ranting of the orators, the solemn rites of the public festivals; and he could be thrilled to his finger-tips by rhythmic utterance and movement, and by music.

In the theatre all his talents found their scope. Doubtless the physical equipment was meagre, compared to ours, but in all ancient drama the physical played a very small part. We have grown up with the picture-stage and the switchboard. To that extent I agree with L. H. G. Greenwood when he says that, compared to ours, a Greek performance resembled a play-reading. But having said that, one proceeds to qualify it. There is a big difference between even a play-reading and a solitary perusal of the text in one's study. If the players learn their parts off, if they wear costumes and move about, we have come a long way towards the fulness of dramatic production. If we add a physical background, however slight, with three real double-doors, two side entrances and a practicable roof—then we have the essential – and all that we moderns have added to this is but frills.

In itself a Roman stage door is simply two panels of wood, turning rather noisily in their pivots. But the simplest physical things can assume importance when worked into the plot and the emotions of drama. Think of the opening scene of the *Curculio*, where the old hag who guards the heroine is tempted to the door by the fragrance of the wine poured by the lover on the threshold – or a little later, when she softly ushers out the heroine:

placide egredere et sonitum prohibe forium et crepitum cardinum,
ne quod hic agimus erus percipiat fieri, mea Planesium.

Come out gently and be careful not to make the door sound or the hinges creak, for fear the boss should notice what is happening here, Planesium dear.

Think of the knocking on the door in the *Rudens*. The girl, speaking in iambic rhythm, knocks somewhat uncertainly at the strange door:

Heus ecquis in uilla est? ecquis hoc recludit? ecquis prodit?

Is anyone in? Will anyone open the door? Will anyone come out?

whereupon the door bursts open, and framed in the doorway
is the boorish Sceparnio, snarling in trochiac rhythm:

Quis est qui nostris tam proterue foribus facit iniuriam?
Who is it who is doing such shameful violence to our door?

These are some of the effects obtainable in comedy. Need I
remind you of some of the scenes in tragedy where we hear
knocking on a door?

In his stage with its limited equipment, its background and
altar, and the occasional use of portable properties, chairs and
tables, dishes, writing-materials, a fishing-net, and the like –
Plautus has his instrument, and he can play on it as a virtuoso on
an old fiddle. As for his aims as a writer, and the way in which
he treated his Greek texts, I think first of the prologue to the
Asinaria:

'There is plenty of fun and merriment in this comedy: it's a piece
that will make you laugh'.

No one doubts his power to make us laugh, but there is also a
remark in the *Bacchides* about another play of his:

'Even in the case of the *Epídicus*, a play which I am as fond of as
I am of myself, there is no play which I see with less pleasure if
Pellio is taking part'.

Finally there are the prologue and epilogue to the *Captivi*, in
which he praises the play for its good moral tone, and says that
poets like himself find few plays of this type, showing good men
becoming better.

I find it equally hard to believe that Plautus altered the structure of his Greek originals and that he did not alter the dialogue,
style and atmosphere. He was a fast, hasty worker – why bother
to change the plot? But the language, the jokes, the topical hits,
the pungent dialogue, the abuse and the endearments, all poured
effortlessly from his pen. The result is, I believe, something
which is different from all the Greek originals which the sands of
Egypt have ever disclosed, or will disclose to our successors.

We are told that Terence was a young man and a foreigner. What does *Afer* mean? Someone has said to me, 'How interesting that the first elegant Latin we possess should have been written by an African!' If there is any truth in the story that he came from Carthage, I would see in him a Carthaginian, of Phoenician stock and therefore racially akin to the Jews. Certainly there is something un-Roman in the intelligence which shines through his work. He had noble patrons – whether these included the younger Scipio is still not agreed; but the rumour that they helped him to write his plays is certainly a slander. Terence's plays bear the stamp of his individual genius.

A young man, of foreign blood, perhaps of swarthy skin, befriended by the great, he has brooded long over this curious new industry which has grown up, the turning of Greek plays into Latin for the entertainment of the Roman public. There are no established rules governing Roman translators; there is nothing corresponding to the French Academy; but certain tendencies are becoming manifest. Terence, watching from the wings, has discerned the weakness in the productions of the Latin Muse. He has made up his mind to beat these *barbari* at their own game. He may pretend to admire the popular favourites, Naevius, Plautus and Ennius; in fact he despises what he calls their *neglegentia*. But there is more behind. He intends to improve not only on the Roman adaptors but on the Greek originals.

This is the central point, the vital secret in Terence's work. He says that his aim was to write plays which would please the people; but he says elsewhere that he aims to give the people plays 'free from faults'. He teases his rival because of the presence of blemishes which in all probability were taken over from the Greek; for example with making the defendant speak first – for which we have a parallel in the *Epitrepontes* – and for showing a crazy youth who thinks, or dreams, that he sees a deer running away from hounds, and begs for aid; which reminds us of Daemones' dream in the *Rudens*.

I do not believe that Terence attached much importance to these charges in themselves. He had been attacked, and he was going to defend himself by attacking the other party – and in terms which could easily be understood, even in the excitement of an occasion in the theatre. But the implication is that faults should be avoided. What is the point of saying this, if Terence conceived of himself as a translator and nothing more? What does he mean when he calls his rivals 'good translators and bad writers'?

We have evidence that Terence did depart from the text of his Greek models. His wholesale dropping of the explanatory prologue – a Greek legacy, and still found in Menander – is itself a criticism of this traditional expedient. The turning of the opening monologue of Menander's *Andria* into a dialogue with a client (whom Terence has invented for the occasion, according to Donatus), the turning of the monologue of the excited young rascal Chaerea in the *Eunuchus* into a dialogue with a friend (whom, again according to Donatus, Terence has invented for the occasion) – these are clear departures from the Greek. Why did he introduce them, unless he thought that they were improvements? But the Roman audience would not have understood him, had he told them that he was improving on the Greek. They had come to hear a play of Menander or Diphilus or Philemon or some other Greek. The fact that a play by Plautus, or even by Caecilius, was *verbally* quite different from the Greek would not bother them – verbal changes were part of the job of translation. It was the changes in *structure* – for example, the addition of a second lover – in the *Andria* which caught the jealous eye of the old rival playwright Luscius Lanuvinus and led to his denunciation of Terence for 'playing about' with his originals.

If keeping close to an original was all that was asked of a Roman dramatist, success would not have been difficult to achieve. But mere fidelity was not what was really wanted, nor would it have guaranteed success. What the Romans enjoyed was a play in their own idiom.

It must not be thought that Terence was indifferent to stage success. The friendship of the great has its value. But it is a poor substitute for the dramatist's real reward, the applause of the multitude. The repeated failure of the *Hecyra* and the querulous tone of some of Terence's remarks in his prologues about the public – *populus studio stupidus* and the like – must not obscure the fact that Terence was a master of stage technique. But his mastery is of a different order from that of Plautus. There is not a play of Terence, there is scarcely a line of Terence, which we could imagine written by Plautus.

Now it is always possible that the difference was largely the result of choice of originals; Plautus liked one sort of Greek play, Terence another. We have learned a good deal from the discovery of the *Dyscolus*. Perhaps other plays will turn up all complete and perhaps it will then be seen that what Terence did was simply to look for originals which had those dramatic qualities which he admired. What these qualities were is, I think, clear: intelligent intrigue and contrast of character.

Intelligent intrigue and contrast of character are scarcely to be found in Plautus. Plautus gives us farce – a succession of fireworks; as one fades another lights up the sky. Terence gives us comedy. The difference between the *Menaechmi* and the *Adelphi* is the difference between farce and comedy.

To see Terence's mind at work, it is natural to turn to his first play, which most people agree to be the *Andria*. Right through the play runs a closely-knit intrigue. Pamphilus has formed a secret union with the poor girl Glycerium. His father Simo intends that he shall marry Philaenium, daughter of their wealthy neighbour Chremes. Davus, the slave of Pamphilus, intends to spoil this plan of Simo. But Davus has so over-reached himself that neither of the old gentlemen is likely to put any trust in anything he says. Glycerium has just given birth to a child – Pamphilus' child. This fact, if known for a fact to Chremes, would put an end to the preparations for his daughter's marriage to Pamphilus. But no statement by Davus would carry conviction. What does he do? Mysis, the woman-servant of Glycerium, is on the stage; Davus brings out the baby and tells her to lay it on Simo's threshold. Chremes is seen approaching; Davus dashes off, leaving the bewildered Mysis alone to confront the astonished Chremes; then Davus returns and accuses Mysis of palming off some stranger's baby as that of Pamphilus. Mysis hotly denies this; Chremes, listening, discerns in her voice the ring of truth. Horrified, he rushes into Simo's house to announce that the wedding is off. Mysis bitterly reproaches Davus for the way in which he has treated her. He replies, 'You silly woman, don't you know what I've been at?' She replies, 'How should I know?' He says, 'That was the father-in-law; it was the only way to let him into what we want him to know.' 'But', she expostulates, 'you should have told me beforehand.' He answers, 'Do you think it makes so little difference whether you say things honestly and naturally, or after preparation?'

Even if we suppose that these words, and the whole scene, come straight from Menander, do they not show a sense of acting as an art? I know no parallel in Plautus, or indeed in Greek drama, to this scene. All the evidence points to one clear fact: Terence was an artist in comedy.

In turning to Seneca, I must ring up the curtain on a different background. We are in Imperial Rome, the luxurious, dangerous atmosphere of Nero's court. On this gloomy stage Seneca appears – the great statesman, philosopher and author.

A cleavage of opinion separates Anglo-Saxon scholars from most European scholars with regard to the purpose for which these tragedies were written. We of the Atlantic Alliance believe that the plays were written for private reading or declamation – not for performance in the theatre. Moreover we think little of them as plays. Here is Mr Barker on Seneca, in the *Oxford Classical Dictionary*: 'In the tragedies we meet no product or promise of a balanced artist-mind, but the primitive thought-forms, rough-hewn idola, and nightmares risen out of a tortured egoist's unconscious mind. Everywhere are traceable the erratic ability and the limitations which are common stigmata of paranoiac abnormality.' This of the writer whom a Continental scholar calls the greatest writer of tragedy in the gulf of time between the death of Euripides and the rise of Shakespeare – two thousand years! Thus the Anglo-Saxons tend to depart not only from Europe but even from our own ancestors and fellow-countrymen of the Elizabethan Age. For it is Shakespeare who describes the repertoire of the strolling players who visit Elsinore by saying that they can do anything from Plautus to Seneca.

I am concerned in the first place with the immediate purpose for which the tragedies were written. They can of course be acted; they were acted in the University in sixteenth-century England. But there are some points which have to be considered here.

We know that in the Imperial age plays were often written for declamation: witness Juvenal, *Satire I*, lines 3–6. We have no certain information of any play being written for performance. The only plays mentioned as being performed in the Imperial age are old plays of the Republican period. We know that the literary class of Rome were self-conscious, that they made a show of despising the entertainments of the people. Seneca himself records the tedium of a visit to the amphitheatre. It is true that we hear of *libretti* written for pantomime by established poets, and earning their authors large fees; but these would, presumably, be *cantica*, songs on stock themes, not at all the same thing as plays.

Some of the scenes in the plays would be difficult to stage. For though the spectator's imagination may supply almost any material want, it is a different matter to ask him to imagine as absent something which is obviously present.

In Seneca's *Hippolytus* the hero's mangled corpse is brought on to the stage, and is pieced together before our eyes by his father Theseus:

> *Be firm, my hands, for your sad purpose now;*
> *Be dry, my eyes, and check the tears that flow,*
> *While I the parts assemble, and employ*
> *My efforts to re-constitute my boy.*
> *What is this ugly, shapeless piece, I wonder,*
> *On every side with gashes torn asunder?*
> *What part of thee it is I cannot see;*

I only know that part it is of thee.
Here will I set it . . . not its proper home . . .
Not . . . the . . . right . . . place, I know . . . but . . . where there's room!

In the *Hercules Furens* the hero murders his wife and children before our eyes; we see his club crashing through their skulls. In the *Medea* the heroine murders her children in full view and throws the body of one down from the roof to his father below on the stage. Perhaps dummies could be used for all these scenes. But what of the scene in the *Medea* where, after a speech has been attributed to Medea, another character asks her why she has been standing in gloomy silence? I am specially puzzled by the scene beginning at line 618 of the *Hercules Furens*. Hercules and Theseus enter dragging with them the monstrous three-headed dog Cerberus. Hercules warns all to avert their eyes from him. News of Lycus' plot summons Hercules from the stage. Does the dog go too? Theseus remains, and in the next two hundred lines gives a detailed account of how they brought the dog from Hades up to earth. I ask myself how this was staged. Why did Hercules ask all not to look? And what is the tragic effect of Theseus' long speech, if all the time he is holding on to the dog? I feel that the dog neither comes on nor goes off. He seems to fade out, like the Cat in *Alice in Wonderland*.

For these and other reasons I cannot believe that these tragedies were meant for performance. But the reading for which they were meant would be declamation – probably by the author in person. He would use all his arts to impress his audience. I imagine that he dressed with particular care, that he gargled and tried out his highest and his lowest notes, on the morning of the great day.

The object was to impress the listeners, but with the hammer-blows of rhetoric. Over-statement is carried to the limit. This is characteristic of the Silver Age. I remember country fairs in which a favourite competition was to show one's strength by bringing a heavy mallet down on a metal plate operating a spring. The force of one's blow was shown by the indicator which ran up the pole. A real snorter sent the indicator up to the top of the pole, a bell rang, and one got one's money back. 'Great Strength', said the notice, 'Returns the Penny.' I am tempted to think of those fairs when I read Silver Latin, always striving to outdo previous records.

In the constant straining for effect the subtle has no place, the simple and the natural gain no marks. Black and white character drawing, ferocious villains, milkwhite victims, ghastly descriptions, Byronic defiance, flamboyant repartee, meet us on almost every page. The reciter is trying, we feel, to go one better than any previous reciter. Furthermore, we are bethumped and stunned by erudition. Juno, surveying the starry heavens, reads there the record of her husband's infidelities. 'Yonder the Bear, high up in the icy North, guards the Argive ships; yonder he shines who bore the Tyrian Europa across the waves; there the Atlantides put forth their band ... here Orion terrifies the gods ... and golden Perseus has his stars; the bright constellation of the Tyndaridae shines yonder, and they at whose birth the unsteady land stood firm.' How many of us, unless we have just edited a Classical Dictionary, would recognize in these lines references to seven distinct amours of Jupiter? There is also the revelling in the ghoulish. Here, in the *Oedipus*, Manto consults the omens. 'With no gentle motion do the entrails quake and shiver, but my whole hand do they cause to tremble. The heart, diseased through and through, is withered, and lies deep hidden, and the veins are of livid hue. A great part of the entrails is wanting, and from the rotting liver oozes forth BLACK GALL!'

And yet we have to admit that these plays, such as they are, were read and admired by the men who created our own drama. Part of what they borrowed was mechanical; at a time when there was nothing with any form in English drama, these plays, with their efficient structure, their five acts divided by choral songs, as laid down by Horace, their famous personages, their thrilling plots, their reflective choruses, had a fascination for the Elizabethans, and indeed for all Europe. But further I find in Seneca a certain sense of the theatrical, of dramatic timing, which may

have been nearer than was Greek tragedy to Elizabethan sensibilities. In the *Troades* there is the scene where Andromache,
trying to save her little son Astyanax from the Greek victor,
conceals him in Hector's tomb, and then confronts Ulysses with
the truthful statement that her son is gone to the tomb and lies
among the dead. The gradual awakening of suspicion on Ulysses'
part, the cunning with which he plays on the mother's fears, till
she calls the child out, her plea for mercy and its failure, the
child's one and only utterance, 'Pity me, Mother!', before he is
led off to death – form together a powerful scene. Again, Phaedra's disclosure of her passion to Hippolytus is quite different
from the scene in Euripides, where it is the old servant who
reveals the secret which Phaedra would have concealed till death.

Is there not something to be said for Seneca's re-casting of the
story? If Phaedra comes out of it more tarnished, is she not also
more real?

In these scenes – the search for the condemned victim, the
disclosure of passion by woman to man – can we not see the
Rome of his day, its informers and the woman-dominated palace
of the Caesars?

A great dramatic moment has something abrupt about it; it
must hit us like a blow. Such a moment we may find in Seneca's
Oedipus, when the king relentlessly forces the reluctant Phorbas
to confess who the child was whom he rescued; and when Oedipus
knows that the child is himself he is still far from knowing the
full horror of his situation. He must still elicit the further point –
'born of what mother?' to which comes the dreadful reply 'born
of your wife'. Here we have the sort of sledge-hammer effect
which impressed the Elizabethans.

The dialogue is often powerful – especially in that Roman
feature, repartee. When the Nurse points out to Medea the weakness of her position:

> *Colchis is far away, your husband lost;*
> *Of all your riches nothing now remains.*

Medea flashes out the swift reply:

Plautus, Terence and Seneca

Medea now remains! Land, sea, sword, fire,
God and the thunderbolt, are found in me!

There are also undeniably moving passages, especially in the choruses, where we see that after all these are the works of a great mind. There is the address to Sleep over the prostrate body of Hercules:

O sleep, conqueror of woes, rest of the soul, the better part of human life, brother of Death; O thou who art peace after wanderings, haven of life, day's respite and night's comrade, who comest alike to king and slave, sweetly and gently soothe his weary spirit.

There is the terrible sense of blood-guiltiness:

What Tanais, what Nile, what Tigris can cleanse this hand? Though cold Maeotis should pour its northern sea upon me, though the whole ocean should stream along my hands, yet will the deep stains cling.

Need I remind you of the famous far-off English echoes of these passages:

Sleep that knits up the ravelled sleeve of care.

Will all great Neptune's ocean wash this blood
Clean from my hand?

Sleepe after toyle, port after stormie seas,
Ease after warre, death after life does greatly please.

W. Beare

PART TWO

EUROPEAN DRAMA

VIII:

'THE SPANISH TRAGEDY' AND 'HAMLET': TWO EXERCISES IN ENGLISH SENECA

IT IS NOT USUAL TO CONSIDER SENECA A GREAT dramatist today. But he was one to the Elizabethans, and his influence played its part in the making of two of the best-known plays of the Elizabethan theatre. Neither *The Spanish Tragedy* nor *Hamlet* is adequately described as an exercise in English Seneca; there is so much more to each of them. Yet they have both derived enough from the Roman tragedian as he appeared to their age to make the description valid in some essential respects.

By the second half of the sixteenth century many educated Englishmen saw Seneca as a fine example of tragedy conceived and written in the high style in accordance with the precepts of Aristotle as these were interpreted (or misinterpreted) by neo-classical critics. Seneca gave outsize personages, five acts and impassioned speeches. He gave a stoic view of the world, showing heroic persons unyielding in their conflict with one another and with Fate. English society did not need encouragement from outside to develop an attitude to revenge. A cult of revenge is inseparable from that of honour in every incompletely civilized community in which law does not dominate. Seneca made the subject of revenge academically respectable in drama. By way of the universities and the Inns of Courts, and to a much lesser extent, of the upper forms of some of the grammar schools, the Roman tragedian helped to develop the popular theatrical *genre*, revenge tragedy or the tragedy of blood.

Seneca did not offer violence and revenge to a society hitherto immune to both; he merely showed the Elizabethans one way (and a way which they enjoyed) of treating themes which were in any case of interest to them. He also supplied them with examples of some of the paraphernalia which became common in popular revenge tragedy, the Ghost demanding vengeance, the prologue, which in the case of *Thyestes* probably helped to develop the later Induction.

To Englishmen who were trying (rightly or wrongly) to create or re-create a vernacular literature by classical example and precept, Seneca was an incomparable model. To them his superb command of language was exercised as a weapon in the service of the stage. For us to understand how they could see him in this light we must disregard certain modern notions about performance and style.

The modern critic observes quite correctly that Seneca did not write for the theatre but for recitation, or what is sometimes called rhetorical declamation; as a result, the argument runs, he was not really a dramatist. Nevertheless, it is undeniable that the Elizabethans certainly regarded him as one and do not seem to have been unduly dismayed by the fact that he wrote for recitation, not for theatrical performance. They did not make the modern distinction between reciting and acting.

Today, to recite is not to act; in the sixteenth century it was. Neither the actor nor the reciter did what we know as recitation, they both acted. The Elizabethan reciting Seneca was as completely identified as the modern Englishman acting Wesker. Whether the Elizabethan recited the words of Atreus or acted those of Hamlet or of Hieronimo, he was completely identified, behaving in each case as if he were the person whom he represented. In rhetorical delivery as in acting it was essential to feel as if one were the imagined character and to communicate thought, feeling and want by means of 'lively action'. Evidence exists to show that the training of boys in 'recitation' involved accustoming them to imagine themselves to have the same need as the speaker to utter the words; emotion must be truthfully and intensely felt and communicated. And some of the practices of the modern acting school which we owe to the influence of Stanislavski were known to the Elizabethan grammar school thanks to the influence of the Roman rhetoricians, notably to that of Quintilian. Elizabethan recitation was acting.[1]

In these circumstances to recite Seneca was in essential elements the same as to act Kyd or Shakespeare. The words had to be

[1] See B. L. Joseph, *Elizabethan Acting* (2nd ed. 1964), pp. 5 ff, 10 ff, 40.

thought in each case as those of the character; they had to be used to communicate his feeling and want to obtain an objective. And trained voice, face and bodily movement were brought into action to these ends. What the audience saw seemed to be the very character come to life, but in such a way that virtuosity of physical movement gave aesthetic satisfaction in its own right. What the audience heard was the sound natural to human beings expressing thought, emotion and desire, but in such a way that the pattern of articulate sound was simultaneously an artist's created relationship of words expressing ideas. I suggest that the difference between Seneca recited by Elizabethans and Kyd performed by them was fundamentally like that between the concert performance and the theatrical performance of opera, or between the radio performance and the theatrical performance of a play. I do not know whether this analogy holds good of the Roman performance of Seneca in his own time. Possibly it does, as Latin writers on 'recitation' agree with the Elizabethans and the moderns on identification and truthful expression of emotion. But we are concerned here with what Seneca was for the Elizabethans.

To understand more fully what he was for them we have to abandon a second modern notion, this time one which concerns style as that is related to the subject known as rhetoric. The Elizabethan was taught to regard 'the figures', 'the tropes and schemes' as a means, not an end. The end was full, clear and elegant expression in which style and subject were one. To make style an end in itself was as alien to the spirit of Elizabethan 'rhetoric' as it is to that of modern criticism. The combination of confusion and sheer ignorance of much modern thinking about 'rhetoric' cannot be better illustrated than by the remark which I sometimes receive from pupils to the effect that the verbal patterns of *The Spanish Tragedy* are simple while those of *Macbeth* are complex. The reverse is true. *The Spanish Tragedy* has verbal patterns which are much more complex than anything in *Macbeth*; but the patterns of meaning in *Macbeth* are much more complex than those of *The Spanish Tragedy*. Our modern tendency is not to recognize the fact that a figure exists when it serves the end of perfect expression, with the result that too often we equate 'rhetoric' mistakenly with bad writing.

As a stylistic model to English writers as a whole, and so to Shakespeare in particular, Seneca contributed to the richness, strength and precision which he exhibits as a user of language. The modern danger is to acknowledge the contribution as it shows itself negatively in Polonius' admission that ' "'tis true 'tis pity;/And pity 'tis, 'tis true" is "a foolish figure".' We all hasten to agree with him; this, it is commonly declared, is an example of the dangers of studying 'rhetoric'. But I have not found anyone making the same sort of judgment on the same figure, *antimetabole*, in Lucius' approval of the seeming youth, Fidele:

> *Thy name well fits thy faith, thy faith thy name.*
>
> (*Cymbeline*, IV, ii, 384)

It is not the figure that is foolish, but the way in which Polonius uses it. He cannot resist its mechanical ingenuity. But in his case, as in that of Lucius, Shakespeare the dramatist uses the figure to create and communicate to us the imagined character. It would be valid to make the generalization that in *The Spanish Tragedy* Kyd is too often dominated by 'figures', but that they always serve Shakespeare's dramatic needs in *Hamlet*. It is not that *Hamlet* is 'less rhetorical' than *The Spanish Tragedy*. As a matter of fact there is more 'rhetorical' ingenuity in Hamlet's, 'A little more than kin and less than kind', than there is in Belimperia's:

> *Accursed brother, unkind murderer,*
> *Why bend thou thus thy mind to martyr me.*

But the complexity of meaning and the flexibility of rhythm of the passage from *Hamlet* are both much richer and more dramatic than those of the passage from *The Spanish Tragedy*.

When we are tempted to deplore the Elizabethan standards which found Seneca a great dramatist and fine user of language, I think we ought to keep in mind the fact that these standards helped to foster the art of Shakespeare, and that by them Ben Jonson was able to find Shakespeare great as well as Seneca. And there were many Elizabethans whose taste may not have been as impeccable as Jonson's but who found much to amuse them in the excesses of *The Spanish Tragedy*.

Hamlet and *The Spanish Tragedy* share some of the obvious characteristics of English Seneca. Hamlet has no induction, but they each have a ghost, a mad or seemingly mad revenger, a female who goes mad and kills herself (even if Ophelia may not be strictly a suicide); they each have a dumbshow (there are two in *The Spanish Tragedy*) and a play within a play. These last two features do not belong to the legacy of Seneca; but he certainly contributed to the violence and bloody slaughter of both plays.

The revenger in each play delays until he is certain of the murderer's identity. Hieronimo distrusts the letter written in blood, 'For want of ink'; Hamlet distrusts the Ghost's assertion that Claudius is a murderer. Some readers might insist that Hamlet does not really delay out of distrust of the Ghost, but makes that the rationalization of his dislike of the deed; but the similarity between the two plots remains. In *Hamlet* the guilty Claudius engineers his own destruction as a result of his plan to destroy his nephew; in *The Spanish Tragedy* Lorenzo unintentionally arranges for his guilt to be betrayed to Hieronimo as a result of his plan to keep it secret for ever. Both Hamlet and Horatio are isolated in a court full of festivity, most members of whom have no idea that a murder has been committed in secret and has to be avenged. And each avenger must throw off the scent the guilty who would so easily destroy him. Hamlet sees a reproach for his own failures in the Player's articulate grief for Hecuba, and in the readiness with which Fortinbras and his men risk their lives for what is no more than an illusion of honour, 'a trick of fame'. Hieronimo feels reproached for his delay by the grief of the Old Man, Don Bazulto, who is 'the lively image of my grief'. A few moments earlier he bade Don Bazulto:

> *Here take my handkercher, and wipe thine eyes,*
> *Whiles wretched I in thy mishaps may see*
> *The lively portrait of my dying self.*
>
> (III, xiii, 83–5)

With such obvious similarities between the plots of the two plays it is not surprising that a number of short passages in *Hamlet* could fittingly be applied to incidents in *The Spanish Tragedy*. Gertrude's state of mind as she hears about Ophelia is well expressed in the couplet:

> *So full of artless jealousy is guilt*
> *It spills itself in fearing to be spilt.*
>
> (IV, v, 19–20)

But this is also a *sententia* with a comment on the nature of guilt in general. And it has an additional particular application to what happens in the second half of the play. It states explicitly what will be true of Claudius' 'jealousy', of his determination not to be caught napping, but to forestall Hamlet. The failure of the attempt to destroy the Prince in England brings him back to a new situation in Denmark, in which Claudius thinks he can use Laertes and the poisoned sword and drink. This 'jealousy' is shown to be 'artless' in essence, when it leads not only to the death of Hamlet, but to that of Claudius himself.

Perfectly as Gertrude's lines belong to *Hamlet* they could be fittingly applied to the attempt made by Lorenzo to keep his guilt secret in *The Spanish Tragedy*. It would be more difficult to find a character so fitted to speak them as Gertrude. Instead of expressing foreboding they would probably have to be used to express Hieronimo's triumph when Pedringano's death reveals what it is intended to hide for ever. Shakespeare's couplet would be an improvement on the lines which Kyd has given his avenger:

> *O sacred heavens, may it come to pass*
> *That such a monstrous and detested deed,*
> *So closely smother'd and so long conceal'd,*
> *Shall thus by this be venged or reveal'd.*
>
> (III, vii, 47–50)

When Claudius has decided to have Hamlet killed in England the intensity of his awareness of the danger in which he stands is expressed in this assertion:

Two Exercises in English Seneca

> *Diseases desperate grown*
> *By desperate appliance are reliev'd,*
> *Or not at all.*
>
> (IV, iii, 9–11)

This might easily be put into the mouth of Lorenzo determining to destroy his accomplices. In each case, without the murderer knowing it, the desperate appliance does not relieve the disease at all.

Some short passages in each play might fittingly be exchanged for equivalents in the other. Isabella insists:

> *The heavens are just, murder cannot be hid,*
> *Time is the author both of truth and right,*
> *And time will bring this treachery to light.*
>
> (II, v, 57–9)

From Hamlet in similar circumstances we hear:

> *Foul deeds will rise,*
> *Though all the earth o'erwhelm them, to men's eyes.*
>
> (I, ii, 256–7)

Hamlet's realization of the monstrous quality of what has gone wrong in Denmark brings from him:

> *The time is out of joint. O cursed spite,*
> *That ever I was born to set it right!*
>
> (I, v, 189–90)

Hieronimo has an equivalent moment of revulsion when confronted with Pedringano's unrepentant levity:

> *O monstrous times, where murder's set so light.*
>
> (III, vi, 95)

Lorenzo replies to Balthazar's refusal to believe that they have been betrayed:

> *A guilty conscience, urged with the thought*
> *Of former evils easily cannot err.*
>
> (III, iv, 14–15)

127

The equivalent in *Hamlet* comes from Gertrude:

> *To my sick soul, as sin's true nature is,*
> *Each toy seems prologue to some great amiss.*
>
> (IV, v, 17–18)

Of course it is possible to explain such similarities by postulating *The Spanish Tragedy* as the source of a conjectural *Ur-Hamlet*. And in his very able Introduction to Kyd's works, F. S. Boas gives a detailed list of passages in support of an argument that the First Quarto of *Hamlet* contains lines written by Kyd which come from the *Ur-Hamlet*. I am concerned with a different connection between the two plays, one that does not rely on proof that Kyd's hand is to be seen in both, or that Shakespeare's *Hamlet* is a later form of something for which *The Spanish Tragedy* served as a source. I think it very unlikely that Shakespeare had not read *The Spanish Tragedy*; indeed I have long conjectured privately that Juliet's Nurse was all the funnier for Elizabethans because her, '"Twas no need, I trow,/To bid me trudge', reminded them of Hieronimo, armed with poniard and rope, declaring: 'Hieronimo, 'tis time for thee to trudge'. There may be the same sort of echo in Lennox's, 'And the right-valiant Banquo walk'd too late; . . . Men must not walk too late' (*Macbeth*, III, vi, 5–7). When the Third Watchman asks Pedringano, 'Why hast thou thus unkindly kill'd the man?' the reply comes, 'Why? because he walk'd abroad so late' (III, iii, 39–40).

The point which I think it is important to make, however, is that what Shakespeare (if he read *The Spanish Tragedy*) found especially significant for his own treatment of *Hamlet* is associated with Revenge's words to the disgusted Ghost of Andrea when Horatio has been killed:

> *Thou talk'st of harvest when the corn is green:*
> *The end is crown of every work well done;*
> *The sickle comes not till the corn be ripe.*
>
> (II, vi, 7–9)

There is a similar passage in one of the Player King's speeches in *Hamlet*:

Two Exercises in English Seneca

Purpose is but the slave to memory,
Of violent birth, but poor validity;
Which now, the fruit unripe, sticks on the tree;
But fall unshaken when they mellow be.

(III, ii, 183–86)

In each play a Ghost urges haste, deplores delay in the vengeance which will give him peace. And in each an avenger delays, partly because of uncertainty as to the identity of the murderer, partly because of his strength in a court which does not even suspect that murder has been committed, and eventually finds himself in a position to strike as the result of the murderer's own actions. The implication is that human beings are involved in something out of their control, something which is nevertheless controlled by a supernatural power, in whose own good time the necessary end will be attained as the result of an inter-action between Fortune and human will. Hieronimo comes near to saying this explicitly when he decides not to kill himself:

Then stay, Hieronimo, attend their will,
For mortal men may not appoint their time.

(III, xiii, 4–5)

And a few minutes later in the same speech:

Wise men will take their opportunity
Closely and safely fitting things to time.
But in extremes advantage hath no time:
And therefore all times fit not for revenge.

(25–8)

As one Ghost relies on Hamlet for vengeance, so the other looks to his friend Horatio. But Andrea's Ghost is astounded when the first move towards his promised vengeance turns out to be the death of Horatio, the apparent avenger. This is the devious way in which Revenge works; this is a spirit which takes human character and Fortune into account, and is confident that the murder of Horatio will lead to the death of Balthazar who killed Andrea; and eventually this is what happens. No matter what the

129

mortals intend, what they achieve is what Revenge has planned. In the words of the Player King:

> *Our wills and fates do so contrary run*
> *That our devices still are overthrown;*
> *Our thoughts are ours, their ends none of our own.*

(Hamlet, III, ii, 206–8)

Andrea's Ghost is avenged because Hieronimo is prepared to wait for his opportunity, because Lorenzo betrays himself in his confident machination, because circumstances allow Belimperia and the Marshal to have their unwitting victims expose themselves 'in jest' to what is murder in reality; Lorenzo learns most unexpectedly how correct he has been in telling Balthazar:

> *Our greatest ills we least mistrust, my lord,*
> *And inexpected harms do hurt us most.*

(III, iv, 4–5)

Hamlet is pervaded with a similar irony. Whatever motivation individual critics see fit to allow the Prince the plot continues to show us a duel between two adversaries each of whom regards the other as highly dangerous. Time after time it looks as if one or the other of them will strike, until with Hamlet unexpectedly back in Denmark, Claudius' guilt, overflowing with 'artless jealousy', demands swift and deadly policy to preserve itself. Like Lorenzo, Claudius is not to be moved from his purpose:

> *That we would do,*
> *We should do when we would.*

(IV, vii, 118–9)

But this very determination, this very refusal to delay, delivers Claudius over to his nephew's vengeance. The guilt which he wants to hide is revealed by the dying Laertes, the treachery with sword and wine is exposed in public; the sword which he prepared for Hamlet pierces Claudius; the wine poisoned to destroy his nephew is poured down his own throat, after both sword and wine have each claimed another unintended victim. So the engineer is hoist 'with his own petar'.

Two Exercises in English Seneca

Like Kyd, Shakespeare does not suggest that these things happen merely as a matter of chance, they are not entirely fortuitous. Shakespeare also sees the events which he imagines in his plot as connected coherently one with another, moving one and all towards the end desired by the Power which dominates men's lives in their revenges as in their more hallowed activities. Where Kyd postulates a spirit, Revenge, in control of events, it seems to me that Shakespeare writes in unassailable confidence that Divine Providence governs both the world of *Hamlet* as he imagines it and the real world of human beings as he lives in it.

In that brief pause as the swiftly moving action seems to gather new breath to hurtle on to the *catastrophe*, Hamlet confides in Horatio: 'Yet thou wouldst not think how ill all's here about my heart'. Yet he will not let his friend persuade him to 'forestall their repair hither'. Hamlet has had enough of trying to assess possibilities, of balancing pros and cons. His recent experiences have taught him better. He can see this moment as the outcome of plans gone astray on both sides, of attempts made or half-made. Neither he nor Claudius has managed to achieve anything more than survive without being able to destroy his enemy. Remembering how the odds were against him when he left for England, Hamlet insists that in a world ruled by Providence rashness ('And prais'd be rashness for it') may often carry a man further towards his goal than the coolest of prudent planning. Earlier he has assured Horatio:

> *let us know,*
> *Our indiscretion sometime serves us well,*
> *When our deep plots do pall.*

The lesson of this for him has been:

> *and that should learn us*
> *There's a divinity that shapes our ends,*
> *Rough-hew them how we will.*
>
> (V, ii, 7–11)

This is the doctrine of a world governed by Divine Providence as it was known to Elizabethan Anglicans and Papists and to many whom we would call Separatists or Puritans; it was certainly accepted by Milton. The ends of Providence are achieved through an inter-action between human Free-Will and Fortune. Claudius willed Hamlet's death in England, but in acting rashly Hamlet preserved himself. In his freely-willed decisions, in those of Claudius, in the chance that brought the pirate ship, in the sudden parting of the two vessels that let Hamlet come back to Denmark, in all these he now perceives the working of Providence. Providence takes cognizance of such facts as that he has once learned 'to write fair' and that he has his father's signet in his purse, 'Which was the model of that Danish seal'. These are not the workings of chance, 'Why even in that was heaven ordinant'.

Hamlet has learned like Hieronimo to wait for his opportunity. Now he relies on the certainty that Providence does not let evil flourish for ever. If Providence intends to use him to destroy Claudius, 'this canker of our nature', whatever he does, whether he fights now or postpones the duel till later, it does not matter, the moment of revenge will come.

That is why Hamlet answers Horatio: 'Not a whit, we defy augury: there is a special providence in the fall of a sparrow'. If the moment for which he waits 'be now, 'tis not to come; if it be not to come, it will be now; if it be not now, yet it will come'. What matters is 'the readiness is all'. In *The Spanish Tragedy* Hieronimo says much the same:

> *attend their will,*
> *For mortal men may not appoint their time.*

Behind the words 'the readiness is all' lies much renaissance thinking and comment on the way in which men and affairs ripen to maturity, on the inability of men to foresee the moment of their own death, on the uselessness of trying to harvest 'when the corn is green', on the need to wait patiently until the moment for action arrives; then, when it has made itself, action must be devastatingly swift against an adversary caught off balance. In this last meaning Hamlet's statement overlaps that made by

Edgar in *King Lear*. For each, 'ripeness is all'; for each, events have worked themselves out under Providence to a moment of opportunity which is about to be taken. Edgar knows that his has come; Hamlet knows that if his revenge serves the end of Providence it will come either now or later, and when it comes he must and will act. In the Good Quarto (1604) he adds: 'since no man of ought he leaves, knows what ist to leave betimes'. This I gloss as: 'since no man knows of anything he leaves, what is it to leave at the right moment – no man knows enough about anything that he leaves to know if he is leaving it at the right moment'. It follows naturally that he ends with the calm decision, 'let be'.

Having learned the lesson, Hamlet serves the end of Providence; Claudius serves the same end although he has not learned the lesson. His planning is used by Providence as much as Hamlet's refusal to plan. For the success of his plan Claudius relies on Hamlet's readiness to meet Laertes and show his own skill; and because Hamlet fights, Claudius is killed. When they are both dead Horatio is left alive in a position at last to

> *speak to th' yet unknowing world*
> *How these things came about.*

The end of Providence has been attained, the eradication of evil, the time has been 'set' right.

It is obvious that *Hamlet* is a better play than *The Spanish Tragedy*. Shakespeare's skill is superior to Kyd's in plot construction, in blank verse, in characterization. But even if Kyd had possessed craftsmanship equal to Shakespeare's this would not have made his play fundamentally better than it is, so long as it continued to be a contrived demonstration of the thesis that Revenge rules the world, working deviously through human beings and Fortune. Where Kyd did not really believe this to be true (as a result of which his play suffers in every respect), Shakespeare writes as if he really did believe that the world as it exists and has existed since the Fall is subject to the onslaughts of evil, but is never out of the control of Providence. Human beings suffer grievously from these evil onslaughts, but through Fortune, through spirits, through men and women, good and bad, God's Providence attains its ends, and these are always good. I suggest that Shakespeare is not primarily concerned to weigh the pros and cons of revenge as a code; he concentrates on the fact that it is harsh, has terrible consequences for individual human beings, yet thanks to Divine Providence, can be used for good – so can everything, no matter how evil it may be. Hamlet is shown as serving Providence in his revenge, however savage that is in itself. He is certain that he will have his revenge only if it serves the ends of Providence. And Shakespeare seems to be affirming his own conviction that in real life, as in this play, nothing happens that does not come within the scope of a special providence, no matter how big or small, how good or bad it may be. I do not hold this view myself; nevertheless, to suspend my disbelief and imagine the world of *Hamlet* in terms of it is a satisfying aesthetic experience. What Kyd inherited from Seneca makes a very imperfect play. Shakespeare utilizes his inheritance to create a first-class tragedy.

B. L. Joseph

IX: TOWARDS

A DEFINITION OF FORM

IN DRAMA

IN RECENT YEARS AFTER ALMOST TWO CENTURIES OF neglect there is apparent among critics of literature and to some extent among writers themselves a growing concern with the questions and problems of form in the literary arts.[1] Evidence for this developing interest in form, especially in drama but also in non-dramatic poetry, could be adduced from many sources but I will mention two books only to which I wish to refer. The first of these is *Form and Meaning in Drama*, published in 1956 by that penetrating interpreter of Greek tragedy H. D. F. Kitto. The second is John Gassner's *Form and Idea in Modern Theatre*, published likewise in 1956.[2] Though Kitto nowhere in his book attempts a complete definition or exhaustive examination of the meaning of form in drama, his analyses and interpretations of Greek and Elizabethan plays and his comparisons of their differing structures do serve to give some fairly concrete ideas of his conception of form and its significance. In fact at the outset in his preface he makes the following revealing declaration:

> I have come to believe more firmly, and I hope to follow more consistently as a principle of criticism, the idea that in a great work of art, whether a play, a picture, or a piece of music, the connection between the form and the content is so vital that the two may be said to be ultimately identical.[3]

As a consequence of this conception, Kitto recognizes the uniqueness of form; that is, no two dramas can have exactly the same form and hence must have different meanings. In support of that point of view, he says: '. . . what does a dramatist "say"? It is one theory – and I think it commands respect – that a work

[1] This paper is based upon a manuscript of a book, which I call *The Third Form of Drama*. In the spring of 1960, in essentially its present form, it was delivered as a lecture in the Humanities Series at the University of Illinois.

[2] (London: Methuen & Company, Ltd., c. 1956; New York: The Dryden Press, Inc., 1956).   [3] P. v.

of art means only itself, that if, for example, we are asked what *Antigone* means, the only answer is that it means the *Antigone*.'[1]

In his *Form and Idea in Modern Theatre*, as in his *The Theatre in Our Times*, John Gassner says that the dominant forms in modern theatre and drama are realism, naturalism, and expressionism. In using the term form to designate these and other examples of composition, which I would call styles, Gassner is not alone among writers on later drama and theatre. In that realism, naturalism, and expressionism may be considered not merely different methods of organization and composition, but also as schools of thought about the nature of reality and of man, they certainly may be viewed as determinants of form. Such a point of view, however, raises the question of the meaning of the word form in drama.

The conception of form as shape is reasonably clear when applied to certain visual arts, such as architecture and sculpture, for these are arrangements in space whose effects or impact is readily associated with the shape of the whole. The conception of form in painting, though complicated by the element of colour, is still not too difficult to comprehend as a shape resulting from an arrangement or composition in space. The appeal is to the eye and through the eye to the imagination and understanding. The eye is the sense that most readily apprehends shape. Drama, like music, however, is a time art whose appeal is dominantly tonal, though in production on the stage its effects are both tonal and visual. This dual aspect of drama, which is to a degree present when the play is read with a kinetic imagination from the pages of a book, complicates the whole question of form. The problem of applying the idea of shape to a sequence that is essentially an arrangement in time is difficult enough; but it becomes even more difficult when we note that the effects of the sequence are dominantly tonal and must be apprehended by the ear. Despite the musical critic's talk of pear-shaped tones, the ear is by no means man's best instrument for the apprehension of shapes. Perhaps if we examine a bit more thoroughly just what is involved in the

[1] P. v.

apprehension of form in a space art, say in a work of architecture, we may arrive at some understanding applicable to the time art of drama.

Without entering into the dialectic necessary for the derivation of the deductions, I should like to present three propositions concerning the apprehension of an art object as form. The first of these propositions is that when we contemplate the form of a building we are contemplating the whole – not a segment, not an aspect, but the whole building as an architectural accomplishment. The second proposition is that as a whole the building has a power, creates an effect, and that the effect is aesthetic, a matter of beauty giving pleasure. The third proposition is that the building as a form, that is as a whole, is made up of parts and that the form is the result of the arrangement of those parts. Each of these three propositions or ideas needs further explanation.

There are various kinds of wholes but every whole is made up of parts and hence is divisible into parts. In consequence, one of the rewarding methods of examining any whole is through a part-whole analysis. One of the kinds of wholes with which we are all familiar is the natural or organic whole, such as the oak tree or the human body. Such a whole comes into full formulation through a process of growth and has within its genetic origin the power that brings it into complete form. The parts of the natural whole are related to that whole, not aesthetically, but functionally. Such wholes have within themselves not only the power of growth into full formulation, but also the power of reproduction. A second kind of whole well known to all of us is a quantitative whole – a bushel of potatoes, say, or a cord of wood. There is no functional arrangement of the parts in such a whole and no comparative relationship of part to part. A bushel of potatoes may be made up of small potatoes, medium-sized potatoes, and large potatoes, so long as the total measure of potatoes weighs sixty pounds. A quantitative whole is still made up of parts but the parts can be of varying size and in any order without affecting the wholeness. Finally, there are artificial wholes or made wholes, such as a shoe, a musical composition, or a play. In such wholes the size, the shape, and the arrangement of the parts are of utmost importance. A shoe is a whole made up of a certain number of parts put together in exactly the right way if it is to have its proper power, effect, or function. Such wholes cannot, like natural wholes, come into being by their own genetically acquired inner powers. They require a maker who through artifice constructs the form by the right arrangement of the parts. Nor can such wholes reproduce themselves. Certain artificial wholes, the shoe for example, have as their end utility and hence their utilitarian function dominates their formulation. Other artificial wholes have as their end or power certain kinds of effects and their formulation is dominated by considerations of beauty in the specific way in which the particular kind of art object can attain beauty and by the function of giving pleasure. The principles of organization of a constructed whole whose primary function is utility are dominated by an end-means relationship; whereas the principles of a constructed whole whose primary function is beauty and pleasure are based upon a form-matter relationship. I hasten to add, however, that both kinds of relationship – end to means and form to matter – may appear in the utilitarian and the non-utilitarian art products.

When a critic considers a play as a whole, he is viewing that play as a form of drama having its proper powers and effects and as no other thing. In such a consideration the form with its powers and effects is the entire justification for the drama without any additional justifications of utility which it may or may not possess. Perhaps this conception will become clearer if we mention some ways in which plays may be examined partially and not as wholes. Shakespeare's plays have been examined and utilized to explain the Ciceronian style of English composition. They are admirable examples of one mode of Ciceronian English. Such a study is thoroughly legitimate but no one would contend that Shakespeare wrote his dramas as examples of English usage. Lily Bess Campbell has written a splendid book on Shakespeare's history plays in which she explores and explains their relations to English Renaissance historiography.[1] That book is a revealing treatment of the conception of history which certainly underlies those plays but, despite their designation in the First Folio, Shakespeare was writing drama and not history. The late Theodore Spenser has given us a masterly study of *Shakespeare and the Nature of Man*, which on the basis of Shakespeare's plays and other English writings clearly and convincingly sets forth the English sixteenth-century conception of man and his place in the universe. Illuminating as the book is, its author would not for a moment claim that Shakespeare was writing philosophy rather than drama.[2] The Chicago historian, Avery Craven, echoing Abraham Lincoln, used to say that *Uncle Tom's Cabin* was a major cause of our Civil War. Considered as a political document *Uncle Tom's Cabin* is the most powerful and effective novel and play ever written in the United States and perhaps in any nation. Considered as a drama, the play is a poorly constructed melodrama of very little artistic merit. One more illustration and I have done. The late Dr Ernest Jones has written a widely-discussed study of *Hamlet* interpreted in the light of Freud's psychology.[3] Revealing as that study may be of Freudian theories, I am quite sure Shakespeare did not compose his tragedy for that purpose. In conclusion, there are many legitimate ways in which plays may be examined and studied and all of these approaches may yield illuminating results. There remains, however, the obligation if we are to understand drama to examine it as a whole, as an art object of a distinctive kind whose artistic quality as a form is its primary justification.

Leaving the second of my propositions, the powers and

[1] *Shakespeare's "Histories"; Mirrors of Elizabethan Policy* (San Marion. California: The Huntington Library, 1947).

[2] Theodore Spencer's *Shakespeare and the Nature of Man* was originally presented in 1942 as the Lowell Lectures at Lowell Institute in Boston. The book was published in that year in New York by The Macmillan Company. A second edition appeared in 1958.

[3] Ernest Jones' first discussion of *Hamlet* as a Freudian document appeared in his *Essays in Applied Psychoanalysis*, published in London in 1922; a second essay on the subject was published in *The American Journal of Psychology*, Vol. XXI, pp. 72 ff. These studies, somewhat revised, appear in Jones' *Hamlet and Oedipus* (New York: W. W. Norton Company, c. 1949).

pleasures of the form, for later discussion in connection with separate forms of drama, I turn to the third proposition, the question of parts that go to make up a whole. When an artist creates a whole, he is faced with not only the problems of inventing the parts but also of ordering and arranging those parts. That is what composition means. Other synonyms are ordering, arranging, formulating – giving form. Plays, like other works of art, may be variously divided into parts, depending upon the way in which the whole is conceived and the principle of division adopted. If we conceive a play as a piece of mimetic art with the emphasis upon the imitation or the rendering, then we can say that the constructed whole has three parts – the object which is imitated, the means by which the object is rendered, and the manner or way in which means and object are joined together. Secondly, a play may be divided into quantitative parts, which in modern discussions we usually refer to as acts and scenes. From the standpoint of form, however, the most important division into parts is the qualitative rather than the quantitative separation. What are those parts which qualify the form? Modern critics state them in different ways. John Galsworthy in his essay 'Some Platitudes concerning the Drama', though he does not specifically call them parts, discusses four – character, plot, dialogue, and 'spire of meaning'.[1] He then argues that the first three are in reality one only – character. He arrives at this conclusion by the argument that in the last analysis plot is nothing more than what specific characters would do in a given situation because by their natures they could not do otherwise and that dialogue is merely the language through which those characters would normally and habitually express themselves in such situations. His qualitative parts are thus in essence reduced to two. Other modern writers usually name four – character, plot, theme, and dialogue – though certain of these writers tend to place theme first among the parts. Such a division seems to me inadequate, for several reasons, in any discussion of drama as a poetic art. One

[1] In John Galsworthy's *The Inn of Tranquillity: Studies and Essays* (New York: Charles Scribner's Sons, 1912).

of the inadequacies appears in this uncertainty concerning the relationship of the parts. Another appears in the matter of definition. What, for example, is meant by theme? Other inadequacies will appear if we turn attention to the examination of a more complete division.

Before stating these, it will be helpful to repeat once again the question involved. Just what are those parts of the whole which the dramatist formulates – that is, orders, arranges, composes – in giving form to a drama? On the basis of his formal definition of tragedy, itself derived from and based upon his examination of the principles of imitation, Aristotle arrived at the division of drama into six causally related and hierarchically arranged qualitative parts.[1] These are in the order of importance, plot, character, thought, diction, music and spectacle. These six parts are variables but are interdependent variables tied together by a dual causal relationship. Read down the list and it will readily be seen that each part is the immediate formal control or cause of the part below it; read up on the list and it will be seen that each part is the material cause of the one above it. Thus the immediate material out of which poets construct plots is characters but the formal determinant of each of the characters is plot. The immediate material out of which dramatists compose characters is thought, including feelings, emotions, passions, deliberations and decisions; but in the constructed whole the formal control of the thought is the kind or nature of the character. Thoughts are materially composed of words but thought formally dictates the choice and arrangement of the words. Diction in the sense of spoken dialogue is made up of harmoniously and meaningfully combined words but the thought and the diction formally dictate the intonation. Music, the intonation of the diction, is basically motion – sound waves – and spectacle in the sense of the agents' actions, which is the spectacle that the poet is chiefly concerned with, is materially movement or motion. The formal relation of

[1] *Poetics*, Chapt. 6. Ingram Bywater, *Aristotle on the Art of Poetry* (Oxford: Clarendon Press; London: Geoffrey Cumberlege, 1920 – and successive reprintings) translates the fifth part as 'Melody.'

music and spectacle is admirably indicated in Hamlet's advice to the Players: 'Suit the action to the word and the word to the action'.

In the formulated play these six parts are so hierarchically and causally related that there is no possibility of including a seventh or *x*-numbered part. Moreover, they represent the whole range from simple movement as mere gesture to the most fully organized and complete human action, which is plot. They are therefore complete and exhaustive.

Plot is the over-all architectonic element of drama. It is the ordering and organizing principle in that without plot the dramatist would not know what characters were requisite to his play, nor how to develop them, nor could he know what thoughts his characters must express, or what words he must compose for their expression. In this sense plot is the first principle of construction. In yet another sense it is the end which the poet in his creative activity is striving to formulate. As the end, plot has the other five parts as means. As the formulation, plot has the other five parts as matter. In its simplest sense plot is the sequence of incidents which makes up the action of the play. But the incidents in a well-constructed play are what the characters, being what they are, would necessarily or probably do, just as their speeches are what they, being themselves, would in such a situation necessarily or probably say. Thus in its broadest sense plot is more than the mere story line of a play. When the dramatist succeeds in moulding the other five parts into a completed plot, he has achieved form.

In formulating a plot the dramatist is engaged in ordering and organizing an action which occurs to and is produced by human agents. Any action occurring to or produced by a human being represents change in the life of the agent and/or the person or persons who suffer the action. All drama, then, deals with change. This change can be dominantly of three different kinds or degrees, though all three occur to some extent in every action organized into a plot. The change can be primarily that which occurs within the agents, such as change of attitude, arousing of emotion or passion, or change in outlook or point of view – all of these are changes in thought. The changes may be somewhat greater and result in a complete change in the natures of the agents; that is, a change in character. In the third and highest degree the change may be entire and represent a completed reversal in the course of the agent's life, that is in his destiny. Such a change, if fully formulated, moves from an inciting or initiating cause or beginning to a dramatically logical – that is probable or necessary – ending. These three elements – thought, character and action – which derive from the object of imitation, represent the three ways in which a plot may be unified or made into a whole.

The plots of *The Trojan Women* and *The Hecuba*, like the plots of certain other Euripidean plays, are primarily unified in terms of thought. The plot of Bertolt Brecht's *The Private Life of the Master Race* is composed of a sequence of disjunctive episodes. What holds this plot together, as in several of his other plays, is primarily thought in the sense of a thesis or an argument. Hence his plays tend to become dominantly didactic. Shakespeare's *King Lear*, on the other hand, is unified in each of the three ways. Lear's division of his kingdom and the consequent banishment of Cordelia and Kent set in train a sequence of events which leads to and culminates in the dramatically logical final catastrophe. In this action antecedents lead with a kind of inevitability to probable consequences; hence the whole play is unified in terms of a whole action. This action results in a drastic change in the character of King Lear and in his thought, whose outcome is that Lear, though he goes down in death, rejoins the human race.

Any significant change within man or in his condition is potentially painful or pleasurable. The most complete change in the human condition is one that moves from one extreme to another; that is from misery to happiness or from happiness to misery. An action involving human suffering and moving from happiness or relative contentment to misery will have different powers or effects from an action moving in the opposite direction, provided the agent or agents are of a certain quality. An action involving an evil man, a Hitler say, which moves from relative happiness to misery and catastrophe would certainly not have the same powers or effects that such an action involving a sympathetic and good man would have. Hence we can readily see that character is material to plot and is a condition of the form. The kind of change which occurs in the action and the kind of man involved in that change are specifications of form. We have customarily called the two categories of form thus far indicated tragedy and comedy but there are other specifications requisite to the genuinely tragic and genuinely comic form. Before examining some of these, I wish to make it quite clear that the terms tragedy and comedy are not evaluative in themselves but are merely designations of form. There are good tragedies, mediocre tragedies, and bad tragedies, and the same may be said of comedy. All are tragedies but tragedies of different qualities. It is necessary to emphasize this, for since the days of the New Humanism in criticism there has been a marked tendency to restrict the term tragedy and thereby make it an evaluative designation. Moreover, it is likewise important to note here that tragedy designates a category of form and that no two plays have exactly the same form. Since form is the result of the ordering of the composition of the parts or elements, it would be impossible for two plays to have precisely the same form. Were they to have the same form, they would have exactly the same parts and composition and hence would not be two separate plays but merely copies of each other. The *Hippolytus* of Euripides and the *Phèdre* of Racine are based upon and tell much the same story but they are utterly different in form and hence different in their powers or effects. The same statement may be made about the *Antony and Cleopatra* of Shakespeare and Dryden's *All for Love; or, the World Well Lost*, and the same contrast applies to the *Antigone* of Sophocles and the *Antigone* of Anouilh, as well as to scores of other similarly paired plays.

All tragedy deals with an immutably serious action but the serious in life is of different degrees and qualities. It is quite serious to a little child to have his box of candy taken from him or to the great business tycoon to have his swollen fortune snatched away. Neither of these situations would make tragedy. The quality of a tragedy then depends in part upon the poet's perception of the nature of high seriousness in the human condition, as well as upon his abilities to render that vision through the proper combination of the parts and elements. The minimum essential of a serious action is twofold; that change must pose a threat to a human being and that human being must be a person of a certain kind of character. In character the person threatened must be sufficiently humane – one like ourselves – to be able to apprehend the threat and sufficiently strong to oppose the threat. Further, he must have qualities of human character that allow us to understand or to sympathize with him in his predicament. He need not be dominantly a good man, though most of the major tragic protagonists are, to win our sympathetic understanding as he suffers the threat to his happiness. He may be as foolish as old Lear and in the progress of his fighting back he may become as evil as Medea or Macbeth. When the tragic protagonist is of such a nature, the effects or powers of the tragic action are quite different from those involving a Hamlet or an Oedipus. To the extent that we the reader or the audience apprehend the threat to the tragic characters and especially to the tragic protagonist, we are emotionally moved to feel varying degrees of uncertainty, ranging from suspense, through apprehension, foreboding and fear. If the threat becomes extreme, it may produce horror and even terror, exaggerated degrees of fear that are usually undesirable in tragedy but acceptable in melodrama. One of the reasons for the restraint upon the element of fear is that it is not included in tragedy for itself alone but as a material basis for pity. The definition of pity, that is tragic pity, reveals the relationship. Pity is that which we feel for another human being; were we in his place we would feel fear. To the degree that we identify and sympathize with the suffering of the person subjected to the fearful situation, to that degree are we able to pity him. There is yet another requirement for tragic pity; it is evoked by a person suffering undeserved misfortune. The only way in which deserts may be determined is by assessment of the character and the action of the victim. To arouse tragic pity then the protagonist must act, must take up such arms as are his to command against the threatening destiny that assails him. Fear and pity are therefore the specific powers of a serious action and they delimit or define the serious. Both the fear and the pity must appear first in the play before they can occur in the audience. Moreover, they will occur in different audiences in varying degrees, depending in part upon factors not truly germane to drama itself. To interpret these powers and catharsis as purely psychological phenomena of audience response is not merely a misinterpretation of their nature but also contributes to the destruction of the idea of form in drama.

The catharsis or purgation must likewise occur in the play before it can affect an audience. How may fear be purged in a serious drama? There are a variety of ways open to the playwright. Remove the threat and the fear disappears, as it does for Orestes in the famous verdict at the end of *The Eumenides*. Conversely, the victim of fear, says Hamlet, may suffer the ultimate consequence of death from the threat. When that occurs, there is no longer fear for Hamlet. Just as the fear occurs in changing form through the play, so does the purgation likewise appear through the whole course of the action. The first great fear for Hamlet appears in his brave resolution to follow the Ghost and that fear is unmistakably in Hamlet and in his companions. When, however, the Ghost does make its full revelation to him and charges him with a threefold obligation, the first fear for Hamlet has disappeared but is replaced by another and stronger apprehension. Since the basic condition of fear arising from a threat is uncertainty, any establishment of certainty in the threatening situation will purge the element of fear.

The catharsis of pity because of the nature of tragic pity is never so complete. Like fear, it occurs in varying modes and degrees throughout the play. We have seen that the condition of pity depends on a kind of person whom we can sympathize with or understand and on his deserts, that is on both his nature and his actions. The fear in Hamlet and for Hamlet are quite tangibly present in the incidents of the play; the pity is a more tenuous result of our sympathetic understanding of him and his predicament. Unlike Ophelia, he never becomes an object of mere pathos. He is made of mettle too strong to allow pathetic sympathy. Tragic pity for a protagonist such as Hamlet or Oedipus leads us to a deeper appreciation of human character as represented by them and to admiration. Thus pity is attenuated and at the end of the play character in the sense of our deeper understanding of man remains. In certain tragedies pity is purged by our perception that though the hero goes down to defeat and perhaps to death, his very downfall asserts a universal moral order.

Catharsis is essential if the play is to be complete. A play in its beginning is entirely the potentiality of change. In its middle change has already occurred but has produced the possibilities and the anticipations of further change. In its end change is complete and a rest from the particular kind of change dealt with is established. Fear and pity as concomitants of the change must in the end, so to speak, be exhausted but exhausted in a way that is both probable and satisfying. That kind of exhausting of their potentialities is catharsis. Fear, pity and catharsis serve to delimit the form of a serious action. A serious action has other powers. For example, like any other action made into an artistic whole, it has the power of arousing interest, of producing anticipations, and of satisfying interest and anticipations. But the particular powers which specify a serious action and no other kind are pity and fear and if that action is given full formulation there will be in it purgation of these.

This highly condensed and therefore somewhat over-simplified attempt to explain the formulation of drama of high seriousness may seem to restrict tragedy to 'character centred' drama, to employ a term often used by Kitto. Such is not the intent, though clarity and brevity limit the exploration of the many different ways in which the dramatist may formulate his conception of the serious nature of the human predicament. The playwright is not merely a thinker and therefore something of a philosopher; he is also, like other artists, an experimenter in formulation. He seeks that combination of the parts which, put together into a completed whole, will best express his vision of the human condition. Let it be repeated again for emphasis, the range of formulation open to him is wide indeed; yet if he is to compose a work of high seriousness, there are principles which he must observe.[1]

There are plays whose action is not in the full and complete sense serious. There come to mind immediately such plays as Ibsen's *A Doll's House* and Chekhov's *The Three Sisters*. Though these plays have form, they are not fully formulated tragedies. Ibsen's play nearly approaches the form of tragedy, while Chekhov's approaches that of modern tragi-comedy. Certain other modern plays, such as O'Neill's *The Iceman Cometh*, are inhibited from full formulation as tragedy by the playwright's nihilistic conception of man and of the universe which he inhabits. Similar inhibitions operate in the case of Samuel Beckett's *Waiting for Godot*. In this play man is a human absurdity awaiting an unknown destiny in a meaningless universe. To the extent that he is absurd, his fate is merely pathetic or serio-comic. Such a drama can obviously contribute little to our understanding of the nature of man and the conception of human destiny. At best it can merely mock both and announce the necessity of a stoic despair. Though man has frequently adopted such a mode in his philosophy, he has never long been satisfied with such an attitude.

The whole action in the sense of its course from a beginning to a certain kind of outcome, the kinds of characters who serve as the activating agents of the change in that action, and the consequent powers or effects are the major determinants of form in a drama. Thus an action that is in any degree ludicrous or absurd in which the agents are a-normal – that is, deviants from normal human beings as generally conceived, without being in their deviations actually harmful or threatening to other sympathetic human beings – and whose outcome is the exposure or correction of the a-normal characters and happiness for the

---

[1] See Elder Olson, *Tragedy and the Theory of Drama* (Detroit: Wayne State University Press, 1961).

sympathetic characters would result in a play that belonged to the category of comedy. Analysis will reveal that the peculiar and distinguishing powers of this form are laughter and ridicule and that either one or the other may receive chief emphasis and thereby establish a type within the form. If the resulting comedy is to be a whole, that is complete as an art form, there must be a purgation of the emotions of laughter and ridicule. As in tragedy, the playwright may effect this catharsis in a variety of ways, but since both emotions are caused by deviations from the normal, the catharsis, however effected, will result in a restoration and assertion of normality. There is a type of the comic tending towards the romantic which chiefly emphasizes laughter – the kind of comedy that Shakespeare wrote. There is another type tending towards the punitative or judicial – the kind for which Ben Jonson is famous. They vary in part in terms of the author's view of his comic personages. Jonson seems to say sternly: 'Lord, what fools *those* mortals be', thus placing himself above and apart from his characters. Shakespeare, on the other hand, seems to say: 'Lord, what fools *we* mortals be, some of the time'. Jonson's approach if carried to extremes will result in savage satire that makes the element of laughter impossible and thus eliminates comedy. Shakespeare's approach in the hand of a lesser artist may result in sentimentalism with an equal fatality to comedy.

There is, I believe, a third major category of form in drama, variously called tragi-comedy, dramatic romance, *drame*, and melodrama. In this form the threat is so intensified that it produces fear. The action which it depicts is seemingly or temporarily serious; hence the threatening catastrophe must be in the end averted. Thus the form must in its best formulation have a double ending – a happy outcome for the sympathetic characters and proper punishment for the antipathetic agents. This form may tend largely towards the comic, as it does in the *Helen* of Euripides and in some of the tragi-comedies of Beaumont and Fletcher. Such a type emphasizes largely the overcoming of threats, obstacles, entanglements, and even dangers in a resultant happy outcome. When the second power, hate, receives the emphasis, the form tends towards melodrama, rather than pure tragicomedy. Since the form has one of the powers of tragedy, fear, it exhibits many of the structural characteristics of tragedy; but when the second power of hate is emphasized, since hate is compatible with ridicule, it also incorporates structural methods of comedy. For example, its characters, like those of comedy, are static in the sense that they have made their fundamental choices prior to the beginning of the action and cannot make successive new fundamental moral choices as the action progresses. Likewise as in comedy, the moral order in which the action transpires remains constant throughout and is not, as in tragedy, subjected to rigorous examination. Space will not permit an examination of other structural and formal characteristics. As Aristotle noted, this third form has been perennially popular in the theatre.[1] It is in itself a perfectly legitimate form of drama and its study will not be advanced by considering it as low or merely popular tragedy.

I should like to conclude with these observations, the first of which is a repetition. The study of drama as form represents the interpretation of drama as drama and no other thing. A play, even a mediocre play, has its own integrity, its significance as a formulated drama, regardless of what may be done to it on the stage. The art of drama is not exactly the same thing as the art of theatre, though the two as conjoint arts may attain their highest expression. Various forces operate upon the dramatist in his formulation of change in the human condition but it seems to me that two determinants are predominant. The first of these two is the playwright's conception of his universe, or rather of that universe in which his action takes place. By the conception of

---

[1] 'After this comes the construction of Plot which some rank first, one with a double story (like the *Odyssey*) and an opposite issue for the good and the bad personages. It is ranked first only through the weakness of the audience; the poets merely follow their public, writing as its wishes dictate. But the pleasure here is not that of Tragedy. It belongs rather to Comedy, where the bitterest enemies of the piece (e.g., Orestes and Aegisthus) walk off good friends at the end, with no slaying of any one by any one' (*Poetics*, Chapt. 13, Bywater's translation).

his universe I mean, of course, not merely the physical universe, but also his socio-political, and, above all, his moral universe. His universe may be as orderly, knowable, and related as is the universe of Sophocles, Shakespeare, or Ibsen – in which case the form of his drama that depicts that universe will be orderly, coherent, clear – a kind of closed form, as it has been called. On the other hand, the universe envisioned by the poet may be as unbridgably divided as that of certain of the German expressionists, as alien and unsympathetic as that of certain of O'Neill's pieces, or as chaotic, absurd, and hostile or inscrutable as that of Genet, Beckett and Ionesco. In such instances it may permit of no well-ordered formulation and demand the open form of the Expressionists of the nineteen-and-twenties or of the modern experimentalists. The fact that the forms of these modern plays do not correspond exactly to the form of any one of the past great plays does not in any sense mean that they are formless. Anyone who has studied intimately the construction of great plays of the past knows how wide and divergent are the forms within the different categories.

The second chief determinant of the form given to a play by a playwright is his conception of the nature of man. When we read or see any of the great plays of the past, we naturally tend to interpret their characters in terms of the psychology, attitudes, points of view and thoughts familiar to us; hence we get the impression that man's conception of the nature of man is constant and fundamentally unchanging. Perhaps there is an aspect of human history in which this idea is true; yet in a larger sense man's view of his nature, as well as his condition, is constantly changing. Drama is one, and perhaps the major, instrument invented by human beings for the exploration and explanation of the nature of man. Paraphrasing Duhamel, we can say that drama is nothing less than a universal picture of the nature of man and an exploration of the varieties of conduct possible to him in the universe which he inhabits.[1] It must, therefore, deal not

[1] Georges Duhamel, *Défense des lettres. Biologie de mon métier* (Paris: Mercure de France, 1937), pp. 280–81.

only with the human condition but also with the question of the relation or lack of relation of that condition to the nature of the universe. How the playwright conceives man and such relations will, as I hope I have shown, influence the formulation of whatever play he writes. If therefore we approach drama as an aesthetic form having its own justification – not justified by utility to the state, to a specific moral code, or to religion, to a social doctrine, or to any other thing or institution outside the drama itself – then we must conclude that form and meaning are inseparable. As Kitto says, if we ask what the *Antigone* means, the only possible answer in this sense is that it means the *Antigone*.

Hubert C. Heffner

X:

NEO-CLASSICAL DRAMA

AND THE REFORMATION

IN ENGLAND

'Seneca cannot be too heavy, nor Plautus too light.'
POLONIUS, *Hamlet*, II, ii.

I

DRAMA TODAY IS STUDIED AND DISCUSSED EITHER AS an aspect of literature or as the end-product of theatrical creative skills, seldom as both. Curiously, much the same may be said of drama in the sixteenth century. The multitude, whom Shakespeare was to compare to Cerberus, whether flocking to the sacred Miracle Cycles of pre-Reformation days in country towns, or packing the public playhouses of Elizabethan London, regarded drama as a festive recreation. The educated minority regarded it quite differently: to them it was a means of education, a form of poetry embodying moral philosophy in emblematic manner or, alternatively, an object for contempt, being morally and politically subversive.

In adopting these attitudes most English divines, school-masters and university dons took their cue from continental example; the apologists from current opinion among scholars and artists in Italy and France, the opponents from the precepts of religious reformers in Germany and Switzerland. Unfortunately the debating of viewpoints derived from these conflicting attitudes on the continent could hardly be carried on in a cool and rational manner in a country that was itself divided on the religious issue. The English apologist for drama, in advocating the writing and acting of plays on grounds of classical precedent in a country that had so recently abjured the rule of Rome in matters ecclesiastical, inevitably found himself at loggerheads with either Church or State or sometimes both.

At the start of the Tudor epoch interest in Roman and Greek antiquity was widespread in government and academic circles and was quickly reflected in artistic achievements ranging from architecture to literature. The interlude of *Fulgens & Lucres* (1497), the work of Cardinal Morton's private chaplain, Richard Medwall, is the first surviving memorial to the effects of this new interest on dramatic art in England. It is to be noted, however, that knowledge of Roman theory and practice advanced much more rapidly than knowledge of Greek equivalents. This is not surprising since Latin was still a living language, used throughout Europe not only by the Church but by government officials in diplomatic, judicial and even domestic affairs: Greek as a language was dead. Those men who read and spoke it like Erasmus, Dean Colet or Sir Thomas More were rare spirits; provision for acquiring a knowledge of it in English schools and universities at the start of the sixteenth century was poor. The quest therefore for Greek and Latin manuscripts which threw light on Greek and Roman attitudes to life was not matched by corresponding skills in translation and interpretation. By the middle of the century, despite rapid improvement in the mastery of Greek, the lead of Latin studies over Greek was so marked as to give Roman thought and practice a virtually unbeatable supremacy. This linguistic pre-eminence of Latin over Greek was paralleled in Western Europe at least by such physical monuments of the two civilizations as remained for the eye to see and the excavator to uncover. The Romans as imperial colonizers had everywhere left evidence of their way of life ranging from ruined but still standing structures as striking as the Colosseum to fragments of pillars or of mosaic pavement and the bric-à-brac of deserted armouries. Not having crossed the Alps, the Greeks had left no visible and tangible memorials to their way of life in Northern and Western countries. Thus, although scholars recognized that much of Roman art was derived from Greek example, even the best of them were not equipped to discern how plagiaristic and debased this derivation was. As a result the worship of false gods became widespread, Horace, for example, ranking higher as a dramatic theorist than Aristotle, Seneca ranking higher as a dramatist than Sophocles, Roman theatres and amphitheatres (in strangely confused amalgam) assuming a greater authority than the genuine θέατρον at Delphi or at Epidaurus. It is these confusions which led directly to the imitations of Terence in Italian, French and English with their curious illustrations, to the building of the *Teatro Olimpico* at Vicenza and the naming of a public playhouse in a dissolved Priory in Shoreditch as *The Theater*. Polonius, although a figure of fun to Hamlet and Horatio, was very much in the academic *avant-garde* in acting the part of Julius Caesar in his university dramatic society and in praising Seneca and Plautus as 'the only men' for 'the law of writ and the liberty': Sir Philip Sidney and Ben Jonson would have agreed with him. How then did Shakespeare dare to risk making these sentiments the cue for laughter? Only because he knew the multitude knew little of them and cared less.[1]

2

Perhaps the most startling consequence of the discrepancy in the pace at which studies of Roman and Greek drama advanced in Italy itself during the sixteenth century was the genesis of what we now term opera. Accustomed as we are to the vast musical forces (and complementary financial subsidies) associated with the operas of Verdi, Wagner or Richard Strauss, it requires a substantial imaginative effort to see any connection between the music dramas of the modern opera house and performances of Latin comedies and tragedies in Florence, Ferrara and Rome: the link is in Florentine efforts of the 1590's to solve in musical terms the problems posed by the Chorus in Greek tragedy.[2] Scarcely less startling to the modern mind is the pre-eminence accorded to the landscape-painter's art in Italian revivals and adaptations of Latin plays which to us appears to involve flat

---

[1] See G. Wickham, 'Shakespeare's "small Latine and less Greeke"', *Talking of Shakespeare* (ed. J. Garrett) 1954, pp. 209–30.

[2] A group of musicians, poets and nobles known as 'the Camerata' used to meet in Florence during the 1580's to discuss how best to imitate and revive Greek tragedy, and in particular the relationship of lyric poetry to music in production. Initially it was admitted that the music must be subordinate to the verse, but by the end of the century this attitude had changed. See H. Leclerc, *Les Origines italiennes de l'architecture théâtrale moderne*, Paris, 1946, pp. 121 *et seq.*

contradiction of Aristotle's views on the place of spectacle in drama. Both of these phenomena derive from the pre-eminence which Latin comedy enjoyed over tragedy coupled with the pre-eminence which all Latin drama enjoyed initially over Greek; for knowledge of Latin drama embraced not only the texts of plays but Vitruvius' remarks on the architecture of Roman theatres as well. When painters and musicians who were themselves men of genius, like Raphael, Leonardo da Vinci or Monteverdi, assisted with these revivals, the original academic course of these studies was submitted to a greater strain than it could bear without shifting its direction. Comedies by Plautus and Terence were being performed in Rome, in Florence and in Ferrara when Henry, Duke of Richmond, defeated Richard III and founded the Tudor dynasty in England: Henry VII had been succeeded by his son before the first Latin tragedy (Seneca's *Hippolytus*) was performed for the edification of audiences in Rome and Ferrara. Although this revival of the *Hippolytus* was an un-doubted *succès d'estime* it did not encourage the immediate revival of other tragedies, whereas the repertoire of comedies was steadily expanding, and several of them were being translated out of Latin into Italian.[1]

Greek studies in Italy began to make some headway early in the fifteenth century as princely bankers began to commission their oriental agents to import Byzantine manuscripts along with other merchandise. In 1423 Giovanni Aurispa returned from Constantinople with a collection of books that included six plays by Aeschylus and seven by Sophocles. Further plays arrived in subsequent consignments, but it took nearly a century for any of them to become available in print. Nevertheless it is worth noticing that at most twenty years separates the publication of the first edition of *Senecae Tragoediae* (1480–90) and that of the

---

[1] Ariosto's *I Suppositi* was performed in Ferrara in 1509 and Cardinal Bibbiena's *La Calandra* in Urbino in 1513.

Machiavelli's *Mandragola* was performed in Florence in 1513. The latter, although constructed in the Roman manner, is wholly his own creation in respect of plot and characters. Raphael provided a backcloth for the production of *I Suppositi*, and *La Calandra*, when revived in Rome in 1518, was presented in a setting designed by Perruzzi.

works of Sophocles (Venice: 1502). May not this fact account in some measure for the evident lack of enthusiasm for Senecan tragedy in performance that followed the revival of the *Hippolytus* in 1509? It is at least significant that in the first published excursion into tragedy in the Italian vernacular, *Sofonisba* (1515), the author, Giangiorgio Trissino, leans more heavily on Sophocles than Seneca in his handling of the Chorus. *Sofonisba* earned Trissino a striking literary reputation, but the play was not performed until 1562, twelve years after his death. Leo Schrade adopts the view that the advent of published editions of Greek tragedy (Sophocles, 1502: Euripides, 1503: Aeschylus, 1518) was at least partially responsible for delaying practical experiments based on Senecan tragedy either in Latin or in the vernacular in Court theatres.[1] The first tragedy in the Italian vernacular to appear on a stage was Giraldi Cinzio's *Orbecche* (Ferrara: 1541). Cinzio himself declared Seneca to be more deserving of imitation than the Greek authors, but the general trend of academic thinking on dramatic theory and practice was gradually moving in the opposite direction. The final triumph of Greek tragedy over Latin was bodied forth in the performance of Orsatto Giustiniani's *Edipo Tiranno* with Choruses set to music by Andrea Gabrielli in the *Teatro Olimpico* at Vicenza on March 2nd, 1585. The text was published that same year, the *Canto Chori in Musica* three years later. The title page of the former is explicit: '*Edipo Tiranno di Sofocle . . . in lingua volgare ridotta. . . .*' Giustiniani's dedication is to Sophocles himself. A dedicatory epistle to Signor Veniero explains the translator's aims and comments on the difficulties encountered.[2] And yet . . . and yet . . . posterity must be excused for harbouring doubts. The *Teatro Olimpico* with its painted ceiling, its Roman style of auditorium and orchestra, its scenic streets modelled in receding perspective and its batteries of oil lamps in coloured glass, still stands to testify to any scholar who cares to visit it that the Latin spirit rather than the Greek was pre-eminent in that notable performance of March 3rd, 1585. Was

[1] L. Schrade, *La Représentation d'Edipo Tiranno au Teatro Olimpico*, C.N.R.S., Paris, 1960, pp. 11–33.   [2] *Ibid.*, pp. 85–9.

it not, one must ask, a desire to dignify Italian literature by harnessing the Greek antecedents of Roman antiquity to the modern language rather than a determination to let Greek culture speak for itself that had prompted both this 'translation' and all its predecessors? This must remain an open question; but it is certain that the related problems of style and versification were those on which academic discussion centred. This of itself suggests a wish on the part of the translators to refine Italian verse forms by recourse to Greek example.[1] Greek tragedy in Greek (or comedy for that matter) was not attempted either indoors or in the open air. Both Greek and Latin tragedy in Italian failed to find a popular following. Patrons, aided and abetted by their architects and painters, moved away from the derivative style of the *Teatro Olimpico* towards a stage of pictorial illusion: actors, perplexed by the problem of finding a rhetorical style appropriate to the recitation of archaic texts in translation, moved away from recitation and towards a combination of intoned declamation or '*stilo recitativo*' and melody or '*aria*'. The problem of the abrupt change from passages for individual actors to those for Chorus was met if not solved by a borrowing of the traditional 'Entries' from the masks and intermezzos of Court festivities, themselves already an excuse for lavish spectacle.[2] The practical realities of stage performance thus came to combine with renaissance theatrical taste to swamp the original objectives of the learned translators (or possibly to expose both the mixed motives and the theatrical sterility of those objectives) and to

---

[1] Schrade (*op. cit.*, p. 24) says of Lorenzo Valla's translation of Demosthenes' *De Corona* following swiftly upon Leonardo Bruni's translation of the same work: 'Le motif d'une telle rivalité n'était pas le désir de donner une traduction plus fidèle, mais l'ambition de polir avec une habileté encore plus grande ce qui avait déjà été porté à un haut degré de raffinement. Ces traductions prouvent clairement que la rhétorique latine les préoccupait davantage que le sens intime des lettres grecques.'

[2] See H. Leclerc, *Les Origines italiennes de l'architecture théâtrale moderne*, Paris 1946, and Enid Welsford, *The Court Mask*, Cambridge, 1927. On the Florentine *Intermezzi*, see A. M. Nagler, 'Theater der Medici', *Maske und Kothurn*, IV (1958), No. 2/3. pp. 168–98, and A. Beijer, 'An Early 16th Century Scenic Design in the National Museum, Stockholm, and its Historical Background', *Theatre Research* IV (1962), No. 2, pp. 85–155.

provide Italians of the seventeenth century with a theatre that was vocally and scenically more elegant than any other in Europe, but which was about as far removed in spirit from the austere simplicity of Greek tragedy as it could be.

3

In one form or another this pattern imposed itself during the course of the seventeenth century on every country in Europe from the Tagus to the Volga. My concern here is with the English variant. The generalization which has dominated school textbooks on both historical and literary aspects of this topic is that the renaissance followed the same pattern in England as in Italy but, being an imported commodity, at a later date. This view seems to me to ignore altogether the impact which the Reformation in England had upon higher learning throughout the country and its repercussions on academic life. You cannot, for instance, dismiss the Latin Bible of the Roman Catholic Church and substitute for it an English version which draws its inspiration from Greek originals without dragging the two languages in question into the wider issues of metaphysical polemic. In other words, as a convinced Roman Catholic you find yourself obliged to defend Latin whatever your personal feelings may be about the Greek authors: for the convinced Protestant there is a similar but opposite compulsion to denigrate Latin as the language of superstition, and to defend Greek as the language of the Evangelists and the Early Fathers. Ample evidence survives from the middle of the sixteenth century to show how adoption of these rival standpoints retarded the progress in both languages which had been made earlier in the century. The damage done to the advancement of classical studies in England during the reigns of Edward VI and Mary I on this account however was small compared to that resulting from the extreme extension of the Protestant standpoint under Elizabeth I: personal inspiration and enthusiasm were elevated to a point where it became a virtue to abrogate academic degrees and dismiss *all* disciplined study as of small consequence when compared to the direct revelations vouchsafed by the Deity to the self-appointed 'saved'. Whole libraries were stripped and destroyed by these zealots, including the MSS. of religious plays.[1] When the effects of this attitude to manuscripts and books are considered in conjunction with those resulting from the earlier dissolution of the monasteries it may readily be seen that the revival of interest in classical learning in England could not possibly follow the course of such studies in Italy. For one thing, no steadily evolving programme of humane studies lavishly and consistently patronized within sheltered academies could be contemplated after 1531. Once Henry VIII had broken with Rome, pursuit of classical studies had either to be conducted publicly in an atmosphere of propagandist debate not unlike that which surrounds diplomacy as conducted today in the General Assembly of the United Nations, or else carried on by isolated individuals in privacy, semi-secrecy and even in exile: the better part of half a century separates the break-up of Sir Thomas More's circle and the re-establishment of free intercourse among humanists in the circle centred on Sir Philip Sidney.[2]

English interest in the revival of Greek and of classical latinity had begun early. The mediaeval passion for pilgrimages to the Holy Land ensured that some contact at least was maintained with Hebrew, Arabic, Greek and Latin during the fourteenth

---

[1] T. Warton, *History of English Poetry* (ed. 1778–81), pp. 607–27, discusses the effects of the Reformation on university life at Oxford and Cambridge with particular reference to the fortunes of Greek and Latin studies. He concludes: 'The study of the classics, together with a colder magic and a tamer mythology [i.e. than those of Gothic times], introduced method into composition: and the universal ambition of rivalling those new patterns of excellence, the faultless models of Greece and Rome, produced that bane of invention, IMITATION. Erudition was made to act upon genius. Fancy was weakened by reflection and philosophy. The fashion of treating everything scientifically, applied speculation and theory to the arts of writing. . . . The lover of true poetry will ask', he says, 'what have we gained by this revolution?' This question and his own answer to it have a special urgency in the twentieth century. 'We have parted with extravagancies that are above propriety, with incredibilities that are more acceptable than truth, and with fictions that are more valuable than reality.'

[2] See G. Wickham, *Early English Stages*, 1300–1660, ii, pp. 13–53.

century: and in the fifteenth century, despite the social and political insecurity that accompanied the Wars of the Roses, determined efforts were made by many Englishmen to acquire in Italy itself the knowledge which could not be obtained in English schools and universities. The reward for this enterprise and industry was high preferment in the Church at Papal hands. Two examples from the middle of the fifteenth century are Robert Fleming and John Free. Fleming acquired Greek, is said by Leland to have compiled a Greek-Latin Lexicon, became prothonotary to Pope Sixtus and was appointed by him to the Deanery of Lincoln c. 1450. Free, who was born and bred in Bristol, was similarly favoured by Pope Paul II, being appointed in 1465 to the bishopric of Bath and Wells. He earned this preferment by translating, among other Greek authors, the works of Xenophon; and his Latin was so good that he received an invitation to compose an elegiac epitaph for Petrarch's tomb. These men and others like them copied, bought, imported and donated MSS. to English libraries in much the same way that Italian princes were enriching their own libraries.

When Henry VII seized the throne in 1485, he quickly recognized the worth of these pioneer efforts and encouraged further initiative by giving Italian artists and men of letters incentives to work in England. Latin received the greatest impetus by virtue of the commission accorded to Polydore Vergil to reside at Court and write an official History of England.[1] Greek however began to be a matter of public as opposed to purely private interest when William Grocyn began to lecture on it at Oxford, albeit on a voluntary basis: with the establishment of a chair at Cambridge shortly afterwards, and the appointment of Erasmus to that chair, all was set for a revival of humane studies in England as vigorous and enlightened as that progressing in Italy. It was in England, we might note, that Erasmus completed his translation of two of the plays of Euripides. No less important for classical studies in general and dramatic art in particular was the reorganization of St Paul's School by Dean Colet in 1512 and the

[1] See Denys Hay, *Polydore Vergil, Renaissance historian and man of letters*, 1952.

appointment of William Lyly as High Master.[1] Lyly had spent five years in Rhodes acquiring Greek and as long again in Rome working in the learned company of Pomponius Laetus and Sulpitius, both of whom were actively concerned with the earliest representations of Latin plays in Italy.

Where Henry VII had moved cautiously, setting an auspicious eye on the efforts of others, Henry VIII and his Chancellor Wolsey vied with one another in bestowing liberal endowments on humane studies in both schools and universities.[2] But here they were acting without reckoning on the forces of reaction, the dons and churchmen who viewed this mad career to new disciplines with ever increasing alarm. Their riposte, when it came, was deadly. 'What men are these' they asked 'who pour scorn on the old scholastic curriculum in divinity and philosophy, if not heretics and even pagan idolators?' We in our turn and at this distance in time may fairly ask what sort of men were those who reproachfully stigmatized Erasmus as *Graeculus iste* and cautioned young priests under instruction: *Cave a Graecis ne fias haereticus!*

In this way the ground was prepared for the forces of academic reaction to rally to the cause of Roman Catholicism with its Latin liturgy immediately Henry VIII had vested in his own person the headship of the Church in England. The dissolution of the monasteries which proceeded piecemeal throughout the last decade of his reign paradoxically strengthened the hand of the reactionaries, for it deprived the provinces of all centres of higher learning other than Oxford and Cambridge. The full effects of this took time to make themselves felt, but were evident enough twenty years later when the Anglican Church of Elizabeth discovered that it lacked sufficient clergy to fill its livings who could be trusted to construct a sermon in English, let alone claim a command of the classics. It is this aspect of the decline in literacy which is touched on by Shakespeare in the character of

---

[1] On the significance of Lyly's appointment, see L. B. Campbell, *Scenes and Machines on the English Stage*, 1923, p. 83 *et seq.*
[2] See Warton, *op. cit.*, pp. 608–10.

Sir Nathaniel who is rebuked by Holofernes for saying *bone* instead of *bene* (LLL, V, i, 30).

At Oxford and Cambridge the classics had come to stay, but pursuit of them there was severely disrupted. Roger Ascham notes with satisfaction that under Edward VI the works of Homer, Sophocles and Euripides were normal reading for undergraduates, but wonders how long this can last and deplores the state of Latin studies in the schools. The founder of Trinity College, Oxford, particularizes in his statutes which Latin authors are to be read and to what end: yet when encouraged by the liberal Cardinal Pole to make better provision for Greek, replies: 'This purpose I lyke well; but I fear the tymes will not bear it now'.[1] Much of the ground made up was, however, quickly lost again under the attacks of the Calvinist exiles on their return to England following the accession of a Queen who prided herself on her command of Greek. It is this type of fanatical ignoramus whom Ben Jonson satirizes in the person of Zeal-of-the-land-Busy who stigmatizes quotation from Horace as 'lists of Latin, the very rags of Rome, and patches of Popery'. To have small Latin and less Greek therefore on leaving school was possibly no bad thing if one had chanced to be born in 1564 and wished to adopt a truly objective standpoint when depicting human nature in dramatic dialogue in the England of Elizabeth I.

To have had no reading knowledge of either Greek or Latin at a time when the Italian *novella* and the literature out of which it was born was being imported into England from so many quarters would have been a crippling disadvantage to any aspiring artist, especially a poet. Yet to have acquired an authoritative mastery of either or both carried with it not only the risk of being branded as a heretic, an atheist or a political revolutionary, but the certainty of isolation from the mainstream of popular attitudes and thought. Heresy and atheism were closely associated with necromancy and witchcraft, papists with political subversion: excessive enthusiasm for Greek or Latin, like the mark of Cain,

[1] See Warton, p. 622. See also F. S. Boas, *University Drama in the Tudor Age*, 1914, pp. 7–8.

served to advertise these criminal tendencies and invited investigation. Only following the execution of Mary of Scotland and the defeat of the Armada were these suspicions relaxed, by which time a formidable attack was being mounted on the theatre in all its aspects. The religious stage had already succumbed: both the popular and the academic stage were fighting for their lives.

4

The facts relating to the revival of Roman and Greek plays in England during the course of the sixteenth century are well known and are clearly set out by F. S. Boas, *University Drama in the Tudor Age* (1914) and by T. H. Vail Motter, *The School Drama in England* (1929). Neither of these scholars concerns himself directly with plays performed by the young lawyers at the Inns of Court, and neither of them devote much attention to the physical conditions in which the plays they discuss were performed. Both of these aspects of the subject, however, are treated by Miss L. B. Campbell, *Scenes & Machines on the English Stage* (1923). Where staging is concerned I have myself felt unable to agree with Miss Campbell in some of her deductions and have argued an alternative case in *Early English Stages* (Vol. ii, Chapter VII). A full bibliography of documents relating to drama at the Inns of Court is shortly to be published by D. S. Bland.

With so much information of a factual kind so readily available it is pointless to retail it here: on the other hand theatre research in recent years has caused us to alter many of the assumptions which served as a background to these earlier surveys of the surviving evidence. Accordingly a case exists now for drawing the reader's attention to those aspects of the subject which appear to warrant reappraisal. In doing this we can at least start from reasonably firm ground; for no one is likely to wish to dispute the fact that during the first three decades of the sixteenth century the same passion for the revival of Roman and Greek plays as

Neo-Classical Drama and the Reformation in England

prevailed in Italy (in so far as technical mastery of the respective languages allowed) was given free rein in England. It is with the start of the Reformation that development of this interest in Italy and in England began to part company. I wish to suggest that where in Italy matters of form and stylistic expression began to assume an overriding importance, in England questions of pedagogical content took precedence. I attribute these developments in part to a sharp divergence in attitude to the virtues of Latin as a language, in part to a marked difference of approach to the religious stage inherited from the Middle Ages and above all to the impact made on both Latin studies and the religious stage by advances in the command and understanding of Greek.

In the early years of the century the study of Roman plays and of Greek plays in Latin dress recommended itself to educationalists as much as a training in the *speaking* of Latin as for the extended knowledge of vocabulary, syntax and grammar that accrued.[1] It was on these grounds that schools and university colleges when given the opportunity to reconstitute themselves or when newly endowed by private benefaction chose to include the annual performance of a play or plays in Latin in their statutes.[2] No such immediate or obvious *vocational* benefit was to be gained by performing Greek plays in Greek. The Reformation, however, occasioned a sharp reappraisal: for with the Latin liturgy and Bible, together with any other overt demonstration of dependence on Rome, translated into subjects of contention, continued performances of Latin plays could scarcely be justified on these grounds alone except by reactionaries.

The dilemma confronting Protestant humanists on this account was resolved by a dawning realization that Greek plays were

---

[1] A notable English work in this context was Nicholas Udall's *Floures for Latine spekynge* (1534–5), culled from three of Terence's plays.

[2] Westminster School, set in order by Elizabeth I in 1560, is particularly important in this respect, Ben Jonson having received his education there. Sir James Whitelock who entered Merchant Taylors School in 1575 says, 'I was brought up at school under Mr Mulcaster. ... Yeerly he presented sum playes to the court, in which his scholers wear only actors, and I on among them, and by that meanes taughte them good behaviour and audacitye.' T. H. Vail Motter, *The School Drama in England*, 1929, pp. 85–104 and p. 110.

Classical Drama and its Influence

possibly to be preferred to Latin ones (at least as texts for reading if not for acting), and by the performance in Germany of Thomas Kirchmeyer's violently anti-Catholic play *Pammachius*, written and performed in Latin in 1535 and presented at Christ's College, Cambridge, ten years later.[1] As a piece of Protestant propaganda, this play suggested that the traditional Miracle and Morality plays could be reformed on lines which combined humanist ideals in respect of scholarly style and education with Protestant ideals in respect of theological and moral content. Such an idea, if carried into action, could not but divorce subsequent development of neo-classical drama in England from its counterpart in Italy; for, in effect, it changed the motive underlying the study and revival of classical plays from being a straightforward desire to imitate and thus refine personal style into one of purifying and thus improving the moral and philosophical content of English drama at large.

Steps in this direction were swiftly taken with the performance at Oxford, c. 1540, of Nicholas Grimald's *Christus Redivivus*. This play opens with the burial of Christ, makes Caiaphas the villain, includes a quartet of comic Roman soldiers and a spectacular Harrowing of Hell, and ends with doubting Thomas's confession of faith. Grimald was a friend of John Bale who was not only a dramatist himself but enjoyed the patronage of Cranmer and Cromwell in turning the religious stage into an instrument of Protestant polemic in the German manner. This of course was a game at which two could play. At Cambridge Thomas Watson and John Christopherson retaliated in defence of the old religion in Latin and in Greek respectively; Watson with *Absalon* (c. 1540) and Christopherson with Ἰεφθάε (c. 1544).[2] Both authors found life difficult under Edward VI, Christopherson going into exile, Watson into prison; both were restored to grace and office under

---

[1] This performance created a scandal involving a sharp exchange of letters between the Chancellor, Bishop Gardiner, and the Vice-Chancellor, Matthew Parker, Master of Corpus Christi College. The accompanying investigation only served to draw the maximum degree of attention to the play. See Boas, *op. cit.*, pp. 22–3.

[2] These two plays are discussed by Boas, *op. cit.*, pp. 43–68. On the subject of performances in Greek see Boas, pp. 16 and 17, and Campbell, *op. cit.*, pp. 86–8.

Mary, but were ruined with the return to power of a Protestant monarch.

The Latin polemical play, whether Roman Catholic or Protestant in spirit, was doomed however like its vernacular equivalent on the professional stage, once the government of Elizabeth I had determined that the security of the realm did not permit of any plays on religious subjects being performed in public or circulated in print. This ban on religious plays of every kind, which was launched shortly after the excommunication of the Queen in 1570, had become fully effective by 1590. The academic stage had therefore to look at itself again and re-examine its *raison d'être*. This it did in the form of violent internal controversy. The question at issue was whether plays Greek, Latin or English should be countenanced at all in centres of learning. It was particularized in the exchange of letters between John Rainolds and William Gager at Oxford in 1592-4 which is treated in full by Boas (op. cit., pp. 220-51). In effect Rainolds brings all the arguments unleashed by Puritan opponents of the professional theatre to bear upon academic performances. Gager counters with the old argument of the training in rhetoric which such performances provided, coupled with the innocent and profitable recreation which they offered to both performers and spectators. Rainolds's letters found their way into print but not Gager's replies or those of his supporters. As public property, they provided the enemies of the professional playhouses with a rich assortment of arguments for their suppression which quickly found their way into sermons, pamphlets and broadsheets and played their part in the ultimate closure of the theatres in 1642.

What then did the English humanists of the Tudor epoch, who risked imprisonment, exile and death to champion a renewed interest in Greek and Roman drama, achieve? Unquestionably they brought a vivid interest in Terence, Plautus and Seneca, derived as much from performance as from textual exposition, into the academic curriculum of the two universities and of all the leading schools. Unlike their Italian counterparts, however, they appear to have lost interest in the problems of stylistic refinement which arose when the verse forms of Latin plays were compared with those used by the Greek dramatists. The Chorus of Greek drama which in Italy aroused the fiercest academic disputes, and which there engaged the attention of musicians as well as scholars, failed to provoke any startling developments in England. A similar lack of concern is noticeable in England in respect of the structural and scenic problems occasioned by strict observance of the unities of place and time which were exercising architects, painters and dramatists in Italy. In this connection it should be noted that where Vitruvius' *De Architectura* was translated into Italian and French early in the sixteenth century, English scholars interested in the Roman theatre had to content themselves with these translations or the original Latin text. No attempt was made to comment on it in English.[1] On the other hand, the English humanists, by adapting Latin plays to meet conditions created by the Reformation, greatly reinforced the didactic element of traditional religious plays inherited from the mediaeval past. In doing this they brought the refinement of their own style, grounded in study of classical models, to bear upon historical narrative and ethical disputation. New characters like the title role of Plautus' *Miles Gloriosus* began to colour the cast-lists of English plays: abstract personifications like those in the early Moralities were softened and given distinctive personalities constructed from the human predicament in which the character was situated. An Interlude like *Ralph Roister Doister* thus looks forward to Falstaff, while the Vice, 'Avarice', of *Respublica* forecasts Volpone: in more serious mood, the deposition scene in Bale's *Kyng Johan*, although conducted by abstract characters, looks forward just as unmistakably to a similar scene in *Edward II* or *Richard II*. These processes of influence and adaptation paved

[1] The first English work on architecture was Sir John Shute's *First and Chief Grounds of Architecture* published in 1563. He acknowledges his debt to Vitruvius and to Philander's commentary of 1544–5, but confines his attention to the five orders. It was 1611 before Serlio's work found its way into English translation.

Vitruvius' *De Architectura* was published in Latin in 1486, in Italian in 1521, in French in 1547 and in Spanish in 1602. An abridged translation into English appeared in 1692.

the way for a professional, secular drama to replace the religious
stage in Elizabethan England without losing sight of traditional
stagecraft and without losing touch with popular audiences.
Revolution, when it came in the next century – scenic and operatic
– was not a native product but a specifically Italian import. In
its arrival it swept poetry out of the English theatre and replaced
the scenic emblems of mediaeval and Tudor stages with pictures,
painted in perspective and properly framed by an arch above
the stage or proscenium.

Glynne Wickham

XI: RACINE'S RESPONSE TO THE STAGECRAFT OF ATTIC TRAGEDY AS SEEN IN HIS ANNOTATIONS

OF ALL THE GREAT TRAGIC POETS SINCE ANTIQUITY, Racine is the one who had the most direct knowledge of the Greek masters. The place given to the study of Greek at Port-Royal is well known, as is Racine's debt – particularly to Lancelot. It has indeed been established that even his own poetic vocabulary is much more marked by Latin than Greek borrowings,[1] but there is nothing surprising about this. Apart from the obvious predominance of Latin influences which was as general as it was inevitable throughout Western Christendom – and nowhere more than in its Romance-speaking lands – Racine's own observations contained in his very substantial 'Remarks on the *Odyssey*', dated April 1662 – he was then twenty-three – show how aware he himself was of the contrast between what was admissible in French, as compared with Greek, poetry.

After summarizing the passage in book V describing how Calypso equips Odysseus not only with an axe with an olive-wood handle and a saw, to make the ship, but 'even with an auger and nails' (this is the equipment Racine singles out from the descriptions in vv. 235–50) – 'so exact is Homer in describing the least particulars' – this (he goes on) 'a bonne grâce dans le grec', whereas Latin is much more reserved 'et ne s'amuse pas à de si petites choses'.

No doubt that language is more barren and does not have words which express things as happily as does the Greek. One might indeed say that there is nothing low in Greek and in it the vilest objects are nobly expressed. Our tongue resembles Latin in this; it has an extreme aversion against stooping to particulars, our ears being sensitive and finding it intolerable that low objects, like axe, saw and auger should be named in serious speech. Italian, on the contrary, resembles Greek and expresses everything – as can be seen in Ariosto, who is in his way like Homer.[2]

[1] Georges May: *D'Ovide à Racine*, Paris and Yale, 1949.
[2] J. Racine: *Œuvres*, ed. P. Mesnard, new edn. 1922, VI, 102–3; for notes on *Iliad* quoted below, ibid. 209–11; and further, on the tragic poets, ibid. pp. 218–65. The

Racine has indeed taken over a number of lines or expressions from the Greek poets (particularly Sophocles) into his plays – borrowings which have been duly noted by critics and commentators; but they are fewer than might have been expected. On the whole they are of the exalted and/or generalized type; whereas in his annotations he renders literally even such Greek expressions as are of a kind which would offend French usage as he understands and interprets it. Thus he presents Electra's ironic question contained in her outburst against her mother (Soph. *El.* 587) in the words: 'Est-ce pour venger ma sœur que tu couches avec Égisthe?'

But it is not my ambition to examine these points which have received detailed and highly competent attention;[1] nor, again, to point out the extent to which Racine sees in Sophocles a tragic norm to which, *mutatis mutandis*, he would himself conform.[2] I would like here simply to single out the things which Racine's comments on the Greek tragic poets show him to have found particularly appealing. It has already been pointed out that they could in a sense be thought of as a sort of Greek stagecraft;[3] the circumstance that he knew his Aristotle, his Horace, his Quintilian – and of course his Seneca[4] – can hardly be held to disqualify him from understanding and responding directly to the Greek poets – sc. Homer, and Sophocles more particularly among the tragic poets – about whom, in fact, his expressions of appreciation are more spontaneous and general than about anything else in

---

annotations are also given in vol. II of Racine's *Œuvres* in the Pléiade edition (ed. R Picard), and includes some new ones first published by R. C. Knight (v. next note).

[1] Particularly in R. C. Knight: *Racine et la Grèce* (Paris, 1950), which is the most serious investigation available regarding all aspects of Racine's Hellenism.

[2] Cf. the present writer's contribution to the Fourth International Congress on Aesthetics: 'Racine, Sophocle et la norme tragique' (Athens, 1960).

[3] Sister Mary Philip Haley: *Racine and the* Art Poétique *of Boileau*, Baltimore, Oxford and Paris, 1938, p. 115; v. also R. C. Knight's pages on 'Racine et la dramaturgie grecque' (op. cit., pp. 210–24).

[4] For the most recent consideration of this question, cf. John Lapp's balanced and subtle assessment in 'Racine est-il sénéquien?' in *Les Tragédies de Sénèque et le Théâtre de la Renaissance*, ed. J. Jacquot, Centre National de la Recherche Scientifique, Paris, 1964, pp. 127–38.

literature. And what engages him most about the latter is the
power of dramatic presentation.

LE LIEU DE LA SCÈNE

Noting that, in Sophocles' *Electra*, the Paedagogus explains
'from the first four lines' both the names of the principal actors
and the whole scene: 'Voilà, ô fils d'Agamemnon, ces mêmes
lieux que vous avez tant désiré voir', Racine makes the general
remark:

> *Sophocle a un soin merveilleux d'établir d'abord le lieu de la scène.*
> Il se sert ici pour cela d'un artifice très agréable, en introduisant un
> vieillard qui montre les environs du palais d'Argos à Oreste, qui
> en avoit été enlevé tout jeune.[1]

And he goes on – in this same note on one of the four editions of
Sophocles in which he made notes on the *Electra* – to remark
on similar beginnings in the *Philoctetes* and the *Oedipus Coloneus*:

> Le *Philoctète* commence à peu près de même: c'est Ulysse qui
> montre à Pyrrhus tout jeune l'île de Lemnos, où ils sont, et par où
> l'armée avait passé. L'*Œdipe Colonéen* s'ouvre par Œdipe aveugle qui
> se fait décrire par Antigone le lieu où il est. *Ces trois ouvertures,*
> *quoiqu'un peu semblables, ne laissent pas d'avoir une très agréable*
> *diversité et des couleurs merveilleuses.*

Similarly he notes, against the opening lines of the *Oedipus Rex* –
which, like most of the plays he annotates, he divides into 'acts'
and 'scenes': 'I. acte, scène 1ère – *Cette ouverture de la scène est*
magnifique: tous ces prêtres suppliants qui viennent implorer le
secours d'Œdipe'.[2]

He likewise visualizes the opening of the *Ajax*, with the goddess 'invisible qui parle à Ulysse, qui entre en cherchant'. The

---

[1] The italics are mine. I have thought it useful to italicize, in these excerpts from
Racine's notes, those parts which express a critical appreciation – as compared with the
passages in which his remarks do not go beyond explanation or interpretation.

[2] In another edition, against the scholiast's commentary of the text (in which he
underlines the words: οὐδ' οἶδε παῖδες ἐζόμεσθ'–l. 32), he notes (to quote him in his
original spelling) that this is a deputation 'de jeunes enfans conduits par un vieux
prestre de Juppiter'.

goddess 'éclaircit le sujet': she alone can know and recount the intention of Ajax, who would have killed Agamemnon, if she had not disturbed his mind. As so often in these notes, he puts himself in the place of the poet when he writes, against line 3: 'Il établit le lieu de la scène auprès des tentes d'Ajax, qui sont les dernières du camp des Grecs'.

THE ROLE OF THE CHORUS

Racine follows the Sophoclean chorus carefully throughout the *Ajax* and the *Electra*, the two plays which he has annotated from beginning to end; and it is clear from his notes that he fully concurs in the desirability of its involvement in the action.

In the *Ajax* he notes that the Chorus, composed of 'vieillards de Salamine, soldats (*sic*) d'Ajax', are asked by Ajax to convey his last wishes to Teucer (567–70); and when he goes out they lament his ill-fortune. He records that Ajax returns to the scene to mislead the Chorus and Tecmessa into thinking he had yielded to their prayers. And at the point where the Chorus dance and 'express their joy at the change of Ajax' (693), he notes, following the invocation of Pan (703), a line intended (so it seems to him) to 'excuser la danse d'un chœur de soldats qui ne doit point avoir appris à danser' (705). Alarmed by the Messenger and Tecmessa, who herself goes in search of Ajax, 'the chorus separates into two bands; and so the theatre remains empty, in order that Ajax may kill himself there, in the full sight of the spectators, with nobody to prevent him from doing so. This is the only place in the Greek tragedies where the Chorus leaves the scene since it has entered; *and it is a fine artifice of the poet, because the last words of Ajax were too considerable to be withheld from the spectator*' (811). The Chorus return from opposite sides and inform one another that they have found nothing. They hear Tecmessa cry out; and she shows them Ajax self-slain. She covers him with a mantle 'for there is no one who has the heart to see him in that condition. *Artifice to hide the blood from the spectator*' (866–913). Later he notes the Chorus counselling

Teucer to hasten the burial of Ajax; and as Teucer goes out he himself enjoins the Chorus to defend Ajax' son (1183). The Chorus goes on to plead with Odysseus in favour of Teucer and praises Odysseus when the latter has prevailed over Agamemnon's hostility to the dead Ajax (1374).

In the *Electra* he notes that the Chorus 'who come to console' the daughter of Agamemnon is of 'daughters of Argos, who approve the grief of Electra, like her detest her mother's crime, but are more timid than she and do not dare to speak freely' (121). They warn her to dissimulate her grief (213), and timidly ask 'if Aegisthus is absent' (310). He notes against line 472: 'Chœur tout seul', but adds: 'Yet it seems to be addressing Electra who does not go into the house during the whole prayer; and it seems likely she is pacing before the door, without going in, as can be seen from Clytemnestra's first line' (516). Witnessing the violent altercation between Electra and her mother, it 'pretends to be neutral' (610). After the shattering announcement of Orestes' death, Electra remains with the Chorus, which enjoins moderation. 'Le Chœur est toujours craintif' (802 ... 990). It supports the counsels of caution of Chrysothemis (1015), but it deplores the 'désordre de la maison de ses rois, la dissension des deux sœurs, et admire Électre' (1060). While announcing the vengeance of Zeus in its ode, 'it does not dare to name anyone' (1066). Later, when Clytemnestra is slain inside the palace: 'Le Chœur frémit de l'entendre tuer' (1408).

While no criticisms of the conduct of the Chorus are to be found in Racine's extensive notes on Sophocles, these are not absent in the much less extensive notes which have survived on texts of Euripides – and particularly concern its irrelevancies. Thus he remarks, in his annotations to the Phoenissae, that the Scholiast is right to indicate 'que *le Chœur s'amuse mal à propos à parler de la Sphinx*, lorsqu'il devait parler de Ménécée'. The latter's death deserved to be recounted at length, 'au lieu de décrire des boucliers' (1026 and 1097). Later he comments '*Ce Chœur est plus du sujet que les autres*' (1290).

THE EFFECT OF THE TRAGIC ACTION

While Racine thus follows the theme and structure of Attic tragedy with due attention to its conventions and a constant concern with 'seeing how it works' in representation, it is not surprising that he pays special attention to what he feels to be the major effects which a tragic action should produce.

In his notes on the *Iliad*, which belong almost certainly to the period when he was composing his own tragedies, he comments on the art of Homer in moving the listener or reader, e.g. (*Il*. XX, 407): 'Homère *se plait à exciter la compassion* pour les enfants de Priam, ici pour Polydore, et dans le chant suivant pour Lycaon', and again with the famous passages (VI, 371-470) describing the last encounter of Hector and Andromache.

Two passages in his notes are particularly interesting, as showing that Racine, like the Greek tragic poets themselves, looked for the tragic intention in Homer and found it:

Hector ne trouve point Andromaque au logis. *Cela se fait pour réveiller l'attention du spectateur*, qui se fâche qu'Hector trouve Hélène qu'il ne cherche pas, et ne trouve point Andromaque. – Leur conversation même devient *plus tragique et plus noble*; elle se passe à la porte de la ville, par où Hector va sortir pour n'y plus rentrer. – V. Plutarque dans la *Vie de Brutus*. Porcie et Brutus.

The other passage, which will be echoed in Racine's own *Andromaque* (1018–99) presents the 'tableau divin' of the actual farewell:

Artifice admirable *d'Homère d'avoir mêlé le rire, les larmes, la gravité, la tendresse, le courage, la crainte, et tout ce qui peut toucher.*

Racine similarly notes the intended effects in the tragedies. Thus, when Chrysothemis comes in the midst of Electra's despair at the (false) news of their brother's death to tell him she has proof that he has come, Racine remarks:

Cela fait un fort bel effet. Car les regrets d'Électre sont interrompus, et sa douleur n'en devient que plus violente. Ainsi la pitié va touiours s'augmentant.

Racine's Response to the Stagecraft of Attic Tragedy

He greatly admires the scene in which Orestes himself brings to Electra, in the presence of the Chorus, the urn in which he says his own ashes are contained:

> C'est le dernier période de sa douleur (Electra's), et *où le poète s'est épuisé pour faire pitié. Il n'y a rien de plus beau sur le théâtre que de voir Electra pleurer son frère mort en sa présence, qui en étant lui-même attendri, est obligé de se découvrir.*

And of the recognition between brother and sister which follows:

> *cette reconnaissance est merveilleusement pathétique et bien amenée de parole en parole, en se répondant tous deux fort naturellement et tendrement.*[1]

He shows a detailed appreciation of Sophocles' presentation of the slaying of Clytemnestra. Electra comes out (of the palace) 'in order not to be present at her mother's death. She tells what is being done within' (1397). 'Reason why Clytemnestra is in the house. She is making necessary preparations for the funeral of Orestes' (1400). 'He (the poet) explains why Electra comes out. To prevent their being surprised by Aegisthus (1402). Cries of Clytemnestra as she is slain. He (sc. Sophocles) makes us hear the cries of Clytemnestra so that, without seeing this death, the spectator shall none the less be present, and in order to dispense with a report. The Chorus shudder at hearing her being killed' (see the French formula quoted earlier) (1402–8). Against the line in which Electra, reacting to the outcry of Clytemnestra, enjoins her brother to strike again, Racine writes: '*Ce vers est un peu cruel pour une fille*; mais c'est une fille depuis longtemps enragée contre sa mère' (1415).

Racine notes each point of the action up to the arrival of Aegisthus. The latter 'orders that the doors be opened. – The doors open and the body is seen, covered. Orestes wishes him to

---

[1] It may be worth noting that the word 'pathétique' is one of the many 'false friends' which are the object of hasty reciprocal misinterpretations as between French and English. In French it simply means 'moving', 'appealing to the feelings' – not 'pitiable'.

uncover it himself, so that he may fling himself upon him at the same time. – This command of Aegisthus marks an overweening man who has no more fear of anything and wishes to be obeyed by all; and at the same time *prepares for the spectator the pleasure of the surprise of Aegisthus,* who in place of the body of Orestes, discovers the body of his wife.'

Racine is thus concerned, as we see from the above examples, with noting how Sophocles achieves an intended tragic effect. Indeed here again we find, despite Racine's approving reference to Aristotle's characterization of Euripides as τραγικώτατος (Preface to his own *Iphigénie*) and the tragic traits that he notes in the *Medea* and the *Phoenissae,* that he shows himself critical on occasion of Euripides' tragic effects. Thus, against the point made by the distraught Medea that music has not been found for soothing affliction he comments: 'Cette moralité est *agréable, mais peu tragique*' (192–7); and on her development regarding the misfortunes of women (238–11) – he comments: 'Tout cela est *plus comique que tragique, quoique beau et bien exprimé*'.

TRAGIC CHARACTERS AND CHARACTERIZATION

A sense of the inseparable bond between tragic effect and character, which underlies the just-quoted comments on Euripides, comes out constantly in these annotations. Thus, against Tecmessa's lines (260–1) in the *Ajax* Racine notes: 'Douleur d'Ajax de se voir cause de ses malheurs'; or again, against the Messenger's speech which reveals to Dejanira at once the unfaithfulness of Heracles and his injustice in destroying Oechalia, he notes that this was because Eurytus, father of Iole 'ne lui voulut pas permettre de coucher avec elle': 'cette injustice d'Hercule (he adds) et son infidélité envers Déjanire sont cause de sa perte, *et l'en rendent digne*' (*Trach.* 360 seqq.).

Racine shows himself constantly responsive to characterization whether it be the general characteristics of a given passion embodied which holds his attention or the trait which marks a character in its ordinarily unchangeable essence. In the *Tra-*

chiniae (436–69) he characterises the pleas of Dejanira as '*Discours admirable* d'une jalouse qui veut apprendre son malheur' and analyses its points.

In the *Ajax* he observes how consistent Sophocles is in his treatment of the character of Odysseus. In the *Electra* he notes the effective juxtaposition of Electra and Chrysothemis:

> Dispute des deux sœurs. – *Leur caractère paraît bien ici.* L'une est intrépide et fière, l'autre timide mais honnête, et sans perdre le respect.

After the scene of mutual recognition between Orestes and Electra, Sophocles (he says)

> représente dans Électra une joie aussi immodérée que sa douleur étoit excessive. Elle ne craint personne, elle s'abandonne à ses transports avec la même intrépidité qu'elle s'abandonne à son affliction.

And, a little later, after the mutual feelings of brother and sister have had full rein, and the Paedagogus blames their imprudence and tells them that without him they would have been taken by surprise, Racine has the remark:

> Sophocle, a voulu marquer l'imprudence des jeunes gens, qui ne peuvent se contenir dans leurs passions, et *afin que le spectateur ne trouve point étrange* qu'on ne les a point entendus à la maison, il fait que ce vieillard, plus sage qu'eux, a fait sentinelle à la porte.

THOUGHT AND DICTION

And just as Racine expresses admiration for the proper integration of characters into the tragic action, so he shows himself sensitive to the close relation between character (*les mœurs*), thought (*les sentiments*) and diction. As Professor R. C. Knight has pointed out (op. cit., p. 211), certain particularly striking lines or expressions have evidently been translated by him because they appealed to him for their poetry. But occasionally we also have the explicit praise, as where 'beau vers' is written against Tecmessa's outcry:

$$\mathring{\omega} \; \delta\acute{v}\sigma\mu o\rho' \; A\mathring{\iota}as, \; o\mathring{\iota}os \; \mathring{\omega}\nu \; o\mathring{\iota}\omega s \; \mathring{\epsilon}\chi\epsilon\iota s.^{1}$$

and against the lines in which Teucer addresses Ajax' son (1171–1172), he writes:

'*cela est fort tendre et fort noble*'.

He notes against line 271 (in Electra's first great opening speech): '*Belle image* de l'état où est la maison d'Agamemnon'. On the whole it is the aptness of expression or image in relation to character or situation which draws his attention. Thus the lofty opening generalizations of the speech in which Oedipus foretells to Theseus that one day Athens and Thebes will be at variance draw the remark: '*Tour admirable qu'il donne à sa pensée*' (*Oed. Col.* 108–28).

Racine's interest in this last-mentioned aspect of thought and diction has been insufficiently stressed. The γνῶμαι or *sententiae* constantly receive his attention. This was to be expected in view of the education he had received at Port-Royal. Among the papers which remained in his library when he died are teaching notes, involving close attention to figures of rhetoric from the hand of his own 'maître en rhétorique' as he has been called, the great advocate Antoine Lemaître, who was also a great lover of poetry.[2] He himself made substantial excerpts from the *Institutions* of Quintilian – who refers to Sophocles as 'sententiis densus.' And it is worthy of note that even where Racine did not otherwise write in commentaries or only very few, he marked the *sententiae* almost throughout in the case of quite a number of the plays of Sophocles, generally by introducing inverted commas against each 'sententious' line in conformity with the earlier practice in printed plays. Here again it is only some of the

---

[1] *Aj.* 924 – one of the few lines of which commentators find a direct echo in Racine's own work – in Monime's outcry when she sees 'the dying Mithridate':

Ah! que vois-je, Seigneur, et quel sort est le vôtre!

[2] Cf. W. McC. Stewart, pp. 62–6 of 'L'Éducation de Racine – le poète et ses maîtres' in *Cahiers de l'Association Internationale des Études Françaises*, Paris, 1953.

sententiae of Euripides of which Racine is critical – not any of those of Sophocles.

We do not have annotations throughout of the *Oedipus* in any of the editions of Sophocles which he possessed and which have survived – and there are four such. In one of the two in which notes on the *Oedipus* occur they only go up to line 623; there is only a brief annotation in the other.[1] But the notes we do have contain ample evidence of Racine's interest in the tragic effect aimed at by the poet.

After saluting the opening (as we have seen above) as 'magnificent', Racine shows how the action reveals the characters. 'In praising Oedipus they (the suppliants) make him known' (33). From the outset the intention to stir pity is shown to be in the poet's mind. Against Oedipus' second speech (58 seqq.) he notes that Sophocles 'représente en Œdipe un prince qui aime ses peuples, *afin qu'il fasse plus de pitié*'. The way in which Oedipus implicates himself is duly noted (236 seqq.): 'Imprécations d'Œdipe contre le meurtrier de Laïus. – *Bel artifice du poète* qui fait qu'Œdipe s'engage lui-même dans d'effroyables imprécations'.

At the point where Tiresias begs Oedipus to send him home and Oedipus ends by pouring abuse upon him, Racine notes that he thus involves Tiresias in telling him truths which he takes for calumnies. '*Bel artifice* (he comments) *pour instruire le spectateur sans éclairer l'acteur.* – Dispute violente d'Œdipe et de Tirésie, et *néanmoins toujours pleine de majesté*' (339 seqq.). He notes how Oedipus' suspicion develops and his jealousy of Creon as the instigator of Tiresias. Yet (comments Racine):

cette mauvaise humeur d'Œdipe *ne le rend point odieux*, parce que l'intérêt public le fait parler; mais *elle le rend digne de compassion*, parce qu'il veut forcer un homme à lui dire des choses qui doivent retomber sur lui (378 seqq.).

When the quarrel has reached its climax and Tiresias counters:

[1] H. Estienne, 1568 (v. *supra*, p.179 , n. 2).

'I seem mad to you; but your father found me wise', and Oedipus answers: 'What father? wait . . .', Racine notes: 'Cette inquiétude d'Œdipe est *admirable*; Tirésie le laisse sans l'éclaircir' (430–8). There follows the altercation with Creon; and against the line

τοῦτ' αὐτὸ μή μοι φράζ', ὅπως οὐκ εἶ κακός.

Racine notes: 'Œdipe ne veut point écouter. *Belle image* d'un homme en colère.'

Fénelon and others have attributed to Racine the plan of an *Oedipus* of his own, 'suivant le goût de Sophocle'; but the internal arguments against Racine's ever having seriously planned such a tragedy are strong. Corneille's unfortunate though at the time not unsuccessful *Œdipe*, with which in 1660 he marked his return to the theatre after the interruption of the Fronde, could only have made Racine feel even more strongly than might have otherwise been the case, how remote was current French tragedy, with its complex plots and its love-interest, from the tragedy of which, as we have seen above, he had considerable direct knowledge and appreciation. The dramaturgy and the stage-conditions of the time make it inconceivable that he could have hoped to realize a tragedy with choruses; and we can at most assume that when the differences between such a tragedy as the *Œdipe* of his much older rival Corneille or such an opera (or 'tragédie lyrique' – as its composer entitled such works) as the *Alceste* of that overbearing collaborator of Molière, Jean-Baptiste Lully, were discussed between Racine and his friends, the poet of *Iphigénie* may well have hinted at his readiness to go beyond negative criticism, of which we have a good example in the preface to his just-mentioned play – and given them to understand that he was tempted by the impossible.

At all events we know that it was only when, twelve years after *Phèdre*, he was approached by Mme de Maintenon to produce something for the girls of the royal foundation of St Cyr, where their production of his *Andromaque* had been found upsettingly successful, that Racine actually conceived and finally produced his Biblical plays, *Esther* and *Athalie*. What his debts were to the

Racine's Response to the Stagecraft of Attic Tragedy

Greeks and to the secular and religious drama and music of the time (tragedy, oratorio, opera) in composing these masterpieces is not the subject of this paper.[1]

But if Racine did not produce an *Oedipus*, it was not that he was averse to drawing a subject from antiquity for contemporary tragedy. All his secular plays but *Bajaʒet* are in part drawn from ancient sources, mythological or historical. And four of them go back, in one way or another, to plays of Euripides: his *Thébaïde*, his *Andromaque*, his *Iphigénie en Aulide*, his *Phèdre*. This circumstance was attributed by his friend Valincour to his not fearing to 'joust against Euripides', whereas 'the lofty idea he had of Sophocles convinced him that he could not imitate him without spoiling him'. The spirit of the age as well as all the conventions which had gradually become established in a live theatre which had produced tragedies, tragi-comedies, pastorals and comedies for a century must in any case have made such imitation appear to him impossible. Saint-Évremond – himself long the friend, defender and partisan of Corneille against the rising Racine and who knew Dryden in the England of his exile – has an interesting passage in his essay of 1672: *De la tragédie ancienne et moderne*, which has a direct bearing on this matter:

> Sans un amour trop grand pour l'antiquité, ou un trop grand dégoût pour notre siècle, on ne fera pas des tragédies de Sophocle et d'Euripide les modèles des pièces de notre temps. Je ne dis point que ces tragédies n'aient eu ce qu'elles devaient avoir pour plaire au goût des Athéniens; mais qui pourrait traduire en français, dans toute sa force, l'*Œdipe* même, ce chef-d'œuvre des anciens, j'ose assurer que rien au monde ne nous paraîtrait plus barbare, plus funeste, plus opposé aux vrais sentiments qu'on doit avoir.

Racine and certain of his most gifted and sensitive contemporaries like Boileau and Rapin did not quite take this view. They accepted the central position given to the *Oedipus* by Aristotle

[1] Cf. W. McC. Stewart: 'La Mise en scène d'*Athalie*' in *La Mise en scène des œuvres du passé* (*C.N.R.S.*, Paris, 1956); 'L'Esthétique du chœur dans la tragédie' in *Atti del III Congresso Internationale di Esthetica*, Venice and Turin, 1956; and 'Le Tragique et le sacré chez Racine' in *Le Théâtre tragique* (*C.N.R.S.*, Paris, 1962).

in the *Poetics* as a model of tragic action; and Boileau in his *Art poétique* presents Oedipus as the very type of the tragic figure:

> Ainsi, pour nous charmer, la Tragédie en pleurs
> D'Œdipe tout sanglant fit parler les douleurs.

Fénelon analyses the subject briefly in his *Lettre à l'Académie* (1714) and emphasizes the effective way it makes its mark, without complexity of plot and excluding artificial love-interest – inseparable from the tragedy of his own time. We have seen that he even attributed to Racine the project of an *Oedipus* of his own.

Whatever the truth of this, we do at least have direct testimony to the effect Racine could produce with the reading out of *Oedipus* to a select gathering of friends. His friend Valincourt recalled in a letter to the abbé d'Olivet (who in his turn recorded it in his history of the French Academy) how one day, at Boileau's home in Auteuil – with Nicole and 'quelques autres amis d'un mérite distingué', they engaged Racine in an interpretation of the *Oedipus* of Sophocles.

> He recited it (sc. read it out) in its entirety, translating on the spot; and he was so moved that all we listeners experienced all the feelings of terror and compassion on which this tragedy turns. I have seen our best actors on the stage, I have seen our best plays; but nothing has ever shaken me as did this reading: and as I write to you, I still think I see Racine with the book in his hand and us all dumbfounded around him ('et nous tous consternés autour de lui').

The scene here described seems to corroborate and authenticate the response to Greek tragedy to which Racine's annotations testify.

W. McC. Stewart

XII: THE

CLASSICAL TRADITION

IN SPANISH

DRAMATIC THEORY

AND PRACTICE

IN THE SEVENTEENTH

CENTURY

'AFTER LUNCH, HE AND MONSIEUR DE BARRIÈRE CAME to take me to see an old comedy which had been revived and which was worthless, although it was by Don Pedro Calderón. I also went to see this author, who is the greatest poet and the best wit they have at present. He is a Knight of the Order of St James and Chaplain of the Chapel of the Monarchs at Toledo, but by his conversation I saw clearly that he did not know much, although his hair is already completely white. We argued a little about the dramatic rules, which they do not know at all in that country, and at which they mock.' This well-known statement was made by François Bertaut, who, in 1659, accompanied the Marshal de Gramont to Madrid to ask for the hand of Maria-Theresa of Austria on behalf of Louis XIV.[1] One wonders what Calderón thought of him.

Ignorance of the neo-classical 'rules' was an accusation that *honnêtes hommes* frequently made against the Spanish dramatists in Bertaut's day. The idea that these playwrights did not know their Aristotle, Horace and the reputable commentaries has haunted many students of European drama, and also many conscientious hispanists, ever since. It would appear to have been behind Moral-Fatio's attempt, when he prepared his edition of Lope de Vega's *New Art of Making Three-Act Plays in Our Own Times*, to demonstrate that, of all the writings on classical dramatic doctrine, Lope used (and knew) only Robortello and Donatus.[2] It survives in *our* own times in the minds of many critics and scholars. We find it in Bray,[3] and it is implicit in many

[1] François Bertaut, sieur de Fréauville, *Iovrnal du Voyage d'Espagne*, ed. F. Cassan, *Revue hispanique*, Tome XLVII (1919), pp. 151–2. The translation is my own, as are all those others in this study, except for certain playtitles which I have adopted from other translators.

[2] See the introduction and notes to his edition of the *Arte nuevo de haƶer comedias en este tiempo*, in *Bulletin hispanique*, Tome III (1901), pp. 365–405.

[3] See René Bray, *La Formation de la doctrine classique en France*, impression of Paris, 1951, pp. 28–33. In the table of contents, the second section of this chapter (Première Partie, Chapitre II) is given as 'Mépris des Français pour l'irrégularité de la poésie

of J. A. Cook's references to seventeenth-century drama.[1] It has led some people to think that the Spanish drama of that age stood outside the classical tradition of the European theatre, that the plays and dramatic theory of the Greeks and Romans had little or no influence on it, and even that writers like Lope and Calderón, who – in their opinion – composed wild, odd, irregular, 'romantic' things which can best be described as tragicomedies, were incapable of writing tragedies.

But what are the facts? Let us begin with the charge of ignorance and thence proceed to the others.

Throughout the sixteenth and seventeenth centuries, Spain and Italy were closely linked, both politically and culturally. The constant going and coming of officers, gentlemen, scholars, writers, churchmen, ambassadors and their households between the two countries made it impossible for the major literary ideas and disputes of either one to be unknown in the other. The plays of the Greek and Roman dramatists, the *Poetics* and *Rhetoric* of Aristotle and the *Poetic Art* of Horace were known in Spain in their original texts long before Malherbe came. So were the Italian commentaries. For those who knew little or no Greek, it was not very difficult to read the *Poetics*, from 1536 onwards, in Paccius' Latin translation or, from 1570, in the Italian of Castelvetro. In the sixteenth century, some Spanish dramatists, University men and others, wrote and published tragedies based on classical models. Hermenegildo has said of the later ones, in his study of the sixteenth-century Spanish tragedians, that they had

---

espagnole et l'ignorance de ses théoriciens'. He observes (p. 32) that 'La littérature espagnole était essentiellement irrégulière'.

[1] John A. Cook, *Neo-classic Drama in Spain. Theory and Practice*, Dallas 1959, *passim*. In this book, which is in its way a useful introduction to the neo-classical drama of the eighteenth century in Spain, the author takes the view, to which I cannot subscribe, that neo-classical doctrines were introduced into Spain in the middle of the eighteenth century. In his preface (vii) he speaks of 'the obvious truth that Spain had reached literary impotence and had produced no works of merit for almost a century before the introduction of neo-classical doctrines'. The first part of his 'truth' is surely disproved by the work of Valbuena Prat, Aubrun and Chapman on Calderón's mythological plays written between 1651 and his death in 1681, and by a reading of any late Calderonian *auto sacramental*. The falsity of the second part will be demonstrated in our argument.

intimate knowledge of the neo-Aristotelian *Poetics* of the Italian theorists but that, although they admired Aristotle, they generally, in practice, followed the Italian imitators of Seneca.[1]

It was during the career of Lope de Vega that Horace and Aristotle became very well known in Spanish. In 1591, Vicente Espinel's translation of the *Poetic Art* was published in Madrid,[2] and Luis Zapata's was issued in Lisbon in 1592.[3] These were followed, in 1596, by the printing in Madrid of a work on which seventeenth-century Spanish dramatists and critics were to look with pride. This was Alonso López Pinciano's *Poetic Philosophy of Antiquity*, a long, careful, point-by-point commentary on Aristotle and Horace, arranged in typical Renaissance fashion as a series of discussions between three thinkers.[4] As Riley has pointed out, the treatise is lucid and intelligent.[5] It is also subtle. To imagine that Lope de Vega did not know it, and reflect on it, is to reject a virtual certainty out of preference for an improbability.

In 1609, four years after the appearance of Cervantes's famous attack on the new way of playmaking (in Chapter 48 of the *First Part* of *Don Quixote*), Lope published his *New Art*.[6] The qualities and content of this work have been underestimated by many modern scholars. Ironic, elliptical in style, it expresses and suggests a remarkable amount of good dramatic theory in its three

[1] Alfredo Hermenegildo, *Los trágicos españoles del siglo XVI*, Madrid 1961, p. 14.

[2] Along with Espinel's *Diversas rimas*, Madrid, Luys Sánchez, 1591.

[3] *El arte poética de Horatio, traduzida de latín en español,*

[4] *Philosophía antigua poética*, Madrid 1596. An edition in three volumes, by Alfredo Carballo Picazo, was printed in Madrid in 1953. There is a review article on this edition, by Robert J. Clements, 'López Pinciano's *Philosophía Antigua Poética* and the Spanish Contribution to Renaissance Literary Theory', in *Hispanic Review*, Vol. XXIII (1955), pp. 48–55. A substantial account of Pinciano's theories is contained in Sanford Shepard's study, *El Pinciano y las teorías literarias del Siglo de Oro*, Madrid 1962.

[5] E. C. Riley, *Cervantes's Theory of the Novel*, Oxford 1962, p. 3. Mr Riley's book is an extremely valuable guide to the problems of literary theory at the end of the sixteenth century and the beginning of the seventeenth.

[6] A serviceable English translation of Lope's *New Art* by William T. Brewster, with an introduction by Brander Matthews, was printed for the Dramatic Museum of Columbia University as *Papers on Play-Making I. The New Art of Writing Plays . . .*, New York 1914. It has been reissued in *Papers on Playmaking*, ed. Brander Matthews (A Dramabook), New York, Hill and Wang, 1957, pp. 2–19.

hundred and eighty-nine lines of verse. Despite Lope's claim that he has rejected 'the Art of the Ancients', the majority of the ideas which he expresses, indeed by far the most important of them, are classical. True, he follows Guarini and the other Italian defenders of 'tragicomedy' when he claims that a mixture of tragic and comic is true to Nature,[1] although he does not say that such a mixture should be made in all plays. True, he follows the tendencies of the Spanish practical dramatists who preceded him and reduces the number of acts to three (*Protasis, Epitasis, Catastrophe*). True, he tells the aspirant dramatist not to worry whether there are Kings in his play or not; he does not advise him to agglomerate personages high and low in every play. It is likewise true that, although he recommends that the events in each act be restricted, if possible, to those of one day, he defends an otherwise untrammelled liberty in the use of time and place. Nevertheless, the rest of the *New Art* is a recital of sound classical ideas: the moral and didactic value of good plays – *Delighting while Profiting*[2] is the Horatian title of one of Tirso de Molina's collections of plays and stories, as well as being the main literary ideal of his age – unity of action; careful construction; exposition, complication and resolution; smooth, continuous action; decorum in characterization, speech and action; verisimilitude; consistency of characters. In fact, what always impresses the intelligent undergraduate when he compares the ideas in Lope's *New Art* with those of the corresponding canto of Boileau's *Poetic Art* is not the differences between them but the great body of doctrine which the two works have in common – the true classical heritage of the seventeenth-century European drama. Even Lope's polymetric system, much more elaborate than those of his Spanish predecessors, is foreshadowed by the Greek tragedians' use of different types of metre for the choral and dramatic elements of their plays.

Defence of a mixture of tragic and comic (or of comic relief in tragedy) is only incidental in Lope's *New Art*. It is quite clear

---

[1] In practice, of course, such a mixture had been used in the Spanish popular theatre since the Middle Ages.   [2] *Deleitar aprovechando.*

that he wrote it in order to defend his own methods and his own plays against criticism. But the work shows, equally clearly, another intention: to advise. It gives advice to those others who would compose plays that would satisfy the audiences of Madrid in 1609, advice penned by a confident authority, by a creative genius who has become tired of the disputes and the hairsplitting of the theorists of Europe, and of Madrid. Don't be put off by their gibbering! Don't hesitate! If you want to mix comic with tragic, mix 'em. If you want to write tragedies with comic relief, write 'em. If you want to make tragedies with 'happy endings', make 'em. And never mind all that unimaginative gabble about unities of time and place. *But*, let me warn you, whatever you write, tragedies, comedies, or what you will, if they are to be successful you must follow your common sense and observe these valuable old maxims: unity of action, careful construction, decorum, verisimilitude, etc. . . . The *New Art* is always worth another reading.

After 1609, commentaries on the drama, containing a clear exposition and examination of the classical and neo-classical theories, continued to be written in Spain, for though many people favoured the 'new art' innovations others did not. In 1617, after Cervantes had changed his opinion of the new drama and turned enthusiastically to extol its virtues in the prologue to his volume of *Eight Three-Act Plays and Eight Interludes* (Madrid 1615),[1] and after Ricardo de Turia, in his *Apologia for Spanish Three-Act Plays* (1616),[2] had vigorously defended what he considered to be all 'tragicomedies', two neo-classical writers stood up as champions of stricter classical ideas. Cristóbal Suárez de Figueroa, in the dialogue of *The Wayfarer*,[3] launched an attack on the new school and, if he conceded that the action

---

[1] *Ocho comedias y ocho entremeses*, Madrid 1615. There is an edition of the prologue in H. J. Chaytor, *Dramatic Theory in Spain*, Cambridge 1925, pp. 33–7.

[2] *Apologético de las comedias españolas*. A. Morel-Fatio edited the text in 'Les Défenseurs de la Comedia', *Bulletin hispanique*, Tome IV (1902), pp. 30–62. His text was later included in Chaytor, op. cit., pp. 43–8.

[3] *El pasagero*, Madrid 1617. The relevant passage was reproduced in Chaytor, op. cit., pp. 48–57.

of a comedy might include the happenings of as many as three days and agreed to its division into three acts, nevertheless advocated the composition of comedies in strict accordance with the doctrines of Horace, which he expounded in some detail. Francisco Cascales, in the discussions which form his celebrated *Poetic Tables*,[1] showed – or, perhaps, appears on the first reading to have shown – very little sympathy for the playwrights of his times. He denied the existence of such a genre as tragicomedy and, with a show of disgruntled impatience, consented to include the 'hermaphrodites', which he considered many Spanish plays to be, in the category of double tragedy.[2] He carefully explained the principles of the two genres that he admitted, tragedy and comedy, and emphasized the importance of verisimilitude and decorum, which he treated rather more intelligently than did the majority of the Spanish neo-classicists.

Whether in Madrid or in the provinces, Lope was at this time by no means surrounded only by supporters. Towards the end of the same year 1617, in an atmosphere of tension between literary men of the two persuasions, there was printed in Madrid *The Sponge*, a bitter Latin satire on Lope by the neo-classicist Pedro de Torres Rámila, friend of Suárez de Figueroa.[3] *The Sponge*, all available copies of which were destroyed soon after it was published, appears to have attacked Lope's literary works in general, and in particular his long pastoral and epic works, but to have said little about his plays except that he committed many ineptitudes in them. With this publication began a heated dispute on paper between Lope and his supporters, on the one hand, and the neo-classical theorists on the other. This dispute could scarcely have left any literary man in the Madrid of 1618, or in the other cities and the Universities of Spain, ignorant of the ideas which the neo-classicists were upholding.

The moral victory in the *Sponge* dispute of 1617–18 went to the

---

[1] *Tablas poéticas*, Murcia 1617.   [2] Ibid., pp. 329–32.

[3] The disputes over the *Sponge* (*Spongia*) are treated by Joaquín de Entrambasaguas in his dissertation *Una guerra literaria del Siglo de Oro. Lope de Vega y los preceptistas aristotélicos*, printed in his *Estudios sobre Lope de Vega*, Tom. I, Madrid 1946, pp. 63–580. This study first appeared in print in 1932.

innovators. After it, Spanish writers went on expressing classical theory. The neo-classicists explained *their* narrow doctrines. The defenders of the Spanish drama, following Lope de Vega in their rejection of some restrictive tenets of neo-classical doctrine, and in their retention and propagation of the fundamentals of classical dramatic theory, continued to champion what one is tempted to call Spanish Aristotelianism, although their ideas were, for the most part, derived from the fusion of Aristotelian and Horatian doctrines.

In 1622 Francisco de Barreda, a prominent jurist who is also said to have been a dramatist, published his book *The Best of Princes, Trajan the August* in Madrid.[1] It contained his fine translation of Pliny's *Panegyric*, together with notes and ten intelligent discourses. The ninth discourse, 'Invective against the Plays that Trajan Prohibited, and Apology for Our Own Ones',[2] is one of the most interesting and lively pieces of dramatic criticism that Spain produced in the seventeenth century. The spirit which inspired it was the pride of Barreda in the great achievements of his nation's drama. Like many of his literate compatriots, he was convinced that, if the Spanish drama was derived from the classical, it had surpassed it in excellence and in virtue. He maintained that comic and tragic elements were not infrequently mingled in classical plays. He argued that classical dramatic practice was often inconsistent with the theories of Aristotle, and he condemned what he found to be lack of decorum in Homer (source of the tragedy), in Aeschylus, in Plautus and in Terence. He pointed out, not unreasonably, that even the best comedies of Plautus and Terence would seem ill-composed, insipid and dull if presented in translation on the stages of Madrid in his day:

> For a time has come when the fortunate boldness of the writers of Spain, the adornment of this century, has decked out [the drama] anew in fine raiment, it has made it discreet and entertaining, and, like a bee that fashions the sweetest honeycomb from the quintessence of the flowers, it has fashioned three-act plays with the

[1] *El meior príncipe Traiano Avgvsto . . .*, Madrid 1622.   [2] Ibid., fol. 120v–141v.

brilliancies of all manner of wit, taking from Natural Philosophy what is most sublime in it, from Moral Philosophy what is most prudent in it, from the Histories what is most suitable, from the Fables, now polished and civilized, what is most profitable, from Eloquence its purest elements. All this in agreeable style, stripped of the severity and roughness in which the Ancients left it to us. Finally, it has come to surpass the plays of Antiquity with its own ones, so that the former seem to be no more than sketches or shadows of the latter. Nor does the moral value of the plays of Antiquity commend them for imitation, for, just as Plato condemned [them] in Homer, the fables on which they founded their plays were scandalous and of pernicious example.[1]

Although Barreda scorned what he considered to be servile, cowardly imitation, he attacked classical drama in defence of his own nation's idea of three classical principles: decorum, verisimilitude and moral value.

Time passed. After the first quarter of the century, we find no hint of serious disputes over the neo-classical 'rules'.[2] Alonso Ordóñez das Seijas y Tovar's *The Poetics of Aristotle rendered in Our Castilian Tongue* was published in Madrid in 1626,[3] long before any French or English version was printed. As far as we know, it provoked no heated comment. Then in 1633, two years before Lope's death, and when Calderón was already famous, came the most notable of the Spanish dissertations on Aristotle, Jusepe Antonio González de Salas's *New Idea of Ancient Tragedy, or Last Illustration of the Singular Book of Poetics of Aristotle the Stagirite*, printed in Madrid.[4] In his useful study of the *New Idea*, Riley has observed of its author that 'few Spanish writers appreciated more than he the enduring significance of Aristotle's *Poetics*, and none could rival him in the scholarly exposition of

---

[1] *El meior príncipe Traiano Avgvsto* . . ., fol. 132v–133r.

[2] One isolated attack on the Spanish drama was, however, printed in 1641, as we shall see.

[3] *La poética de Aristóteles dada a nuestra lengua castellana.* . . . The work was reprinted, with textual alterations, in 1778.

[4] *Nueva idea de la tragedia antigua, o ilustración última al libro singular de poética de Aristóteles Stagirita.* A second edition, in two volumes, was made in Madrid in 1778.

that beguiling and difficult work'.[1] As well as being an erudite classicist, he was a friend of Quevedo, in collaboration with whom he had begun the translation of Seneca's tragedies. He included in his book his translation of the *Troades*, examples from which he employed to illustrate many of his ideas. Also, he 'had relations with all the great Spanish men of letters of his day, as well as many foreigners'.[2] It would require some ingenuity to imagine serious reasons why Calderón might not have read the *New Idea*. Our evidence for forming a judgment on such a question is in the plays alone, and they tend to encourage the opinion that Calderón knew his González de Salas well.

The tone of the *New Idea* is quite different from that of the polemic writings of the 1605–25 period. It is, for the most part, a tranquil work. Except when he attacks obscure, complicated and inflated verse, Salas shows no ill-feeling for the Spanish poets of his time, and he is glad that the comic poets are less affected than the others by 'this pestilential influence'.[3] In fact, he shows no animosity towards the dramatists of the period. He shows respect and admiration for the best of them and grants that they are acquainted with fundamental principles of classical theory. He accepts the genre of 'tragicomedy' and finds praiseworthy ingenuity in the way in which his contemporaries have united the tragic and the comic and raised the comedy to a much higher level than that of the Ancients.[4] He states that their division of plays into three acts has proved to be an apt one, shows that there is no lack of authorities to support it, and simply advises them to be careful to follow closely Donatus's counsel in their movement from *protasis* into *epitasis* and thence to *catastrophe*.[5] One never gets the impression that he is writing for the ignorant. Often, it seems that he is just reminding, digging deeper, and elaborating or clarifying, instead of revealing. He *does* challenge, by providing a solid basis for the comparison of contemporary and classical

---

[1] See E. C. Riley, 'The Dramatic Theories of Don Jusepe Antonio González de Salas', *Hispanic Review*, Vol. XIX (1951), pp. 183–203. For our quotation, see p. 184.

[2] Ibid., p. 183. [3] *Nueva idea* . . ., Madrid 1633, p. 85.

[4] Ibid., pp. 184 and 85. [5] Ibid., pp. 184–5.

theory and practice. The disputes in Spain between strict neo-classicists and defenders and exponents of a new art were over long before 1633. Exactly how petty or how violent they were we shall probably never know. We have only the written word to judge by. Before 1633, the new art had given ample proof of its worth in practice, the supreme test of dramatic theory. All sectarian passion had been spent in the reasonable dramatic theorists. A period had begun in which a man like Calderón could well be no more than bored by a man like Bertaut.

And after 1633? Only one more long treatise on the aesthetic doctrines of the drama appears to have been composed before the end of the century. Nevertheless, we have the critics, and they reveal how classical ideals were alive in the minds of those who thought seriously and reasonably about dramatic aesthetics. When the Royal Chronicler Joseph Pellicer de Tobar Abarca wrote his *Idea of the Castilian Three-Act Play, Deduced from the Dramatic Works of Doctor Juan Pérez de Montalbán*, which was printed in 1639 in a volume of posthumous tributes to the play-wright,[1] he judged his plays systematically, according to classical precepts: moral and didactic worth; decorum of style, action and characterization; skill in plot-construction; verisimilitude. And he found them to be good. These canons of judgment are like-wise apparent in the *Approbations* written by responsible church-men and laymen to give justification for the publication of vol-umes of plays. The classical heritage in seventeenth-century dramatic criticism is strikingly obvious in the most famous *Approbation* of them all. It was composed in 1682 by Father Manuel de Guerra y Ribera for the fifth *Part* of Calderón's three-act plays.[2] Guerra, who finds a great deal that is repre-hensible and indecorous in the plays of the Ancients, observes of Calderón:

> Without offering any slight to as many distinguished poets as have
> made and are making the theatre of the world, and of this Court,

---

[1] *Idea de la comedia de Castilla, dedvƶida de las obras cómicas del doctor Ivan Pérez de Montalbán,* in *Lágrimas panegíricas a la temprana muerte . . .,* Madrid 1639, fol. 146r–152r.

[2] *Verdadera quinta parte,* Madrid 1682, pp. ¶¶¶r–¶¶¶¶ 8v.

illustrious, I must be permitted to say that our Don Pedro Calderón would on his own have been sufficient to ennoble the drama and free the theatre from all scruple. This man of great judgment, learning and intelligence trod the summit of dramatic art so heroically and majestically that he has left only Envy capable of desiring to imitate him. It is not my love and respect that say so. It is his plays.

Who has married the extreme delicacies of plot to verisimilitude of incidents? It is a web so delicate that it snaps as one weaves it, because the danger in what is very subtle and involved is lack of verisimilitude. Let the eye examine all his plots in wonderment and it will find every one handled with such equal skill that they may well dispute the prize for supremacy. His Saints' plays are of fine example, his histories bring disenchantment, his plays of pure invention are innocently entertaining and free from moral danger. The majesty of the sentiments, the nobility of the ideas, the purity of the speech he maintains so rigidly that he keeps them intact even in the midst of the witty shafts of humour. He never slips into puerilities, he never falls into baseness of sentiments. He maintains such a lofty majesty in the argument which he is pursuing that, if it is about a Saint, he makes his virtues even more noble; if it is about a Prince, he inspires him to the most heroic of actions; if it is about a private person, he makes his sentiments more pure than they are in reality. When he writes of a Saint, he brings honour to his throne; when of a Prince, he elevates and kindles his spirit; when of a private person, he wipes his disposition clean.

This prodigy of intellect achieved many things which seemed impossible. Observe how many. He wedded, with sweetest artifice, verisimilitude to illusion, the possible to the fabulous, the feigned to the true, the amorous to the decorous, the majestic to the accessible, the heroic to the intelligible, the grave to the pleasant, solemn moral observations to everyday conversation, ingenious conceits to clear ideas, doctrine to pleasure, morality to sweetness, humour to discretion. He gave his warnings with moderation, his reprehensions without wounding, his admonitions without causing annoyance, his information without tediousness, and, finally, his disenchantments so soothingly, and his blows so softened, that only *his* understanding could achieve the impossible in so many matters.[1]

[1] Ibid., ¶¶¶¶ 6v–7r. I am open to criticism for my rendering of the last clause of the fourth sentence in the second paragraph of the quotation, *sus materias* [*son*] *de inocente*

Classical Drama and its Influence

There is certainly no lack of classical training in this critic. Nor did he find any such lack in Calderón.

The last important work of dramatic theory and criticism produced in Spain in the seventeenth century was by the only dramatist of the Calderonian 'school' who left for us his reflections on his art. Francisco Bances Candamo, official playwright to Charles II, was, as I have found, a remarkably subtle political dramatist. In 1690, stung into action by a Jesuit's attack on the theatre, he began to write a treatise in defence of the Spanish drama. By 1693, he had developed it into the *Theatre of the Theatres of Past and Present Centuries: History of the Greek, Roman and Castilian Stage: Precepts of the Spanish Three-Act Play Drawn from the Poetic Arts of Horace and Aristotle, and from the Usage and Custom of Our Poets and Theatres, and Made Fitting and Reformed in Accordance with the Opinion of the Angelic Doctor and Fathers of the Church.*[1] Unfortunately he left it incomplete when, apparently for political reasons, he resigned from his position and withdrew from Court. Nevertheless, as Professor Wilson has remarked, Guerra's *Approbation* of Calderón and the *Theatre of the Theatres* represent the most profound expression of Spanish dramatic criticism in the seventeenth century.[2] Bances's treatise is also the first systematic attempt to write a history of the Spanish theatre and to show it to be, in large measure, a development of the classical theatre. The title itself is significant. It indicates the three main elements of which seven-

---

diuersión, sin peligro. This may well mean simply 'his materials [are] innocently entertaining and free from moral danger'. Nevertheless, it appears to me that here there is an analogy to be drawn with other parts of the passage, and that, as in them, he is making a distinction between three things.

[1] *Theatro de los theatros de los passados y presentes siglos: historia scénica griega, romana y castellana: preceptos de la comedia española sacados de las artes poéticas de Horacio, y Aristóteles, y de el vso y costumbre de nuestros poetas, y theatros, y ajustados y reformados, conforme la mente de el Doctor Angélico y Santos Padres.* It is contained in MS. 17459 of the National Library, Madrid. Only certain fragments of this work have been published up to the present time. I am preparing, as part of a study of Bances' work, a critical edition of the complete text, as it survives.

[2] E. M. Wilson, 'Las "Dudas curiosas" a la aprobación del maestro fray Manuel de Guerra y Ribera', *Estudios escénicos. Cuadernos del Instituto del Teatro [de Barcelona]*, 6 (1960), p. 50.

teenth-century Spanish dramatic theory and methods of play-writing are a fusion: classical theory, techniques derived empirically out of practice, from the Middle Ages onwards, before the audiences of the public and Court theatres in Spain, and moral doctrines of the Church. Bances' principal object of concern, in writing a treatise on dramatic art for his contemporaries, is not any theory of the mingling or uniting of comic and tragic, or any method of treating time and space on the stage. As far as such matters are concerned, he takes for granted our acceptance of his predecessors' techniques. He sees that the general standard of playwriting, and particularly of Court playwriting, has declined since the death of Calderón in 1681. He wants to raise it again. Therefore he sets out to follow, like González de Salas, an Aristotelian plan of discussion: argument, contexture, episodes, customs, doctrines, forms of speech, personages, music, dances, interludes, machines, contrivances, players and theatres. It seems that he stopped writing before he had gone far along this path, but the fragments of the treatise which have survived are most valuable.

When, in the 1690 version, he makes his historical survey of the development of the Spanish drama, Bances reveals sound criteria of aesthetic judgment and a thorough knowledge of a great number of the plays which his predecessors wrote. The particular plays which he uses to illustrate his ideas are carefully selected. He sees that both Lope's and Calderón's playwriting improved as they matured. He also is aware that considerable progress was made in dramatic art between early Lope and mature Calderón. He is undoubtedly rather hard on Lope at times, as when he says:

> Don Pedro Calderón de la Barca . . . was the man who gave decorum to the boards and established the norm for the three-act play in Spain, in the nobility of his personages, in the circumspection of his dramatic arguments, in the ingenuity of his intrigue and structure, and in the purity of his style. Until his time the Spanish drama lacked majesty.[1]

[1] National Library MS. 17459, fol. 56r.

This does not, however, mean that he despises Lope or under-estimates his great part in the formation of the Spanish drama. Indeed, for him Lope is 'a writer in whom Apollo distilled, with perennial fecundity, all the torrents of his influence'.[1] It is simply that Bances, after careful study, has perceived what we ourselves can see, that as the seventeenth century advanced 'the very taste of the people gradually, day by day, filed and polished as it censured'.[2] He observes two important facts. The first is that sixteenth-century drama, and Lope's early plays, contained much that was stylistically crude and that did not conform to the peculiarly Spanish conception of literary decorum that became a norm in the seventeenth. The second is that great artistic progress was made between the sixteenth century, when the playwrights often created individual dramatic scenes well but failed to con-struct well-knit, effective plots, and the maturity of Calderón, whose skill in construction became remarkable. The influence of classical doctrines in both of these developments is obvious and profound.

Let us deal briefly here with the classical influence in the improvement of plot-making. An excellent source of information for this study (and for all aspects of the study of classical in-fluences in the Calderonian drama) is Dr Sloman's book, *The Dramatic Craftsmanship of Calderón*, in which he demonstrates how, in making eight fine plays, the dramatist refashioned eight earlier and less effective ones.[3] Dr Sloman points out that:

> The history of the Spanish drama in the last decade of the sixteenth century and the first two decades of the seventeenth is largely the history of the development of a *comedia* lacking unity of action to one in which that unity is achieved. Lope's later plays have dramatic unity; so have the best plays of Tirso de Molina and his contem-poraries. But most of the plays written between, say, 1590 and 1610 are carelessly and loosely constructed. Calderón's sources are plays of this kind, and by a variety of means he transformed them.[4]

[1] National Library MS, 17459, fol. 56v.   [2] Ibid., loc. cit.
[3] Albert E. Sloman, *The Dramatic Craftsmanship of Calderón. His Use of Earlier Plays*, Oxford 1958.   [4] Ibid., pp. 278–9.

Now surely it cannot be by sheer chance that the movement towards dramatic unity took place precisely in a period in which, as we have seen, there was quite heated dispute over the neo-classical principles and the techniques of the new art. This is coincidence, but it would, perhaps be naïve to imagine that it is fortuitous coincidence. Coming after the publication of López Pinciano's *Poetic Philosophy* (1596), and clearly not uninfluenced by it, Cervantes's attack on wild, formless plays of the 'new school' in the First Part of *Don Quixote* (1605) must, because of the book's immediate and growing success, have been exceedingly annoying and embarrassing for the dramatists. *It* may have sparked off the disputes. It must certainly have caused *some* spectators to look more critically at the plays that were being presented to them, and *some* playwrights to reflect more critically on their art. It must also have given the neo-classicists an excellent opportunity to give tongue. One cannot doubt that there were disputes in Madrid before 1609, or during 1609. The tone of Lope's *New Art* shows that quite clearly. In this work, which, in its way, can be seen to be a plea for better playwriting, Lope advises dramatists to follow the basic precepts of classical theory (not all those of neo-classical theory), and then, from 1609 to 1624–5, the years in which the series of polemic writings of a passionate nature ends with Tirso de Molina's praise of Lope in *The Country-houses of Toledo*[1] and Mira de Amescua's enthusiastic *Approbation* to *Part Twenty* of Lope's plays,[2] playwriting in Spain improved. Would it be absurd to suggest that this improvement was caused not only by the demands of an ever more demanding kind of audience but also by the influence of the literary disputes, and of the ideas debated in them, on the thinking of both dramatists and public? Or that Cervantes relented and gave his allegiance to the new art because he saw that it was at last producing well-written and effective plays? Or that, however

---

[1] *Los cigarrales de Toledo*, Madrid 1624. The relevant passage was reprinted by Morel-Fatio, with an introduction, in 'Les Défenseurs . . .', pp. 30–44. Most of it was then included by Chaytor in his book, pp. 58–63.

[2] *Parte veinte de las comedias de Lope de Vega Carpio . . .*, Madrid 1625.

loudly and however frequently Lope exclaimed that he was not writing in accordance with the art of the Ancients, the influence of the *New Art* on his fellow-dramatists may have been one of the main influences for the 'classicizing' of the Spanish drama of the seventeenth century? Dr Sloman has shown that at least as early as 1628 Calderón was 'classicizing'.[1] The tendency did not begin with Calderón. We find it in the ironic Lope. Far as they were from being neo-classicists, Lope de Vega, Tirso de Molina, Calderón and the other good dramatists of the seventeenth century were, in their own fashion, classicists.

When we turn to study their plays, we have three most useful guides, Professor Parker's *The Approach to the Spanish Drama of the Golden Age*,[2] his article 'Towards a Definition of Calderonian Tragedy',[3] and Mr Pring-Mill's introduction to Jill Booty's translation of five fine plays by Lope de Vega.[4] The five principles which Professor Parker has seen to govern the structure of the drama of this period are perfectly consistent with classical theory. To what these scholars have said we might add the following observations, on decorum, verisimilitude and genre.

Perhaps the most important of the classical doctrines is that of literary decorum – seemliness and appropriateness in all things, in characterization, actions, sayings, style. It is also a cardinal doctrine of the Spanish drama of the seventeenth century.[5] I

---

[1] Op. cit., p. 297.   [2] Hispanic Council, *Diamante* No. 6, London 1957.

[3] *Bulletin of Hispanic Studies*, Vol. XXXIX (1962), pp. 222–37.

[4] *Lope de Vega (Five Plays) Translated by Jill Booty*, New York 1961, vii–xxxvi. The plays in this collection are *Peribáñez, Justice without Revenge, The Knight from Olmedo, Fuenteovejuna* and *The Dog in the Manger*.

[5] Mr Riley, in his book on Cervantes, has an interesting section of a chapter (pp. 131–45) on 'Style and Decorum'. The concept of literary decorum is also treated by Professor A. A. Parker in 'History and Poetry: The Coriolanus Theme in Calderón', published in *Hispanic Studies in Honour of I. González Llubera*, Oxford 1959, pp. 211–24. Unfortunately I have not yet seen Herman Cleophus Hudson's doctoral dissertation, *The Development of Dramatic Criticism in England and Spain during the Elizabethan Period and the Golden Age*, accepted by the University of Michigan in 1962. In the abstract, which indicates that this is a work of considerable interest for our study, he states that 'Classical concepts of decorum and verisimilitude were strongly entrenched in both countries and those who wished to depart from them felt obligated to justify their doing so'. (*Dissertation Abstracts. Abstracts of Dissertations and Monographs in Microfilm*, Vol. XXIII, No. 1 [July 1962], Michigan 1962, p. 235.)

would venture to add, as a sixth principle to Professor Parker's five, the increasingly strict observance of literary decorum as the century advances. In fact it would seem to be, in many ways, the most important principle of all. The mature Lope, Tirso and Calderón, all in the Horatian tradition, agreed wholeheartedly with Landinus's 'seruetur denique in omnibus rebus decorum'.[1] The importance which decorum had for Lope in 1609 is indicated in his *New Art*. And after him this importance grew, in what a British ambassador called 'this graue Nation'. One need only reflect on the stiff, sombre, elaborate etiquette of the Court at Madrid to see why this was necessary when, during Calderón's time, the Court theatre became the true centre of dramatic activity, for which most plays were written. But it was not only the Court that demanded decorum in the drama. The towns-people had deep moral and social sensibilities also, and strict ideals of conduct. As Bances shows us, they were capable of hissing a play because it presented a state of affairs which shocked them. Of course the most frequently repeated demands for decorum in the theatres came from the Church, and its power was great.

Rennert observed, with justice, that the Spanish plays of this period 'were cleaner and on a higher moral plane' than those of the rest of Europe.[2] This we might expect of a nation that considered that it had a religious mission to carry out. Moreover, many seventeenth-century Spanish critics object strongly to immorality and lack of decorum in Greek and Roman drama, and, when we look at it from their point of view and according to their standards, we can only agree with them. Gods and Princes should not be presented to the seventeenth-century Spaniard with what, for him, are morals and conduct only to be

---

[1] Christophorus Landinus, *In Q. Horatium Flaccum commentaria* (printed in the Basle 1555 edition of the works of Horace), p. 920. Quoted by Marvin T. Herrick in *The Fusion of Horatian and Aristotelian Literary Criticism, 1531–1555* (*Illinois Studies in Language and Literature*, Vol. XXXII [1946], No. 1), p. 50. Herrick's fifth chapter, on decorum (pp. 48–57), is useful.

[2] Hugo Albert Rennert, *The Spanish Stage in the Time of Lope de Vega*, New York 1909, pp. 120–1. See also his observations on p. 266 and in its footnote 2.

expected of the basest peasant. Some critics went very far indeed in their idea of how strict decorum in the theatre should be. Pellicer, for example, believed that:

> There are, in the histories, events, and in the invention there are situations, which are quite unsuitable for public divulgence in the theatre. Such are tyrannies, and sedition of vassals against Princes, which must not be disclosed before the eyes of any century. Still less must one invent examples of lawless men in power who, confident in the majesty of their position, brazenly and despotically dare to commit violent outrages and affronts, violating its gravity with their base deeds.[1]

The dramatists were not, of course, as strict as Pellicer, for from the sixteenth century to Bances Candamo in the 1690s they used and presented such situations for moral and political purposes, as the educators of the people and of the Court. But, after the first years of the seventeenth century, when official control of the theatre became well established and dramatic taste became refined, they selected such situations skilfully and carefully, and they presented them *decorously*. As Bances saw, it is not difficult to find in sixteenth-century drama, and in early Lope, matter that is extremely indecorous by seventeenth-century standards. Despite Cotarelo y Mori's attempt to 'whitewash' it, Lope's *The Witticisms of Matico* (composed not later than 1604) is a pretty scurrilous piece of work by present-day criteria, let alone by those of Spaniards of the late seventeenth century.[2]

The Spanish ideas of decorum in the period with which we are dealing are by no means identical with the Greek ideas of τὸ πρέπον or the Roman *decorum*. Nor are they identical with the French *bienséances* or the English *seemliness* of the seventeenth century, or with the ideas of decorum which obtain today in our own society. Like all these other ideas, they are an expression of

---

[1] Op. cit., fol. 150r.

[2] *Los donaires de Matico* was selected by Bances Candamo (National Library MS. 17459, fol. 56v.) as a clear example of lack of decorum in early Lope. In his prologue to Volume IX of the second series of works by Lope published by the Spanish Royal Academy (Madrid 1917), in which this play is printed, E. Cotarelo y Mori tried (xxvii–xxviii) to convince his readers that it is rather better than it is in reality.

the social, religious and moral ideals of the particular civilization which has moulded them.

A remarkable number of the errors for which personages are punished in the drama of Lope, Tirso, Calderón and their contemporaries are offences against the seventeenth-century Spanish ideals of decorum in conduct. The Commanders in Lope's *Fuenteovejuna* and *Peribáñez* and the Captain in Calderón's *The Mayor of Zalamea*[1] all demonstrate clearly this kind of violation of ideals of behaviour. Even from the first moments of the play, the Don Juan of Tirso's *The Deceiver of Seville*[2] provides the supreme example of it, in his anarchical disregard of the ideals which he ought to fulfil as nobleman of high degree, as subject of his King, as son, as friend and as creature of God. And Sigismund, in *Life is a Dream*,[3] is put back in the tower because his actions at Court are extremely indecorous; they fall far below the ideal of behaviour that the seventeenth-century Spaniard expected of a Prince. After the beginning of the century, the dramatists, as they matured, gradually became more and more adept and sensitive in their selection or creation of such violations for their plays, learning to avoid those which would shock profoundly, and they became more skilful in the art of presenting in as decorous a manner as possible those which they did elect to use. Spaniards in that age were extraordinarily sensitive to subtle class distinctions which, for us, are not always easy to perceive at once. For each class – in the playwrights' view – there appears to have been a set ideal pattern of behaviour to which the individual was expected to conform. It should go without saying

---

[1] *El alcalde de Zalamea.* A free English version of this play was made by Edward Fitzgerald and published in his *Six Plays of Calderón, Freely Translated*, London 1853. The six versions were included in the old No. 819 of Everyman's Library, *The Rubáiyát of Omar Khayam. Six Plays of Calderón.* . . . An excellent study of the play is contained in Professor Sloman's book, and another in a notable article by Mr P. N. Dunn, 'Honour and the Christian Background in Calderón', *Bulletin of Hispanic Studies*, Vol. XXXVII (1960), pp. 75–105.

[2] *El burlador de Sevilla.* On it, see Parker, *The Approach* . . ., pp. 12–14.

[3] *La vida es sueño.* Good studies on this play, in English, are contained in the introduction to Dr Sloman's recent Manchester University Press edition of it, and in his *The Dramatic Craftsmanship.* . . .

that age and sex are important determinant factors in the elaboration and modification of these patterns. A person could move outside the pattern expected of him, or her, by aspiring to fulfil the ideals that corresponded to a higher group, by virtue of which fulfilment he, or she, might, like Peribáñez, become a member of that higher group. In the case of such elevation, a good dramatist will then make the character acquire the language and manners of the higher class, as Professor Wilson has shown in his study of *Peribáñez and the Commander of Ocaña.*[1] This kind of elevation may take place without the personage's willing it, or even by accident. Nevertheless, some sort of corresponding elevation in style and manner is given, even when, as often happens, a dramatist is using temporary elevation in order to poke fun at contemporary manners or for other more seriously ironical purposes. But woe betide the person who, on the contrary, betrays the ideals of his group and acts in a manner that would be expected only of a member of a lower group. The Commander in *Fuenteovejuna* dies like a dog – and Lope decorously spares us the horrifying details of the killing, described in his source in the chronicle, by having it carried out off-stage, as is the subsequent torture of the villagers by the justices. In *The Mayor of Zalamea* the Captain is put to death like a delinquent peasant – but Calderón does not allow us to witness his execution, though he horrifies us just enough and no more by the 'discovery' of the seated corpse. In *Peribáñez* the death of the Commander – by the sword of the nobleman, the former peasant, whose honour he has assailed – is a decorous one; therefore Lope permits us to see it on the stage. And in all three cases Spanish monarchs who are known to be good appear at the end to ratify the justice of the killing. 'I am who I am!' – *¡Soy quien soy!* – is the most common catchphrase of the Spanish drama of the seventeenth century. But it is not to be scorned for being so. Its ring is deep and evocative. . . . It is the cry of self-determination, the self-reminder of a person who finds himself in difficulties, in

[1] E. M. Wilson, 'Images et structure dans *Peribáñez*', *Bulletin hispanique*, Tome LI (1949), pp. 125–59.

a dilemma, in circumstances which even seem to make it inevitable, in some cases, that he betray the ideal he knows he must fulfil, and who in the moment when he utters it resolves to avoid self-abasement, to use all his heart and all his ingenuity in order to remain true to that ideal. A very great part indeed of the drama of this age is concerned, above all else, with just such problems, great and small.

But individual men, social groups, or even society as a whole, may be mistaken in their conception of the true nature of the ideals which they strive to uphold. Their view of these ideals may be distorted, and the distortion may lead them into tragedy. The best dramatists knew this well and carefully sought to correct such distortions. We see this in the ironic, often satirical manner in which Lope presents many noblemen in his plays. We see it in his sombre tragedy *Punishment without Vengeance*.[1] As Professors Wilson and Parker have shown us in an illuminating series of studies, we can see it in Calderón's deeply ironic honour-tragedies, *Secret Vengeance for Secret Offence*, *The Doctor of His Own Honour*, *The Painter of His Own Dishonour* and similar works.[2] In such plays, strained, self-tortured protagonists, when confronted by real or imaginary dishonour, act decorously, in the sense that despite their own feelings they force themselves to act in accordance with the dictates of what they take to be a worthy and inviolable ideal of honour. But their ideal, their decorum, is in some ways a dangerously faulty ideal, incompatible with Christian decorum, with what is truly worthy and honourable.

[1] *El castigo sin venganza.* Miss Booty (*op. cit.*) translates this title as *Justice without Revenge.*

[2] *A secreto agravio, secreta venganza; El médico de su honra; El pintor de su deshonra.* On the first, see E. M. Wilson, 'La discreción de don Lope de Almeida', *Clavileño*, No. 9 (1951), and Dunn, op. cit. Of the second an important edition has been made by C. A. Jones (Oxford 1961), and Roy Cambell's translation, under the title of *The Surgeon of His Honor*, has been published with an introduction by Everett W. Hesse (Madison 1960). The third, of which Fitzgerald published an English version (*op. cit.*), has been studied by Professor Parker in 'Towards a Definition . . .', and by Dr A. I. Watson in '*El pintor de su deshonra* and the Neo-Aristotelian Theory of Tragedy', *Bulletin of Hispanic Studies*, Vol. XL (1963), pp. 17–34. Important observations on these tragedies are also contained in Professor Wilson's 'Gerald Brenan's Calderón', *Bulletin of the Comediantes*, Vol. IV (1952).

For this reason the sensitive dramatists carefully and subtly lead their seventeenth-century audiences, and us, to feel the horror and the tragedy of this false decorum, of this unsound idea of what is fitting. If Kings sanction the justice of these characters' actions, they are Kings who are known to be harsh or untrustworthy. As Mr Dunn has remarked in a notable paper, in plays of this nature

> Calderón uses character and situation so as to make demands on the moral awareness of his audience, and lead it to a critical attitude towards the code of honour.[1]

He leads us away from a morally and humanely invalid concept of decorum towards a truly worthy ideal of decorum.

At the summit of the ideals stand together the perfect Monarch and the Saint. It is in the treatment of Kings and Queens, Princes and Princesses, that we may perceive most clearly how much progress was made between early Lope and mature Calderón in the observance of the Aristotelian precept of the moral embellishment of characters, to which González de Salas devoted a substantial part of his treatise,[2] and which Guerra and Bances lauded in Calderón. 'Our Seneca', the Spaniard, exercised a very great influence on the Spanish drama in this age, but he did so much more profoundly as the Stoic philosopher than as the tragedian.[3] His tragedies and their Renaissance progeny did leave deep traces in the seventeenth-century drama – many a horrific 'discovery' of gory heads, of enthroned, couched or mangled corpses and the like testifies to them. But these horrors are most frequent in the plays of the early decades of the century, and from its first years onwards the extent and nature of such horrors appear to be progressively limited by the exigencies of the Spanish concept of decorum. There could be no *Thyestes* on the Spanish stage. Nor could one present an *Oedipus*, or a *Phaedra*. Subjects

---

[1] Op. cit., p. 79.

[2] Ed. cit., pp. 69–79, 'De las costumbres, i de la Sentencia'.

[3] No comprehensive study of Seneca's influence on the Spanish seventeenth-century drama has yet been published. Some aspects of it are treated by Cecilia Vennard Sargent in *A Study of the Dramatic Works of Cristóbal de Virués*, New York, 1930, and by Raymond R. MacCurdy in *Francisco de Rojas Zorrilla and the Tragedy*, Albuquerque 1958.

like these were much too repulsive to be capable of expression, even in the most decorous manner. Lope – not Calderón – could still, in his maturity, venture to show, in *Punishment without Vengeance*, an incestuous duchess, whose husband ruled over a duchy. But a duchess is a duchess, and a Queen is a Queen. A Queen or a Princess had to be painted with an even finer touch than was necessary for a mature King, or for an impetuous young Prince in training for responsibility. Calderonian drama could portray a wicked Queen, decorously, but, as in the case of Henry VIII's Anne in *The Schism of England*, it could be permitted only to hint very discreetly at her sexual depravity.[1] After the very early drama of the century, an unmarried Queen or Princess may be honourably in love with a worthy nobleman, and she may even tell the audience so in eloquent but decorous 'asides' which reveal her struggle between passion and the need to fulfil the ideal that she represents, but she must never avow her feelings openly to her beloved, or to any other personage in the play. She cannot go beyond arousing the gallant's hopes with subtle hints and discreet allusions. If he is indiscreet enough to show clearly that he understands these, she will be very angry at his unseemly boldness. Queen Elizabeth, in Coello's *The Earl of Essex*, demonstrates these attitudes well.[2]

Lope could openly show, as protagonists, young Spanish or Portuguese Kings who fall below the ideal of kingship, with disastrous consequences for their subjects. The mistress-besotted Alphonso VIII of Castile in *The Peacemaking between King and Queen*[3] and, later, the insecure, suspicious, hard John II of Portugal in *The Duke of Viseo*[4] are good examples. Lope's contemporaries, such as the unknown author of *The Star of*

---

[1] For this play, see Professor Parker's 'Henry VIII in Shakespeare and Calderón. An Appreciation of "La cisma de Inglaterra"', *Modern Language Review*, Vol. XLI (1948), pp. 327–52.

[2] *El conde de Essex*. Legend has attributed the composition of this tragedy to Philip IV. Again, the choice of this play to illustrate the principles of decorum is Bances's (National Library MS. 17459, fol. 77r–v.).

[3] *Las paces de los reyes.*

[4] *El duque de Viseo.*

Seville, could do the same.[1] And later, a politically impassioned writer *might* be so bold as to do so. Diamante, when he refashioned Lope's play on Alphonso (and perhaps also one of Mira de Amescua's) into that unjustly despised political tragedy, *The Jewess of Toledo*, could, in the King's final speech, suddenly horrify and terrify his audience, previously trusting and confident, with the realization that here is a Monarch who has not learned his lesson and that the national tragedy will continue and grow even more fearful and pitiful.[2] Calderón, however, keeps bad peninsular Kings in the background. He uses them only for decorous allusion. His protagonist Monarchs who fall below the ideal are either foreign or imaginary, and even them he embellishes, for despite their follies they are Kings. In his writing we are very far from Lope's Matico, the pretty peasant lad who turns out to be not only a woman but the runaway daughter of the King of Leon. Besides making a countess of Aragon blush with obviously obscenely intended riddles, she does her best to tear off her clothes and expose her breast to her abducter Prince (no more estimable than she) and to the audience!

In the last years of the century, Bances, in *The Duel against His Lady*,[3] could suggest the baring of a noblewoman's breast. Henry of Lorraine, who wrongly believes that his lady, Margarita, has been unfaithful to his love, scorns her and eludes her as, dressed like a man, she pursues him determinedly and frustrates his attempts to woo Matilde, Countess of Flanders. Finally, Margarita contrives to challenge him publicly to a duel. For Henry to fight against a woman would be unthinkable! But how can he avoid it? He demands, as a condition of the duel, that, like the warriors of primitive times, they fight stripped to the waist,

---

[1] *La estrella de Sevilla.* Henry Thomas' English translation, *The Star of Seville*, was printed at the Gregynog Press in 1935. A revised version was printed by Oxford University Press in 1950. Although this tragedy has been attributed to Lope de Vega, it does not appear to be his. A good study of it, in English, is J. L. Brooks's '*La estrella de Sevilla*: "admirable y famosa tragedia"', *Bulletin of Hispanic Studies*, Vol. XXXII (1955), pp. 8–20.

[2] It is quite possible that *La judía de Toledo* was written with political intention, as a warning to Philip IV, or as a commentary on his amorous adventures.

[3] *El duelo contra su dama.*

with, as a concession, only a thin covering of gauze over the upper half of their bodies. At this, naturally, Margarita bursts into tears, to the amazement of Matilde's Court. Henry, touched, relents, reveals that she is a woman and decides to marry her. Bances has decorously suggested something that we might take to be intrinsically indecorous. There are many such decorous hints in the drama of this period. But they *are* decorous. Decorum in literature is largely a question of the manner in which an idea is presented, and the Spanish dramatists handled it ironically, subtly and suggestively.

Of verisimilitude let us say little here. Like the Elizabethans, the Spanish 'new art' theorists and playwrights rejected the neo-classical unities of time and place because they were absurd restrictions, insults to the imaginative agility of any theatre audience, as quick to skip delightedly in time and space as any child at play. Yet, from people who treat *The Skin of Our Teeth* very seriously, we still occasionally hear, when the Spanish drama is mentioned, the snigger for which Cervantes and Boileau played when they talked of Spanish dramatic works in which the hero is an infant at the beginning, a grown man in the middle and a greybeard at the end. The modern drama has produced good plays of this sort; so did Lope. A fine case in point is his excellent tragedy, *The Bastard Mudarra*.[1] At the time of the bitter, ironical first act, in which the slaughter of his half-brothers, the seven Infantes of Lara, is treacherously plotted and prepared in Castile, Mudarra has not yet been thought of. At the end of the second act, when his father Gonzalo Bustos is stricken with horror, pitiful remorse and grief in Córdoba at the sight of their seven bloody heads, Mudarra is in his mother's womb. In the third act he is shown to us for the first time, in Córdoba, as a strong young man, the image of the youngest and fieriest of the Infantes (played by the same actor), and, having learned the truth about his parentage, he journeys to Castile to wreak vengeance on the perfidious Ruy Velázquez and Doña Lambra, to comfort

---

[1] *El bastardo Mudarra* (1612). This is a fine tragedy of treachery within a family. Aristotle would have enjoyed it.

his aged father and to restore harmony. The plan of this impressive play – and of several other tragedies by Lope – is trilogical. Aeschylus had a whole day, from dawn to evening, in which to present a trilogy to his audience. Lope, when he wished to produce the same effects, had under three hours of one afternoon, and only one play.[1] And so we may see that when he recommends, in the *New Art*, that the events of each of the three acts be restricted, if it is possible, to those of one day, he is doing, for all practical purposes, exactly the same as Aristotle, who tells us that a single tragedy 'endeavours to keep as far as possible within a single circuit of the sun, or something approximate to that',[2] and who proffers no time-limit for a trilogy. And the more often I read Cascales, the more I wonder whether he is not sometimes talking with his tongue in his cheek. He makes his Castalio mock at a play in which Saint Amaro goes to Paradise, remains there for two hundred years and returns to earth, to find new places, new peoples, new dress and new customs.[3] An ecclesiastical Rip Van Winkle! I do not know the play, but the idea is magnificent.

And verisimilitude of costume in the public theatres? If you want to show a King of Egypt to a seventeenth-century townsman of Madrid or to a peasant of the Alpujarra, show him as these persons know a King looks. A Velázquez portrait, plus a crown. Or an image from a Spanish emblem-book. If you dress him in accordance with the findings from your archaeological researches, he may well confuse: he may be taken for some sort of monk, and a presumptuous one at that. And the Devil who looks like everyone else, except that he wears red hose? Just as effective, and as credible, as – and, it may be, even more sinister than – what one takes to be the image that many people who today believe

[1] That is, if he decided to produce a trilogical effect in one day's performance in the theatre. Otherwise, he could write a *Second Part*, to continue a story which had just begun in one play. In theory, there is no reason why he might not even compose a *Third Part*, to be acted on a third afternoon. Performances of more than one play on one day were rare, and they took place normally in the Court theatre.

[2] Aristotle, *Poetics*, Everyman's Library No. 901, London 1963, p. 11. The new version prepared by John Warrington for this edition is based on Ingram Bywater's translation.

[3] Op. cit., pp. 346–7.

in a personal Devil have of him, that of Chaliapine in Gounod's *Faust,* or of Christoff in Boito's *Mefistofele.*

And so to genre. At once we have a vision of that sacred cow of not a few modern critics, Tragicomedy. But, when we approach the Spanish drama of the seventeenth century, let us put her out to grass. True, she will come lumbering back and low to us merrily in many of the hundreds of plays we have to recreate – in indifferent plays by bad dramatists and bad plays by good ones. But from many which are worthy of close attention, and of admiration, she is absent. Up to this point in our study we have avoided the unfortunate Spanish term *comedia*. Whatever its origins may have been, it became current in its wider acceptation during a period of terminological confusion, and nowadays it tends to mislead, as indeed it did then. We must not assume overconfidently, as Martinenche, Bray and many other critics have done, that the *comedia* is 'an essentially mixed genre', that all the three-act plays of the period which we are investigating are 'tragicomedies'. We would not call *Hamlet* or *King Lear* 'tragicomedies', and each of them contains more humorous elements than many a Spanish *comedia* has. Lope – or his printer – describes *The Bastard Mudarra* as a *tragicomedia,* but there is no witty jester in it, nor is there anything at all that is intended to be comical. Its main characters are great nobles, ladies, generals, and a King. The few personages of lower rank who take part in it are sober accessories. When Lope calls a play a 'tragicomedy', he means that it is a tragedy in which order and harmony are finally restored – as they are in an Aeschylean trilogy or in a Euripidean tragedy. His contemporary Carlos Boyl defines 'tragicomedy' in a roughly similar manner: 'Tragicomedy is a principle, the plot of which (although it ends in events of good fortune) begins in mortal misfortunes'.[1] When Lope calls a play a 'tragedy' – for example, *The Duke of Viseo* and *Punishment*

---

[1] *Don Carlos Boyl a un licenciado que deseava hazer comedias,* in Chaytor, op. cit., p. 38. An interesting study of Lope's use of the term *tragicomedia* is contained in the beginning of E. S. Morby's paper, 'Some Observations on "tragedia" and "tragicomedia" in Lope' *Hispanic Review,* Vol. XI (1943), pp. 185–209.

without Vengeance – he appears to mean that it ends in the profound misfortune of the hero or the protagonist, either in his own death or in the death of some person or persons that he loves or cherishes. This is the sort of tragedy that we might be tempted to call Sophoclean. Such a distinction between 'tragicomedy' and 'tragedy' could in reality have very little to do with any but the most naïve kind of theory of 'combination of tragic and comic'. And there is no such naïvety in Lope. It would merely seem that Lope suffers as a categorist, although certainly not as a creative writer, from the modern-literature theorist's hastiness, his haziness and his tendency to oversimplify, when he attempts to form and express a clear idea of the nature and limits of the Greek and Roman genres. His distinction does no more than indicate, in rather confused and confusing terms, the difference between certain categories within the genre of tragedy. Lope is a brilliant and fecund composer of tragedies and of comedies. We ought not to expect him to be a brilliant categorist as well.

Of the seventeenth-century writers, it is Pellicer who provides the most concise suggestion of what the genres are, and of what the term *comedia* means, in his time. He says of Montalbán:

> He was not ignorant of the fact that, although all kinds of action that are played in the theatre, be they historical, novelesque, or fabulous, are in common usage embraced by the seemingly generic name of *comedias*, not all of them are comedies. For, as we have already said, that action which depends on elaborate stage effects is a fable. That action into which a King, or sovereign Lord, is introduced is a tragedy. That in which the hero, who is the 'male lead', dies is a tragicomedy. And the only action which is properly called a comedy is that which consists of affairs which occur between private persons, without the intervention of an absolute Prince. Montalbán discussed these considerations with me on many occasions.[1]

Pellicer does not distinguish between his categories merely by separating what modern critics tend to consider to be 'tragic

[1] Op. cit., fol. 150v.

elements' and 'comic elements'. Moreover, his idea of 'tragi-comedy' is different from Lope's. It is a play which ends in misfortune and in which there is not a King or sovereign Lord (although in practice there is usually one when a play treats a subject of this nature). If a King or sovereign Lord does appear in such a play, then it is not a 'tragicomedy' but a tragedy. And in his view of comedy, which takes place between private persons only, it goes without saying that the ending is not characterized by misfortunes for the hero. Like Lope, Pellicer is in reality talking of only two genres, of tragedy and of comedy. In addition, he indicates clearly what the term *comedia* signifies. It is often used in the seventeenth century to designate the genre of comedy or a play which is of this genre. But it is most commonly used to designate not a genre but an art-form: a dramatic structure divided into three acts. A remarkably adaptable structural unit, which may be used as a vehicle for one genre or another.

Apart from those persons whom we have consulted, how did the practising men of the theatre divide their plays into categories, for practical purposes, when asked to describe them? They appear usually to have divided them into two. According to Suárez de Figueroa there are 'three-act plays of body', which show Kings, Princes or Saints, and 'three-act plays of wit, or of cloak and sword'. Salas Barbadillo talks of 'three-act plays of elaborate stage effects' and 'three-act plays of cloak and sword'. Bances Candamo divides them into two, and then he goes on to sub-divide:

> We shall divide them into only two classes: amatory, or historical (for Saints' plays are also historical and not a separate species). The amatory ones, which are pure invention or ideas without foundation in truth, are divided into those that are called 'cloak and sword plays' and those that are called 'plays of invention'. The 'cloak and sword' ones are those whose characters are only private persons of the minor nobility, like Don John, or Don Diego, etc., and the events in them are reduced to duels, to jealousy, to the lover's hiding and the lady's veiling her face, and, in short, to the more domestic, everyday ups-and-downs of a courtship. The 'plays of

221

invention' are those that carry some particular intent to be proved with the story, and their characters are Kings, Princes, generals, dukes, etc., and pre-eminent personages, [all of] whose names are indeterminate and unknown to the histories. Their artifice consists in divers chances of Fortune, long peregrinations, duels [worthy] of great renown, noble conquests, elevated loves, and, in short, happenings strange and more lofty and extraordinary than those that come to pass in the episodes that a moment ago I called everyday ones. ... The argument of those plays that we call 'plays of invention' is usually a contest between Royal persons for the hand of a Princess, with that majestic decorum which is appropriate to the personages who are presented, especially if they are Kings or Queens, or Palace ladies, for even if they belong to the Palace of China, simply because of their name the poet takes great care to make the allusion decorous, venerating through images even the shadows of what may be called Royal. ... The historical three-act plays are, for the most part, examples intended to teach with the most efficacious result, in verse, in order to produce relief.[1]

And along with the sacred and profane histories Bances groups those plays which deal with the fables of classical mythology.

Several points emerge from Bances's description of the categories, and also from his reflections on them. On one hand we have plays which are drawn entirely from the imagination. On the other we have plays which are built up on material taken from histories, pseudo-histories, known legends and the classical myths. These latter plays are tragedies. They may sometimes be bad tragedies, but tragedies they are. The former, as Bances describes them, are comedies.

The 'comedies of cloak and sword', in which Calderón excelled, are quite clearly the Spanish, decorous version of Plautine comedy. They are light-hearted, often even frivolous; we are expected to laugh gaily in them. Their incidents are presented in such a way that we are led to treat them all light-

---

[1] National Library MS. 17459, fol. 75r–77v. I have, for the sake of brevity, omitted Bances's reflections on these descriptions. For Suárez de Figueroa's division, see Chaytor, op. cit., p. 49. Salas Barbadillo's distinction is contained in his *Coronas del Parnaso y platos de las Musas*, Madrid 1635, fol. 33v.

heartedly. What's a duel between two people we know are quite safe and are going to be reconciled in the end? The 'comedies of invention' – of which there are many in the Court drama – are a sort of *comedia togata*. Bances's *The Duel against His Lady* is a good example. They resemble the type of play of which Aristotle says, while talking of tragedy,

> The pleasure here is not that of Tragedy; it belongs rather to Comedy. The most determined enemies in the play, e.g. Orestes and Aegisthus, march off good friends at the conclusion, and no one is slain by anyone.[1]

Rather less light-hearted than the 'comedies of cloak and sword', but also detached from historical reality and from the seriousness that is accorded to classical myth, they are intended to produce more subdued amusement and also wonderment and admiration, but not pity and fear. All the ideals are preserved in the end, the audience is never led to imagine seriously that they might be violated, and it can feel secure, unaffected by harsh realities except in those brief moments in which a quick stab is directed at some contemporary social abuse, and which, because of the rapid pace of the play and its tone, are quickly relegated to unimportance.

Nevertheless, just as tragedy, if handled carelessly and clumsily, may turn into bad comedy, so comedy, if handled carefully and skilfully, may turn into good tragedy. Bances knew this. So did Lope, Tirso, Calderón and other competent dramatists of their times. A good playwright may lead us into a situation which appears to be a happy one, and then, quite suddenly, by a twist of our imagination, he may make us feel the tragedy of what we are witnessing. Or he may, amidst all that is *prima facie* happy, or comical, gradually create in our minds a doubt, an increasingly grave doubt, that what is seemingly a situation of good fortune is so in reality. In other words, he may – slowly or abruptly – disenchant us. A jolt, by the introduction of a known historical figure, a patently serious violation of an ideal, or a

[1] *Poetics*, ed. cit., p. 23.

telling allusion, may be quite sufficient. So the playwright may lead us into a 'tragic sense of life'. It needs no more than one deft and sure touch. Quite suddenly the beautiful, harmonious universe, in which one is safe as long as one takes the trouble, and has the ingenuity, to fulfil the ideals, may dissolve into the world of human reality, in which these ideals become in every successive moment more elusive, more ethereal in comparison with our capacities, and therefore all the more poignantly desirable. *Timor vitae, timor mortis conturbat me*. What century, in modern history, could be more sensitive to disillusionment, to the crumbling of ideals, than the seventeenth century in Spain? And then, from that moment of disenchantment, if our dramatist is skilful and we are willing to be led, we shall look back on what it seemed we should giggle at, and we shall see that we were wrong – or, at the least, that we should have giggled with less confidence, and with more understanding. Moreover, from that moment, if our dramatist is skilful and we are willing to be led, we shall go on to see in a new relief, in a new perspective, all that our play will show us that, at a hasty glance, might seem to be frivolously comical. And if we laugh at such things, our laughter will be the frenetic laughter of the alleviated spirit, or else it will be sad, ironic laughter. If it is neither, it will be the guffaw of a cocksure fool. In good Spanish tragedies of the seventeenth century, the humour is of a kind that is appropriate to tragedy. It is not humour which is mixed with tragedy. It is humour which is fused with tragedy. This appears to have been glimpsed by one adversary of the drama, who disapproved of the simultaneous occurrence of the tragic and the comic. In a satirical and moral work, *Heraclitus and Democritus of Our Century*, published in 1641, Antonio López de Vega complained that:

> The comic [writer] ... is confused with the tragic, and, being neither one nor the other, not only does he alternate in one and the same plot the buskin and the sock but he also puts simultaneously one foot in each and draws them on together. He weeps and laughs on the selfsame occasion.[1]

[1] *Heráclito i Demócrito de nuestro siglo*, Madrid 1641, p. 174.

For López de Vega this was a grave fault. But when intelligently
and subtly contrived, as it is in many Spanish tragedies, it does not
diminish the tragic effect; rather does it enhance it.

There are still critics who, when they approach Spanish
tragedies of the seventeenth century, finically pick out – like
canaries picking at their seed – scenes, incidents and phrases
which they take to be 'pure comedy' and therefore unworthy
of inclusion in tragedy. The consistency of a tragedy is, however,
rather more dense than that of bird-seed. What is truly important
in a tragedy is not the apparent nature of any of its constituent
elements in isolation, but the effect which it produces as a dramatic
whole.

Moreover, there are still critics who object to the appearance
of personages high and low, each with his or her appropriate
style, together on the stage on terms of near-equality. They
forget that the Spanish drama's greatest original contribution to
the European tragic tradition is, precisely, its demonstration, in
plays such as *Fuenteovejuna, Peribáñez* and *The Mayor of Zalamea*,
that even the peasant may be a truly tragic hero or heroine. For
the Spanish dramatists of this period, all men are, as moral beings,
equal in the sight of God. Their position in society is merely lent
to them as a means of working their salvation, and it may be taken
away at any moment. Rank and power are the vestments donned
by the actors in the great theatre of the world. They may be cast
off, and others may be donned in their place, during the performance or at its end. Those who wear them are all players, no
more, no less.

Also, it must be said that, unlike specialists in the study of
classical drama, many specialists in that of modern drama tend to
limit their idea of tragedy to the type which ends in deep misfortunes. We might say that they are of the 'Sophocles or nothing'
school. Yet fear and pity can be produced, with lasting effects,
during the course of the action of a tragedy, whatever the ending
of this action may be. Let us be content when we find that they
are produced in us. In an excellent study of the genre, Spain's
finest tragic dramatist of the present day, Antonio Buero Vallejo,

Classical Drama and its Influence

has shown the futility of narrowing excessively our ideas of tragedy.[1] Those of the classical dramatists are wide. So are those of the Elizabethans, the Stuart tragedians and the Spaniards of the seventeenth century. Professor R. C. Knight's fascinating observations have shown us that the French seventeenth-century tragedians subscribe to a significantly more ample concept of the genre than that which we tend to adopt nowadays.[2] The disenchanted Spain of that century left to us many tragedies. Each of the eight plays of Calderón which Dr Sloman has treated in his book is, in its own way, a tragedy, and a good one. So is the same dramatist's *Jealousy, the Greatest Monster*.[3] So are many Calderonian plays that Professors Wilson and Parker have studied for us. So are more, which have yet to be adequately considered. Tirso's *The Deceiver of Seville* is a great social tragedy. His *Condemned for Lack of Trust in God* is a profound double tragedy,[4] and he composed other good plays of this genre. And Lope? We have indicated the tragic nature of several of his plays – in particular, of *The Bastard Mudarra* and *The Duke of Viseo*. In addition, *Fuenteovejuna* is an admirable tragedy, and *Peribáñez* is one of the best examples of double tragedy that we have. Lope wrote others that do honour to the genre. The Spanish drama of the seventeenth century was by far the most prolific of the three great national dramas of the classical tradition in that time. And it was by no means the least fertile, moving and subtle in the tragic genre.

The drama works in us partly through the head. As Luís de

[1] Antonio Buero Vallejo, 'La tragedia', in *El teatro. Enciclopedia del arte escénico*, ed. G. Díaz-Plaja, Barcelona 1958, pp. 61–87.

[2] See R. C. Knight, 'A Minimal Definition of Seventeenth-Century Tragedy', *French Studies*, Vol. X (1956), pp. 297–308.

[3] *El mayor monstruo los celos*, also called *El mayor monstruo del mundo* and *El tetrarca de Jerusalén*. See Professor Everett W. Hesse's introduction and notes to his edition of the partly holographic manuscript of this play (Madison 1955), and also his article 'El arte calderoniano en "El mayor monstruo, los celos"', *Clavileño*, Año VII, Núm. 38 (1956), pp. 297–308. Professor A. A. Parker's *The Approach* ... and 'Towards a Definition ...' also contain studies of other good Calderonian tragedies.

[4] *El condenado por desconfiado*. On this play, see T. E. May's excellent paper, with the same title, in *Bulletin of Hispanic Studies*, Vol. XXXV (1958), pp. 138–56.

Morales said, the Spanish drama of the seventeenth century is 'a banquet which the understanding gives for the ear, and for the eye'.[1] But the drama also works in us, and even more powerfully, through the sinews and the spirit. We must approach the Spanish plays of that century humbly. From the publication, in the sixteenth, of the first translations of that splendid tragedy, *The Tragicomedia of Calisto and Melibea*, known as *The Celestina*, to those of Gracián's treatises on wit and other matters late in the seventeenth, Englishmen sought in Spanish literature not only adventurousness but also intellectual brilliance and subtlety. Lope, Calderón, Tirso and other playwrights of their time, all 'subtle Spaniards', have better minds than most of us have. We must let them lead us where they will. They have, in their tragedies, made more than one intelligent man sob, with fear and pity. Let us not, when we go to them, commit the sins of our great-great-grandfathers.[2]

Duncan Moir

BIBLIOGRAPHICAL NOTES

For English versions of Spanish plays, see Remigio Ugo Pane's *English Translations from the Spanish, 1484–1943. A Bibliography*, New Brunswick, Rutgers University Press, 1944. In Jill Booty's volume of translations of Lope, Mr Pring-Mill gives an excellent selected bibliography (xxxvii–xli) of works on the drama in Lope's time, and of studies of the five plays. The following collections of translations have appeared in recent years:

The Classic Theatre, edited by Eric Bentley, Volume III, *Six Spanish Plays*, New York, Doubleday Anchor, 1959. (It contains an

[1] Luis de Morales Polo, *Epítome de los hechos, y dichos del emperador Trajano . . .*, Valladolid 1654, fol. 61r. He makes this statement on the *comedia* in the course of a discussion, closely modelled on that of Barreda, on Trajan's prohibition of plays.

[2] Apart from the sources which I have acknowledged, my debt, for basic information, to M. Menéndez Pelayo's *Historia de las ideas estéticas en España* and to Margarete Newels' *Die dramatischen Gattungen in den Poetiken des Siglo de Oro* (Wiesbaden 1959), is considerable. I am also indebted to Professor A. A. Parker, Professor O. N. V. Glendinning and Professor G. D. Trotter for helpful comments on this study.

adaptation of Mabbe's translation of the *Celestina*; Roy Campbell's versions of Cervantes' *The Siege of Numantia*, Lope's *Fuenteovejuna*, Tirso's *The Trickster of Seville*, and Calderón's *Love after Death* and *Life is a Dream*; Shelley's translation of scenes from *The Wondrous Magician*.)

Spanish Drama, edited and with an Introduction by Angel Flores, New York, Bantam Books, 1962. (It includes *Fuenteovejuna*, *The Rogue of Seville*, Juan Ruiz de Alarcón's *The Truth Suspected*, and *Life is a Dream*.)

Calderón de la Barca, *Four Plays*, Translated and with an Introduction by Edwin Honig. With an appendix on Spanish Golden Age Customs and Drama by Norman Maccoll. A Mermaid Dramabook, New York, Hill and Wang, 1961. (It contains *Secret Vengeance for Secret Insult*, *Devotion to the Cross*, *The Mayor of Zalamea* and *The Phantom Lady*, as well as a useful bibliography.)

Calderón de la Barca, *Six Plays*, Translated by Denis Florence Mac-Carthy, with revision by Henry W. Wells. New York, Las Américas Publishing Company, 1961. (It contains *Life is a Dream*, *The Wonder-Working Magician*, *The Constant Prince*, *The Devotion of the Cross*, *Love after Death* and *Belshazzar's Feast*.)

The following are useful studies:

R. D. F. Pring-Mill, 'Sententiousness in *Fuente Ovejuna*', in *Tulane Drama Review*, Vol. 7, No. 1, September 1962.

A. A. Parker, *The Theology of the Devil in the Drama of Calderón* (The Aquinas Society of London Aquinas Paper No. 32), London, Blackfriars Publications, 1958.

XIII: THE NATURALIST
AND THE CRITICAL VIEW
OF DRAMA

A LTHOUGH GOTTHOLD EPHRAIM LESSING HAD SCANT
patience with the fussiness of neo-classic drama theorists
– 'The only unpardonable fault of a tragic poet is this,
that he leaves us cold; if he interests us he may do as he likes with
the little mechanical rules'[1] – he was no critical enemy of the
principle of verisimilitude on which Renaissance theories were
based. One passage he wrote in the *Hamburg Dramaturgy* is a
revealing illustration of the traditional anthropometric argument,
the appeal from natural law in justifying dramatic aesthetics. The
'large body of people' is the chorus:

> For since their actions required the presence of a large body of
> people and this concourse always remained the same, who could
> go no further from their dwellings nor remain absent longer than
> it is customary to do from mere curiosity, they were almost obliged
> to make the scene of action one and the same spot and confine the
> time to one and the same day.

While it might be argued that chorus members did not 'change
being' in a Dionysian sense, that fact cannot entitle them to
humane considerations withheld from the actors who did. There
is nothing of the 'actual' about a fixed number of Theban Elders
chanting choral poetry in unison; nothing actual in their stylized
and patterned movements, their prophetic wisdom and their
carefully structured response to the dramatic action. To imply
that Greek playwrights cut action to the measure of the attention-
span of the chorus' curiosity, or to the length of time its members
might be distant from their homes or places of business, is to
mix apple with pears. The chorus is a *convention*, not an actuality
thrust into the midst of a fiction. If men could take the part of
women, dance, chant, deliver sentiments in lyric poetry, they
certainly had it in them to be anywhere, and to stay there as long

[1] Unless otherwise noted all passages quoted may be found in Barrett H. Clark's
European Theories of the Drama, Crown Publishers, Inc., New York; revised edition,
1947.

as they wished – or as the playwright wished. The notion that audiences might have grown uneasy had Theban Elders been kept from lunch or committee meetings by an inconsiderate tragic conflict is absurd. In at least one instance – if we are to be literal-minded – the chorus stood around all night waiting for something they had no way of knowing was going to happen – and there is no record of audience dismay. Study of Sophocles' *Antigone* reveals that the action of the play is credible only if a night is presumed to intervene between the first and second burial of Polynices. Francois Ogier noted this necessity in 1628 in his *Preface to Tyre and Sidon*:

> Whoever will carefully consider the *Antigone* of Sophocles will find that a night intervenes between the first and the second burial of Polynices; otherwise, how could Antigone have deceived the guards of the body of this unfortunate prince the first time, and avoid being seen by so many people, except in the darkness of the night? For on the second occasion she comes to the body aided by a heavy rain which causes all the guards to retire, while she, in the midst of the storm, buries her brother and pays her last respects to him. Whence it happens that the tragedy of *Antigone* represents the events of two days at least; since the pretended crime of that princess presupposes Creon's law which is proclaimed publicly and in broad daylight, on the stage and in the presence of the elders of Thebes.

Ogier is right. A considerable lapse of time must be supposed during the chanting of the second choral ode – a matter of some forty-four lines of approximately ten minutes in stage time – for it is the period that separates the first and second announcement by the guard of Polynices' burial. Furthermore, two of the three Greek tragic playwrights extant were not so concerned about distances the chorus could travel as Lessing supposes they must have been. In the *Ajax* and the *Eumenides* where the playwrights need to change scenes, they simply dance the chorus off and then dance them on again. Same chorus, different place: elapsed stage time, negligible. If more Greek plays avoid change in place than indulge in it, what more plausible reason than that the interruption breaks the tension? If Sophocles' chorus of Salaminians could be whisked from in front of Ajax' tent to a lonely place on the sea-shore, so could any chorus from any city.

Measurement of the fictional against the actual is of course pointless. There is nothing natural, for example, in placing the whole of a Greek tragic action in front of a palace door; it is merely expediential. Greek tragedies were written for performances in a large open-air circle on the circumference of which stood a small robing hut or sometimes a Dionysian temple which served to house the actors' masks and costumes. Although the players probably entered and left through the door of this edifice, thereby localizing it as a palace, it would have been impossible for an audience to see through this temple to an action played inside. Hence all action was conceived as taking place in some open space – whether the location was heaven, hell, the wilderness or mid-air. The 'messenger', like the prophetic Cassandra in *Agamemnon*, was a dramatic invention, a device for reporting inside doings, not an idiosyncrasy of Greek national mores translated onto the stage.

The convention of off-stage death has suffered equally from the naturalist interpretation. Greek practice was to march those marked for death into the robing hut and there despatch them. To heighten the spectator's pleasure in the deed, blood-curdling shrieks and vivid verbal description could be added, the excitement reaching a climax when the palace doors were thrown open to reveal the dead bodies for all to see. But the killing and dying remained hidden. Why? Shall we say: because the viewer knows death is not really happening; he could not 'credit' it if he saw it? Horace seems to say it in *The Art of Poetry*: 'Let not Medea murder her sons before the people; nor the execrable Atreus openly dress human entrails; nor let Procne be metamorphosed into a bird, Cadmus into a serpent. Whatever you show to me in this manner, not able to give credit to, I detest.' Julius Caesar Scaliger in his *Poetics* (1561) is more nature-oriented still, fearing all sorts of 'violence to truth'.

Therefore neither those battles or sieges at Thebes which are fought through in two hours please me, nor do I take it to be the part of

233

a discreet poet to pass from Delphi to Athens, or from Athens to Thebes, in a moment of time. Thus Aeschylus has Agamemnon killed and buried so suddenly that the actor has scarcely time to breathe. Nor is the casting of Lichas into the sea by Hercules to be approved, for it cannot be represented without doing violence to truth.

Jeane de la Taille in 1572 clearly says it when he insists: 'no murders or other forms of death, pretended or otherwise, for the audience will invariably detect the trick'. Dryden has Lisideius put it this way in *An Essay on Dramatick Poesie*:

> ... dying especially is a thing which none but a Roman gladiator could naturally perform on the stage, when he did not imitate or represent, but do it; and therefore it is better to omit the representation of it ... When we see death represented, we are convinced it is but fiction; but when we hear it related, our eyes, the strongest witnesses, are wanting, which might have undeceived us.

Ogier conjectured that on-stage blood-letting was offensive to the religious feelings of the Greeks. He may have been right. But if he is not, there is still a more cogent reason for their apparent delicacy than that offered by Horace and his naturalist followers. It is not dying that offends nature and reason, but the coming to life of the dead actor. Greek dramatic festivals took place in daylight. No means were available for 'blacking-out' an action; no curtain was handy to cover the actor's return to life. If the character 'died' in the orchestral circle he had either to get up and walk away at the close of the play, shattering the suspension of disbelief, or in Shakespeare's ugly phrase, someone had to 'lug the guts' across the entire area and out of sight. The Elizabethans could locate deaths within the inner stage or within some other conventional tented or veiled area developed from the curtained sepulchre of early church drama; but the Greek dramatists enjoyed no comparable device. On the face of it, a dead actor is no more credible than a dying one, and the Greeks found nothing to offend nature in the sight of dead bodies. What mattered was that palace doors could be closed upon those dead bodies at the conclusion of the play thereby preserving rather than undoing the fiction of death.

Neither custom nor expedience can be expected to account wholly for the idiosyncrasies and conventions of Greek drama nor for those of the Romantic. But certainly in the origins of both they exerted a greater force than did a philosophy of the theatrically verisimilar. Mediaeval drama was not conceived as art by artists, but as living ritual by churchmen. They used what readily came to hand, developing the first dramatic experiments within the church service itself in a manner consistent with the practices and conventions of Catholic worship. They juxtaposed the sacred and the vulgar. They conventionalized time and distance not from patterns observed in nature but to clarify an idea. The space that separated the fields where the shepherds were visited by the angel and the manger where the infant Christ lay had no significance. Only the relation between Christ's birth and the lot of the lowly shepherds had meaning, and a few paces sufficed to make the spatial connection. What mattered was Noah's devotion to God, not the forty-day and forty-night duration of the flood. Enacted on an English pageant wagon or in the town squares of Continental cities, the deluge would descend and the waters recede – frequently with remarkably realistic effect – within the time it took the players to recite twenty-five lines. In the Wakefield *Second Shepherd's Play* what mattered was the contrast between despair and hope illustrated by the farce of Mak and the glory of the announcing angel, not an artistic loyalty to nature's changeable moods. Later, the rationalization appears – as if the practice would be intolerable without her validation. Victor Hugo wrote:

> ... everything in creation is not humanely *beautiful* ... the ugly exists beside the beautiful, the unshapely beside the graceful, the grotesque on the reverse of the sublime, evil with good, darkness with light.

And clinched it with:

> Hence it is time to say aloud – and it is here above all that exceptions prove the rule – that everything that exists in nature exists in art.

Classical Drama and its Influence

If it could be shown that the principle of the verisimilar had been firmly authorized in primitive practice, were it evident, for instance, that Aeschylus had determined duration and place anthropometrically, as it appears Lessing thought, it is doubtful that the principle could have achieved greater popularity. The drive toward internal naturalism in the dramatic phenomenon seems to have something of historic determinism about it, as if the living flesh of the actor were overpoweringly coercive. From Jean Chapelain's rules which were 'a necessary corollary to the verisimilar without which the mind is neither moved nor persuaded' to Zola's characters who were not to play but live before an audience, the movement has been relentless. It is even no great surprise that the theorists of the Theatre of the Absurd should see in the aesthetic of Ionesco, Genet and Becket not a convention formed to construct an idea about life but a door opening into a direct experience of life itself. Martin Esslin has written:

> The Theatre of the Absurd has renounced arguing *about* the absurdity of the human condition; it merely *presents* it in being – that is, in terms of concrete stage images of the absurdity of existence. This is the difference between the approach of the philosopher and that of the poet; the difference, to take an example from another sphere, between the *idea* of God in the works of Thomas Aquinas or Spinoza and the *intuition* of God in those of St John of the Cross or Meister Eckhart – the difference between theory and experience.[1]

While the anthropometric or naturalist principle has dominated dramatic theory since Castelvetro re-wrote the *Poetics*, an alternate metric has been touched upon, but left undeveloped, in the writings of a number of critics. Aristotle in suggesting a measure for magnitude had said:

> And to define the matter roughly, we may say that the proper magnitude is comprised within such limits, that the sequence of events, according to the law of probability or necessity, will admit of a change from bad fortune to good, or from good fortune to bad.

[1] *The Theatre of the Absurd*, Anchor Books, Doubleday and Company, Inc., Garden City, New York, 1961; p. xx.

The Naturalist and the Critical View of Drama

Here he views dramatic composition in terms of an inner logic. Yet in an earlier paragraph he had written of magnitude as a function of psychological tolerance, from the position of the subject's response, that is, as opposed to the object's plausibility:

> Hence a very small animal organism cannot be beautiful; for the view of it is confused, the object being seen in an almost imperceptible moment of time. Nor, again, can one of vast size be beautiful; for as the eye cannot take it all in at once, the unity of sense of the whole is lost for the spectator; as for instance if there were one a thousand miles long.[1]

It is revealing that Butcher, in noting the distinction in his commentary, should acclaim the aesthetic of inner logic as 'the more truly artistic principle'. The appeal of 'natural process' (Butcher's 'natural development of the story') has the expected stronger appeal. Still, as early as 1563, the Italian Churchman Minturno had emphasized Aristotle's second order of evaluation in defining duration:

> Not less than three hours nor more than four; lest neither too great brevity rob the work of its beauty and leave the desire of the hearers unsatisfied, nor excessive length deprive the poem of its proportion, spoil its charm, and render it boresome to the beholders. And indeed the wise poet should so measure the time with the matter to be presented that those who hear the work should rather deplore its brevity than regret having remained too long to listen.

But it is Lessing who first acknowledges that a legitimate criterion in dramatic aesthetics is the response which the audience will make. In a remarkable passage from the *Hamburg Dramaturgy* he confronts the principle of artistic verisimilitude with the reality of human response:

> My chief thought is this: it is true and yet not true that the comic tragedy of Gothic invention faithfully copied nature. It only imitates it faithfully in one half and entirely neglects the other, it imitates the nature of phenomena without in the least regarding the nature of our feelings and emotions.

[1] Butcher's translation.

In nature everything is connected, everything is interwoven, everything changes with everything, everything merges from one into another. But according to this endless variety it is only a play for an infinite spirit. In order that finite spirits may have their share of this enjoyment, they must have the power to set up arbitrary limits, they must have the power to eliminate and to guide their attention at will.

Look again at this sentence: '. . . it imitates the nature of phenomena without in the least regarding the nature of our feelings and emotions'. Lessing has here placed concern with natural process where in dramatic art – perhaps in all art – we intuitively sense it belongs: in the responder, in the configuration of emotional attitudes, tensions, physical and psychological drives that constitute the apparatus of human reaction. In this notation he laid the corner-stone of a revolutionary aesthetic; then walked away from it. A half-dozen paragraphs from paper number seventy of his monumental work – 'I will throw out a few thoughts, which if they are not thorough enough may suggest more thorough ones' – and the matter was dropped.

But not without reverberations; the Frenchman, Francisque Sarcey, heard him. In sharp dismissal of Hugo's 'Sublime/Grotesque' thesis Sarcey extended the German's few thoughts into a major exposition in Part IV of his *A Theory of the Theatre* (1876). He announced categorically: 'There is nothing more legitimate than the absolute distinction of the comic from the tragic, of the grotesque from the sublime'. The playwright, he said: '. . . is not concerned in the least to know whether in reality laughter is mingled with tears'. Nature is in the audience not on stage:

> . . . When these twelve hundred spectators are entirely overwhelmed with grief they cannot believe that joy exists; they do not think about it; they do not wish to think about it; it displeases them when they are torn suddenly from their illusion in order to be shown another aspect of the same subject.

In his critical reviews Sarcey was proud to represent the bourgeois play-goer of his time. He quotes Molière's famous remark, 'There is no other rule of the theatre than that of pleasing the public', and supports it with a weighty dictum of his own: 'The audience is the necessary and inevitable condition to which dramatic art must accommodate its means ... from this single fact we can derive all the laws of the theatre without a single exception'. It is a flattering pronouncement from so eminent a critic, recalling Samuel Johnson's equally flattering line: 'The drama's laws the drama's patrons give' and anticipating the cruder 'giving the audience what it wants' of contemporary parlance. But regrettably Sarcey does not carry out the promise of his pronouncement. Apart from his laughter/tears argument, he leaves his readers to 'derive all the laws of the theatre without exception' for themselves. He rests his anti-naturalist case on the assertion that drama is not the mirror of nature but an aggregate of conventions; but what principles can be derived to guide the selection of those conventions he leaves unmentioned.

In his laughter/tears passage Sarcey draws an aesthetic judgment from what he supposes to be a psychological truth. If the supposition is sound, that is, if in a large measure it can be generalized, there seems no reason – if we accept the method as valid – to reject his conclusion. So too can other suppositions be made about human nature which, if allowable, carry aesthetic implications.

As warm-up examples, we can assert that it is an intolerable experience to have our natural desire to see and hear what is before us frustrated (we are willing to disbar the other senses as a convention of 'witnessing'). We would have no hesitation in rejecting as unaesthetic any performance failing to satisfy those senses. Equally natural is our urge to understand, to follow and to anticipate; and any dramatic work with its logic, order and conjunction of parts so devised as to render it unintelligible can be legitimately judged as aesthetically poor. Unless, that is, by means of some transcendent technique, we have been led to suspect a significance in our failure to understand.

As basic as these suppositions is Minturno's, regulating length. We would probably not disagree that the outside tolerance limit of an audience whose attention is required to remain fixed upon a narrow area is three or four hours. Yet within this generous limitation there is considerable margin for difference in the attention-fixing power between one play and another. One playwright's long may be another's short. Shaw and O'Neill have kept audiences in their seats far longer than William Inge or Genet would dare to. Nor is the quantum of talent the sole consideration; the nature of the material itself can be the determining factor. For example, stark tragedy such as *Oedipus Tyrannus* brings us to exhaustion quicker than a pleasant romance by Phillip Barry, even were the two playwrights judged equally gifted. So does what we might call non-logical order, the apparently haphazard or obscurely connected episodes that comprise Beckett's *Waiting for Godot* or Genet's *The Maids*, for example. The mental energy of an audience *groping* for understanding flags quickly, particularly when it dawns upon them that understanding of the conventional sort may not be forthcoming even by the end of the play. A shorter sitting would improve Ionesco's *The Chairs* for that reason alone. His *Rhinoceros*, on the other hand, does not oblige a grudging attention; it continues to tantalize hope throughout its three acts.

We might conclude, then, that a play is of proper length, that it has aesthetic magnitude, when its duration corresponds to a vigorously maintained attention span in the audience.

More elusive than the aesthetics of duration, audibility and order, are those associated with notions of rhythm, tempo and contrast, all of which a good work of art is traditionally presumed to possess in some mysterious degree or quality. We arrive at 'good' in respect of these three when, in all three respects, the play, and our natural response, are perfectly in step. That is, we experience pleasure when we find natural needs of ours structured into the composition of the work of art. Together, rhythm, tempo and contrast serve as an antidote to monotony, which, prefiguring death or deadness, the body in its experiencing seeks to overcome. A rhythmless concatenation of units, for example, is hypnotic and acts as an irritant upon the alert organism wishing to remain alert. A rhythmic movement, on the other hand, is one wherein the repetition of connected units is relieved by a sudden surge or accent, like the down beat in a measure of music. The body responds to such accenting pleasurably; it gives itself energetically to the periodic surge, receiving, in reward, full value from those units which receive no accent.

A definition of proper tempo is similarly governed by the body's prejudice in behalf of its own vitality. If events pass so quickly that they elude apprehension, again the condition of hypnosis is approached, and the body, in revolt, indignantly refuses its attention. If the events pass too slowly, anticipated conclusions outdistance actuality, and again attention is vacated – the psyche always searching out a condition in which it can experience its own aliveness.

Sarcey's rejection of the sublime/grotesque mixture points to the larger question of propriety in contrast. Abstractly, contrast is neither desirable nor undesirable. Its proper employment in the theatre depends upon relating the dramatic material (and the playwright's point of view toward it) to the presumed needs of the audience. Each play must discover its own formal character, not only in respect to such extremes as laughter and tears, but in all dimensions where juxtapositions are possible.

Sarcey's example, however, serves his point. When twelve hundred spectators are 'entirely overwhelmed with grief' they resist being 'torn suddenly' from it and precipitated into a laugh-provoking situation. But it is the *resistance* that renders the aesthetic undesirable, not a *disbelief* on the audience's part that joy exists, as Sarcey suggests. Emotional recovery from an empathic experience of deep grief is not a split-second operation. If it is necessary to a dramatic fiction that joy follow sorrow, then the playwright must artfully construct a period of convalescence; otherwise emotional tissue will be torn, and the resulting defence against a repetition of the experience may vitiate the play's effectiveness. We can enjoy an extended vicarious experience of grief; it produces a kind of pleasurable pain. All that is asked, is that the experience be terminated before an audience feels pressed to terminate it by leaving the theatre. Emotional convalescence will follow in its own time after the curtain has fallen. Interjected amusing moments, say in *Oedipus Tyrannus*, would be psychologically alienating. There is no pleasure to be had in the wrench from commitment.

We tolerate sharp juxtapositions only when they compose an image which successfully reinforces the dominant tone of the play – the fool in *King Lear*, for example, or the Wagner parallel in *Doctor Faustus*. To be successful, the contrasting element must act as a rhythmic device: it must claim no commitment to itself. As Lessing observed, the alert organism is highly selective in its receptivity; it turns aside at every moment masses of stimuli that dislocate concentration. Particularly it rejects any stimulus with competitive power sufficient to divide and thus neutralize the committed attention. If for example the colour red of the same area, hue and intensity is placed near green, a poor aesthetic contrast has been created, for the red does nothing to accent the green, it simply increases the rate at which fatigue is induced. As aesthetic contrast respects the organism's propensity to select and focus. Its purpose is support, not relief; it recharges attention and lends strength to the object of focus. In the drama such a contrast would bear a similar relationship to the dominant style or mood, as in painting a smaller purple area of softer hue and weaker intensity would bear to green. Unsupporting contrasts of humour and pathos have become highly fashionable in contemporary realistic drama, an aesthetic drawn less from Hugo's principle than from the supposition that audiences are not attracted to serious drama unless they are assured it need not be taken seriously. Vapidity, of course, is the price – a legitimate charge, too, if the supposition is correct.

T. S. Eliot's *The Cocktail Party* provides some striking examples of functional contrasts; the play's lighter moments – and they are numerous – never subvert its serious statement. They substantiate it by forming an ironic shadow to the characters' pointless lives. Yet in *Murder in the Cathedral* the same author commits an uncharacteristic aesthetic blunder. A wrenching contrast between parts one and two cracks the tonal unity of the play, producing an effect precisely the opposite of the one Eliot intended. The fumble is not catastrophic; the play survives nobly despite it. But it does point to further suppositions from which aesthetic inferences might be drawn.

In the play, Thomas à Becket speaks a language that is a far cry from conversational prose. In the total composition, his diction and the metre he employs are appropriate parts of the theatrical reality. The device of the Chorus of Women, the elusive and mystic expressions of the Archbishop at the moment of his death, the very presence of the Tempters, are all acceptable as theatrical conventions, consistent with the conventionalized verse of the dialogue. Suddenly, the implied contract that has authorized this stage reality is broken. In an Interlude the Archbishop delivers a sermon in prose as distinct in style and diction as the surrounding verse had been from ordinary speech. The contrast was not fortuitous. Eliot had a reason for it. In his essay, *Poetry and Drama*, he explains: 'A sermon cast in verse is too unusual an experience for even the most regular churchgoer: nobody could have responded to it as a sermon at all'.[1]

Here we have Eliot, like Lessing, concerned quite properly with the experience of the audience. Conscientiously he adjusted the formal character of his play in regard to 'the nature of our feelings and emotion'. As churchgoers, we could not, he felt, respond to a sermon in verse. But it is precisely what we can do as *audience*, and as witnesses to his play that is all we are. Verse had become the established linguistic convention of the play, and as such, anything and everything is expressible through it. We do not find Romeo's and Juliet's love-making in iambic pentameter 'unnatural' because at one time or another in some degree we are all lovers. We cherish them for teaching us how to love.

Yet even were Eliot's supposition defensible, it is not controlling. The controlling supposition, I believe, Eliot overlooked. It might be put this way: in any contrast where abruptness is likely to be a factor – as it is in this instance – the organism resists

[1] Harvard University Press, Cambridge, Mass., 1951; p. 30.

movement from the conventional to the unconventional. Conversely, it feels security and therefore finds pleasure in a movement from the unconventional to the conventional. Coming where it does, the prose sermon in *Murder in the Cathedral* shatters the reality of the surrounding verse, by forcing the unconventional – in this case prose speech – into the midst of the conventional. The prose travesties what had become integral to the statement, and suddenly the whole effect of the play is dimmed.

The conventional is a manner or style which is established and acceptable, a status either assumed to be so *a priori* or earned in the course of the work by the playwright's commitment to it. The verse in *Murder in the Cathedral* earns its conventional status. The dominant realism of Tennessee Williams' *The Glass Menagerie*, in contrast, is a granted convention and Williams wisely precedes the established style with the unconventional appearance of Tom as the play's interlocutor. Had he reversed the order, as Eliot did, giving us first the conventional and then introducing Tom's choral function, the play would have come to an abrupt halt as we made our adjustment to an aberrant theatrical manner. We would in some curious way have felt tricked by a device; we would have felt that the preceding material were somehow insubstantial, not meant to be what it had appeared. As Williams handles it we slip easily from Tom's introduction into the body of the play with a feeling almost of coming home, of coming to safety. When from then on, he talks directly to us, we have him safely within the context of the prevailing realism. Thornton Wilder manipulates his devices in *Our Town* with equal care. The unconventional stage manager speaking to the audience precedes the semi-realism of the subsequent dialogue and action. When he participates later in the play as drug-store owner, a further unconventional step has been taken which in turn prepares for the unusual, yet less unconventional, graveyard scene in the last act. At no point do we feel startled out of something: we are always eased into it by Wilder's masterful structure.

The supposition that we move comfortably from the unconventional to the conventional invites further suppositions of the same order. From dark to light, for example. Assuming conditions to be normal, we take more pleasure as a rule in seeing the sun appear from behind the clouds than in watching the clouds obscure it. We are, it might be said, psychologically heliotropic. The eye, and the spirit it windows, readily follows colours and design that directs it from the obscure to the clear, from the shrouded to the explicit, from cold to warm. Similarly (and perhaps it is axiomatic), we are happier with the direction of pain to pleasure, danger to safety, tension to release than we are with the reverse. The former state *calls* for the latter in each instance (indeed, frequently with some urgency) and again, the objective dramatic corollary of the desirable direction flatters the spirit, reassures it, confirms, so to say, its self-directed prejudice.

Yet a little danger, pain and tension are pleasurable experiences, so long as the mind can pre-picture ultimate safety and peace. Our eagerness to explore, to discover, our delight in surprise (when it does not demote the ego) are available to the playwright to direct and reward.

Finally, the body's urge to climax has obvious and powerful aesthetic implications. In all doing there is expectancy of completion. The word 'start' implies continuation and finish. A play, moving as it does through time, is never apprehended as a totality until its movement is officially halted by the last curtain; our experience is always of a work in progress. Yet it is not enough to *know* a play must end as an article of faith; we need to sense its inherent wholeness, its 'beginning, middle and end' as we experience its parts. We can anticipate the outcome of a story line; boy generally gets girl, heroes more often than not overcome obstacles. I don't mean that. I mean we need to *feel* a structured rhythm in the formal life of the play steadily satisfying our instinct for climax. That experience is itself the clue to completion that unifies the play in transit.

Earlier I mentioned that while we all share a drive to understand, it may be to the playwright's point to have us *not* understand in the conventional sense. He may be using our non-understanding ironically, as a catalyst to some larger meaning – as

I believe Ionesco does in *The Bald Soprano*. He may, that is to say, thwart the natural impulses *as an aesthetic device*. He may deny organic empathy so that its absence shall itself become a statement.

If a playwright's purpose, let us conjecture, were to shock us out of emotional commitment, he might well employ Eliot's method in *Murder in the Cathedral* to achieve it. Another might devise a rhythmless progression, or draw us from light to dark as a formal reinforcement of an idea. The tragic playwright, a Sophocles or an Anderson, dares reverse the natural direction only as a device. Ultimately, light must appear from out the darkness, a useful positive must emerge from the constructed negative. If it does not, our inclination to stamp the product rejected is as justifiable as it would be had the performance been inaudible. In short, each desirable direction can be reversed, each desirable quality inverted if the end served invigorates the imagination or creates a transcendent value. It is a difficult art to practise, unquestionably, this countermanding of natural impulses, and a miss in it is as good as a mile. Its success depends as much upon the spectator's willingness to take pleasure from pain in the cause of profit as upon playwriting skill.

Hamlet's understanding of dramatic art was wholly consistent with his limited purpose in having the players reconstruct the circumstances in which he believed his father was murdered. Drama conceived as history revisited is a useful device for catching the conscience of a king. But drama does more than that. It creates conscience. It is a construct, not a mirror held up to nature. It reveals no truths; it proposes them. Like a hammer or saw, dramatic art is strictly utilitarian. It is used to think with, and to feel with. With the equipment of art we control the world around us. We fashion the world in its image.

Cultural habits are difficult to break, as every Abstract Expressionist painter has learned, particularly when they are reinforced by a dogma of inherent necessity. There is something highly attractive in Hamlet's '. . . to show virtue her own feature, scorn her own image and the very age and body of time his form and pressure'. Yet three major negative effects have resulted, I believe, from the naturalist principle in dramatic criticism.

First, it has directed a misreading of dramatic history by imputing to the aims and procedures of Greek and Mediaeval dramatists ideals constructed in the Renaissance. Second, it has established as a corollary the principle that the drama reveals reality rather than constructs it, with the result that playwrights either conform to the prevailing notion of nature or are obliged to invent such mystiques as surrealism, or speak of 'levels of the real' to justify departures from the verisimilar. Third, and most important, the naturalist principle has imposed itself upon the spectator's genuine aesthetic source, subverting faith in that source and, in consequence, inhibiting his freedom of judgment.

Despite the importance given to the nature metric in the annals of dramatic theory, the spectator, I am persuaded, does not in fact respond to the play in its terms, or would not unless trained to admit no other criterion. If he has been convinced that the character drawing, motivation, order and plausibility of the stage must reflect satisfactorily contemporary conventions for appraising the natural, that conviction will limit strictly the perspective from which an approving judgment can be made. Lessing's belief that the Greek playwright devised duration in tragedy to accommodate the human needs of the chorus would force him to consider faulty any play which disregarded that convention or obscured an extended elapsed time, as in the *Agamemnon* and the *Antigone*, by elision. Had he instead viewed duration as he later viewed the mixture of the sublime and the grotesque, from the perspective of the responding organism, much drama that on principle would have to be judged as faulty he might have judged as good. Released from principle, human response has a wider range of artistic pleasure and interest than, until recently, the playwright has felt authorized to explore. Such naturalist shibboleths as order, proportion, logic, necessity, unity, for example, have not only constricted the dramatist, they have also withheld from the spectator dimensions of experience. For

R   247

while it is true that one can respond happily to art patterned in orderly sequence, we are also capable of pleasurable response to disorder, distortion, disproportion and illogic – and it is totally irrelevant that either order or disorder are manifest in the world around us.

Edwin Burr Pettet

XIV: THE FAIR THEATRES
OF PARIS
IN THE
EIGHTEENTH CENTURY:
THE UNDERMINING
OF THE CLASSICAL
IDEAL

IT IS A COMMONPLACE OF LITERARY HISTORY THAT THE classical ideal dominated French drama from the mid-seventeenth century until 1830. Moreover, because France set the literary standards of Europe, the French ideal was an international one until about 1800. Thus, as late as 1776, Voltaire could state what he considered an unanswerable argument for the supremacy of French tragedy: that it was universally accepted, whereas Shakespeare's plays were admired only locally. His evidence was correct, even though his conclusions were soon disproved, for in 1776 Shakespeare was just beginning to be known outside of England, while French tragedy had long been imitated throughout Europe.

Yet the standards which Voltaire defended so vehemently were to be rejected even by the French in the following century. Most historians depict this reversal as beginning with the publication of Mme de Staël's *Germany* in 1814 and being completed with the production of Hugo's *Hernani* in 1830. But the Romantic 'revolution' can be seen more truthfully as the culmination of trends which had begun as early as 1700. This earlier movement has been neglected, because it is associated with the minor theatres of the French fairs. Nevertheless, experiments with dramatic forms at the fairs were instrumental in undermining the classical ideal and in preparing the way for the Romantic drama of the nineteenth century.

Before surveying the developments of the eighteenth century, it might be well to review the basic tenets of French classicism. Although they cannot be examined in detail here, they may be summarized briefly: Comedy and tragedy were regarded as the only legitimate forms, and no mixture of the two was allowed; they were to observe the unities of time, place and action; scenes of violence and death were to be kept offstage, and the liaison (or careful bridging) of scenes maintained. The demand for verisimilitude was even more important. Basically, it required that subject matter be restricted to that which is empirically possible (except when a supernatural element was an accepted part of a myth), that the moral significance of events be emphasized, and that 'norms' be observed. The concept of 'norms' is based upon the belief that ultimate reality is to be seen in those qualities which all phenomena of the same class share in common. Thus, the playwright was expected to confine himself to the typical, rather than the individual or accidental, in his drawing of character, treatment of incidents and use of language.

These strict critical requirements were paralleled by a stringent control over theatrical production. After 1680, by the order of Louis XIV, exclusive rights to present comedy and tragedy in Paris were held by the Comédie-Française. Similarly, in 1672, Louis gave Lully, the Director of the Royal Academy of Music and Dance, a virtual monopoly on musical performances in Paris. Although the King did not specify the limits of the grant, Lully chose to interpret the patent as extending to any performance which required more than six musical instruments and two trained voices.

Lully's monopoly also extended to ballet and complex stage spectacle. The inclusion of scenic effects is explained by two facts: first, the Comédie-Française needed no elaborate machinery if it remained true to the classical ideal; and second, spectacle was an integral part of contemporary opera. Of seventeenth-century opera, one author has said:

> After the austere restraint of the classic tragedies, in which the mise en scène was a negligible factor, the French were delighted with the spectacular effects produced by the elaborate mechanical contrivances of the opera. . . . Every means was employed to enhance the brilliance of the spectacle – not only elaborate staging and costuming, but subjects were chosen which would lend themselves to dazzling effects, such as mythological themes, with a superabundance of gods, spirits, demons.[1]

The only exception to the monopolies held by the Comédie-

[1] V. B. Grannis, *Dramatic Parody in Eighteenth Century France* (New York, 1931), pp. 112–13.

Française and the Opéra were made for the troupe of Italian players which had been performing in Paris since the middle of the seventeenth century. This company used the stock characters of the *commedia dell' arte* (such as Harlequin, Pantalone and Columbine) and had originally played in Italian, using improvised dialogue. By the last quarter of the seventeenth century, however, the Italians had begun to use written scripts and to perform in French. Their plays almost always employed parody and satire; they were topical, frequently impertinent, always exuberant. The Italians were expelled from Paris in 1697, however, because one of their plays, *The False Prude*, was thought to contain a satirical portrait of Mme de Maintenon. It was at this point that the Fair theatres came into prominence, for they attempted to take over the position vacated by the Italian players.

At this time Paris had two Fairs of major importance, the St-Germain and the St-Laurent. The St-Germain Fair ran from February 3 till Easter, and the St-Laurent from the end of June till about the first of October. Consequently, they were open for a combined total of five to six months each year.

Traditionally, entertainment at the Fairs had been provided by acrobats, tightrope walkers, trained animals and freaks. In the late seventeenth century, however, dramatic interludes began to appear. One director surrounded his acrobatic acts with short scenes of dialogue which introduced and tied together the various performances. Since this innovation appeared to increase the popularity of the booth, others seized upon the idea. Soon marionettes were performing *commedia dell' arte* plays. All of these early attempts were crude and almost all were heavily indebted to the Italian comedy. It was only natural, therefore, that, when the Italians were expelled, the Fair troupes should see this as an opportunity to improve their status.

About 1698, then, entrepreneurs at the Fairs began to produce plays similar to those previously performed by the Italian company. The Comédie-Française and the Opéra, however, had viewed the expulsion of the Italians as eliminating the one exception to their monopolies, and when the crowds began to

throng to this new attraction, a war of the theatres began which
was waged intermittently until the French Revolution. Out of
this struggle between the official theatres and the Fair troupes
grew many of the experiments with dramatic form in the eighteenth century.

When the Comédie-Française instituted legal proceedings, as
they were to do many times during the century, the Fairs showed
themselves adept at manœuvring. Being ordered to close their
theatres in 1698, they appealed to the Paris Parlement, or high
court, which did not reach a decision until five years later.
Meanwhile, the troupes continued to perform and to enlarge
their repertoires. They also added music and dance to their plays
and thereby offended the Opéra as well as the Comédie-Française. During these years the Fair companies built up substantial
audiences drawn from all classes.

As might have been expected, the courts ruled against the Fair
theatres and reconfirmed the monopolies of the Opéra and the
Comédie-Française. The Fairs were loath to give up so profitable
an enterprise, however, and they set about to find forms of drama
which would legally circumvent the monopolies.

In casting about, they seemed to reason that, although plays
were forbidden, isolated scenes were not. Furthermore, according
to the accepted critical standards of the day, all legitimate drama
had to observe the unities, bridge scenes carefully and avoid
violence on stage. The Fair troupes began to present works,
therefore, which violated all of the accepted canons of criticism.
For example, *The Abduction of Helen, the Taking and Burning of
Troy*, written by Fuzelier in 1705, was composed of a series of
episodes covering a span of ten years, set in a great number of
places, and showing several battles and deaths on stage. Furthermore, the episodes were separated by incidental entertainment
such as tightrope dancing. The Fair theatres apparently reasoned
that the Comédie-Française would have to abandon its own
critical standards before it called such a work a play. This double-
pronged counter-attack was typical of the Fair troupes throughout
the century: while deliberately subverting orders, they managed

to ridicule their opponents and thereby make the defiance even more galling. Such devices endeared the Fair theatres to the Parisian public, which kept returning to see what audacity the troupes would commit next.

To win the important legal battle, however, the Comédie-Française was willing to abandon its critical standards, and, despite the lack of orthodox artistic merits, the Fair's new creations were forbidden by the authorities. More important here, however, is the deliberate defiance of accepted canons of dramatic form. Few persons at the time would have applied the same standards to the repertoire of the Fair theatres as to that of the Comédie-Française. No doubt the majority looked upon the Fair companies as entertaining upstarts without artistic pretensions, and consequently they tolerated much that would have been hissed off the stage at the Comédie-Française. Nevertheless, it is from such continued violations that a popular acceptance of the so-called irregularities was gradually established.

The court ruling, by implication, defined the monopoly of the Comédie-Française as extending to any dramatic entertainment using spoken dialogue. One of the experiments which was next tried resulted in a kind of pantomimic silent dancing by Harlequin and other *commedia* characters. This innovation is of more than passing interest for, according to Disher, it gave impetus to the development of English pantomime. Some of the Harlequins of the French Fairs went to London, where their performances were billed as 'Italian Night Scenes'. These dances were elaborated by such men as John Rich into pantomime, one of the most popular dramatic forms of the eighteenth century in London.

It was not the comic dancing which disturbed the Comédie-Française, but a new kind of drama advertised as 'comedies in three acts in monologues'. The term 'monologue' was used merely to indicate that only one speaking actor was on stage at a time. The other actors (of which there could be any number) might whisper their speeches to the speaking actor, who would in turn repeat what they said for the benefit of the audience; or the speaking actor would interpret the pantomime of the others to the audience. At times an even more bizarre arrangement was used. One actor would address another and then step offstage; the remaining actor would then reply and step offstage, whereupon the first would return and answer. Although lacking in verisimilitude, this procedure delighted the audiences, who welcomed each new ruse employed by the Fair actors.

But again the Comédie-Française appealed to the police. Much of the evidence about these battles comes from the legal records of the period. A delegation from the Comédie-Française would file a formal written complaint with the authorities, who would then investigate the charges by attending a performance and recording what they had seen there. These reports were then used as a basis for whatever legal action was to be taken. Here is a report of the performance of a monologue:

> We went on the said day, March 2, 1708, at 6 p.m. or thereabouts, to the enclosure of the said fair of Saint-Germain, to the place of business of the said Dolet, where we found a very large public theatre inside which was a large number of persons. After the tightrope walking, a man and woman appeared and performed tumbling on the slack rope. After this, the tightrope dancers spread a cloth on the stage and performed somersaults. Then the curtain was raised and several actors and actresses performed the comedy *Harlequin, Linen Draper of the Palace* in three acts. In each scene one actor spoke aloud and the others responded by gestures which were then explained to the audience by the first actor, all of which presents the comedy. ... The play over, an actor came forward to announce another comedy which will be performed tomorrow.[1]

In addition to the description of the production, some additional points in this report should be noted. First, the Fair theatres remained true to their origins and continued to present tightrope dancing and acrobatics, usually before the plays or as entr'actes. The petitions of the Comédie-Française never referred to the Fair performers as actors but always as tightrope dancers, and the authorities were repeatedly asked to restrict the Fair troupes

---

[1] Reprinted in: Émile Campardon, *Les Spectacles de la Foire ... depuis 1595 jusqu'à 1791* (Paris, 1877), I, 257–8.

to their rightful profession. Secondly, the plays were always in one, two or three acts. Although the Fair theatres were not the first nor by any means the only ones to use the three-act form, they unquestionably helped to popularize it.

The 'monologues' were soon forbidden, and some troupes turned to *pièces à la muette* (mute plays), a designation which again was inaccurate since all of the actors spoke. But what they spoke were nonsense syllables measuring out to perfect Alexandrine lines which parodied the plays in the repertory of the Comédie-Française. Furthermore, the actors imitated the vocal and physical mannerisms of the better known performers at the Comédie-Française. The audience followed the story, not by the speech, but by the pantomime. Thus, the Fair troupes again struck a double blow by performing plays and ridiculing their enemies simultaneously. This new attempt illustrates well two perennial interests of the Fair troupes – parody and satire. Here the repertory and acting style of the Comédie-Française were parodied, but later any well-known play, opera or literary type might be the target. Contemporary controversies and other current topics might also be treated satirically.

Before the mute plays were suppressed, another complication was introduced. The Opéra had become so financially insecure that it sold the privilege of using musicians, dancers and scenic machines to one of the Fair companies. The Comédie-Française considered this a betrayal and filed a complaint against both the Fair troupe and the Opéra. Consequently, on April 17, 1709, the Council of State put an end to the mute plays and forbade the Opéra to sell its privileges. This ruling is illustrative of the interest engendered by the battle of the theatres, for the Paris Parlement and the King's Council deliberated on it seventeen times between 1705 and 1711.

After the Royal order of 1709, the Fair troupes had to start over again. This time they initiated experiments which eventually led to two important minor genres: *comédies-en-vaudeville* and comic opera. In 1710, however, there was little in the productions which suggested these later outgrowths. The new genre was originally called the *pièce à écriteaux* (play with placards or writing). At first the actors used the rather clumsy device of writing their speeches on scrolls, which were rolled up and carried in the right pocket. When a scene required dialogue for clarity, the actor took a scroll from his right pocket, unrolled it, held it up for the audience to read, and then put it in his left pocket. This device proved too awkward and soon an improvement was found. Two young boys, dressed as cupids and suspended above the stage, held placards on which couplets representing the actors' speeches were printed in large letters. These couplets were set to popular tunes, and confederates were placed in the audience to sing them when the orchestra played the melodies. Soon members of the audience joined in and, in effect, performed the dialogue which the actors were forbidden to speak. A police report on a performance in 1711 states:

> We went on Saturday, August 8, to the performance held at the St-Laurent Fair, and there noted that there is a stage elevated about four or five feet, with chandeliers above and an orchestra below the said stage, in which there were seven or eight performers on instruments such as violins, basses, and oboes; that upon the said stage came actors and actresses dressed either in French costumes or as Harlequin or Pierrot or other disguises; that they performed silent scenes on different subjects with placards which were held by two small boys suspended in the air, who were raised and lowered by means of ropes and machines; that the said placards contained songs which were sung by several persons in the audience as soon as they were given the tune by the violin; which songs, written on both sides of each placard, served as a rule as responses one to another and thus gave an explanation of the silent scenes. The play was composed of several acts in which there were dances and ballets performed by various actors and actresses who danced sometimes alone and sometimes as a group of eight or twelve.[1]

This report was made as the result of a complaint by the Comédie-Française, although the offended party was the Opéra, for it is

---

[1] Reprinted in: Émile Campardon, *Les Spectacles de la Foire . . . depuis 1595 jusqu'à 1791* (Paris, 1877), I, 91.

clear that in the use of more than six musical instruments, of scenic machines and group dances the troupe was infringing upon the monopoly of the Opéra. The complaint strongly implied that the Opéra was in complicity with the Fair Company. At any rate, no action was taken, and the Fair theatres produced these 'plays with placards' from 1710 to 1714 without interruption.

In 1714 the Opéra, once more in financial difficulty, received permission to sell the privilege of using dance, music and spectacle to one of the Fair companies. As a result, the placards could be dispensed with, for the actors themselves could now sing the couplets. This was the only actual change wrought by the Opéra's sale of its privilege, for the Fairs were already using dance and music. Beginning in 1715, the new form was called *opéra-comique*, probably to signify its legality stemming from the Opéra's dispensation and to suggest the essentially comic nature of the plots. After this time, any troupe which could purchase the privilege of using music and dance from the Opéra called itself an *opéra-comique* theatre.

By 1715, however, spoken dialogue had begun to creep into the new form. At first, there was only an occasional line, but soon short scenes were given almost entirely in dialogue. A police report of July, 1715, describes one of these productions:

> There was presented ... a play entitled *The Useless Precaution; or Harlequin Newsmonger of Holland*, in three acts, composed of several scenes which were sung by the actors and actresses. And during the course of the said play all the said actors and actresses ... spoke to each other in short speeches ... which tied the songs together.[1]

The use of spoken dialogue allowed much greater flexibility in the form. The number of popular tunes was limited and their frequent repetition made for monotony. The use of spoken sections not only cut down on the number of songs, but, since the relative proportion of speaking to singing could be manipulated, the plays gained in variety as well.

[1] Ibid., II, 354-5.

By 1718, the *opéra-comique* which had grown out of the 'play with placards' had assumed all of its essential characteristics. The perfection of this dramatic type can be attributed primarily to Alain-René Le Sage, one of the great literary figures of the eighteenth century. Le Sage began his playwriting career with the Comédie-Française, but, having quarrelled with that group, had no place to turn except the Fair theatres. He brought with him the outlook which is so evident in his earlier plays and in his novel, *Gil Blas*: a penetrating understanding of human weaknesses and an ability to turn them to ridicule. When he came to the Fairs in 1713 the only form being presented was the 'play with placards'; so well did he develop this type that he came to be called the 'Father of Comic Opera'. He has left a ten-volume collection of *opéras-comiques* written between 1713 and 1730. An *opéra-comique* at this time was a comedy, in one, two or three acts, in which the action was presented through an alternation of spoken dialogue and lyrics sung to the tunes of popular songs. In the introduction to his collection, Le Sage said of the form:

> The reader must not look for complicated plots. Each play contains one action so simple, so compressed in fact, that it does not require those dull bridging scenes which must be endured in the better comedies. . . . Some authors of tragedies and lyric poems have already said, in noting the simplicity of our subjects, that it would not be difficult to write them. They could not be more mistaken. It is not easy to find the middle point between the high and the low. . . . Not all plots are suited to the Opéra-Comique, which has, the same as other forms, its particular demands. . . . One ordinarily finds the marvellous in it, but the marvellous is always joined with natural sentiments and satiric portraits which please those who ask for morality.

The use of *commedia dell' arte* characters, with their farcical stage business, was another typical feature.

Although the history of *opéra-comique* is uninterrupted after 1710, the Fair theatres by no means led a quiet existence.[1] In

---

[1] The best general treatment of the Fair theatre is: Maurice Albert, *Les Théâtres de la foire (1660–1789)*, (Paris, 1900).

1715, following the death of Louis XIV, the Regent recalled the Italian players from exile. From 1716 to 1718 they performed in Italian, but, finding this unprofitable, in 1718 they turned to French. This change in language immediately brought them into conflict with the Fair troupe, since both used the same stock characters, many of the same theatrical tricks and the same type of parody and satire. The Italians, however, did not present the new *opéra-comique*. The Comédie-Française and the Comédie-Italienne were brought together by their mutual opposition to the Fair theatres and, through their combined efforts, the Fair companies were suppressed in 1718.

The Italians did not experience the upsurge in popularity which they had expected, and, thinking this was a matter of location, they moved to the Fairs in 1721. The suppressed theatres, which had been playing surreptitiously, took the move as a sign that performances were now to be allowed at the Fairs and began to produce their plays openly. The Regent complicated matters further by allowing a Fair company to perform a play called *The Fair Revived* at the Palais-Royal. But the Comédie-Française insisted upon its rights, and the Fair theatres were once more reduced to playing monologues. As in earlier years, these were monologues only in name, for the stage was crowded with characters who revolved around one speaking actor.

The Fair theatres were not long forced to play monologues. In October, 1722, Louis XV was consecrated and soon made his sentiments on the theatre controversy evident by inviting one of the Fair companies to perform at the palace. As a result, the Fair theatres resumed their old repertoires in 1723. Louis rewarded them by attending the opening of the Fair theatre in 1723 and refusing to attend the Comédie-Française in the same week. After this, the official theatres did not dare to object, and although the order against the Fair theatres was not revoked, it was universally ignored. The situation was further improved when the Italian company became an official troupe in 1723, receiving a subsidy and the title *Comédiens ordinaires du Roi* (although it was popularly called the Comédie-Italienne). At this time the Italians moved from the Fairs and left the field to its original inhabitants.

By 1725 the popularity of *opéra-comique* was assured, and by that time even the Comédie-Française was giving short plays as afterpieces complete with Harlequins, in imitation of the genre which the Fair theatres had perfected. The Italian troupe, of course, had been presenting such works all along, though both official companies were restricted because they did not have permission from the Opéra to use complex music and dance. In 1726 the Fair companies satirized their imitators in a play called *The Pirate Players*. In this work the actors of the Comédie-Française and the Comédie-Italienne meet on an island to waylay the Fair actors, for both groups are in danger of losing their livelihoods. They capture the Fair troupe and steal its costumes.

C.F. What's in this pack? *Opéra-comique*. Here is the treasure. Open it – this will do for us.

Ital. And I will take this pack of Parodies of the Opera. They belong by right to the Comédie-Italienne.

C.F. Ho, ho. What's this? *The Favourable Obstacle*, a play of intrigue in one act. That will do for us. Let's see what this is. *The Disguised Lovers*, a play. . . .

Ital. Ah, it's a parody. Give it to me. . . .

C.F. We can't content ourselves by taking the plays of the Opéra-Comique. We'll have to make them act some of them for us so that we can capture their style.

Fair. What, thief, isn't it enough that you steal our merchandise? Are we forced to sell it for you too?

C.F. Yes. It's only at that price we will let you go on living.

In spite of this competition, however, the Fair had a relative monopoly on *opéra-comique*, and, except for minor difficulties, the troupes continued a peaceful and profitable existence until 1745. The new controversy which arose at that time came about primarily as a result of innovations in *opéra-comique* itself. In 1740 *opéra-comique* was still much as Le Sage had left it: exuberant, farcical, satirical. After 1740, however, under Charles-Simon Favart, the more delicate and sentimental tendencies of the eighteenth century began to dominate. Favart disdained complicated intrigue, any kind of low humour or *double-entendre*, and was interested primarily in subtle gradations of feeling, much in the manner of Marivaux. Consequently, his comic operas bore little resemblance to LeSage's except in the alternation of song and dialogue. In 1744, Favart's *Acajou* was so popular that riots occurred over the difficulty of obtaining tickets. *Acajou* was a fairy tale rather than an Harlequinade, almost entirely lyrical, with very few spoken passages.

The success of *Acajou*, however, brought the downfall of the *opéra-comique* troupe. The manager of the Opéra argued that *Acajou*, since it made only slight use of *commedia* characters and was almost entirely set to music, was not *opéra-comique* but simply popular opera. Under this pretext, the privilege granted to the Fair theatre was cancelled, and the Opéra itself began producing comic opera at the Fairs. This action elicited so violent an objection from the Comédie-Française that *opéra-comique* was suppressed altogether between the years of 1745 and 1751.

As usual, the resourceful Fair theatres turned to other genres, and it was during this period that the popularity of pantomime was established. To meet his commitments, Favart leased his theatre to an English actor named Matthews, who produced with tremendous success a series of pantomimes in the English manner.

These pantomimes had several standard features: Harlequin, the central character, was presented with a magic wand by a god or magician; by means of this wand he transformed objects or places at will; this, in turn, motivated a great amount of scenic display through magical transformations; the plot, based on mythology, popular legend or well-known events, was composed of alternating comic and serious scenes which afforded material for satire on contemporary situations. This mixture of the comic and serious, of fantasy and realism, of music, dance, and spectacular scenic display was at the opposite pole from the strict formalism of neo-classical tragedy.

Between 1745 and 1751 the pantomime became the most popular dramatic type of the day. Innumerable pieces were given under the varying designations of pantomime, ballet pantomime, pastoral pantomime, parody pantomime, heroi-comical ballet and so on. This new genre was never absent from the Fair theatres after this time and the Comédie-Italienne was soon offering it as well. It remained a favourite of Parisian audiences until well into the nineteenth century.

In 1751, Louis XV authorized a return to *opéra-comique*, and the next few years saw several developments of importance. The first of these is related to the physical theatre. Jean Monnet, one of the producers at the Fairs, took a French troupe to London during the years when the *opéra-comique* was suppressed. He returned determined to build a modern theatre, for at that time all those in Paris were outmoded. In 1752, Monnet, with the aid of Arnoult, Machiniste-Ingénieur du Roi and Boucher, the court designer, built at the St-Laurent Fair a theatre which remained a model for the rest of the century. This event illustrates how the Fair theatres, which had begun as simple stages in booths, had passed to a position of leadership in theatrical spectacle. After 1752, the Fair theatres frequently outstripped the Opéra, the traditional home of scenic display, in the lavish mounting of productions.

A second development came from another innovation in *opéra-comique*. Vadé began to write his *comédies poissardes*, or comedies of low life. This new type soon became so popular that the *commedia dell' arte* characters gave way to Parisian types: fishmongers, laundresses, soldiers and wigmakers. These characters were costumed realistically and talked in their own jargon. They were natural, frank and colourful. Local colour and the lower orders of society were emphasized in these plays long before they were to be found in the regular drama. Although the extreme vogue of the *comédie poissarde* waned after a few years, it remained a regular part of the repertory for the rest of the century.

Another event of importance was the production in Paris of Pergolesi's *La serva padrona* in 1752. It initiated such a craze for Italian music and opera that the Fair theatres set out deliberately to supply the new demand. As a result, original music in the Italian manner was commissioned for the *opéra-comique* plays.

This innovation moved *opéra-comique* still one step further away from its origins. From this time on the tradition of setting the lyrics of comic operas to already-existing popular tunes was abandoned. Since the *commedia* characters also were gradually replaced, only the alternation of song and speech remained as a link with the original *opéra-comique*. In its new guise, it had become what is still called comic opera.

The introduction of comic operas in the Italian manner precipitated still another crisis for the Fair theatres, since the Comédie-Italienne viewed the innovation as a violation of its rights (presumably on the basis of the Italianate music) and it sought the absorption of *opéra-comique* into its repertory. Other motives may have been involved, however, since the Italian company was in debt for 400,000 livres at the time. In 1762, in spite of protests, the Comédie-Italienne was awarded exclusive rights to the production of *opéra-comique*. In its new home comic opera continued to grow in popularity until it replaced almost all other genres at the Comédie-Italienne.

The absorption of *opéra-comique* by an official troupe was a serious blow to the Fair theatres, for a genre which they had nourished over a period of fifty years was now lost to them. But, as usual, they were resilient, and they now returned to an older version of *opéra-comique* – that which used songs set to popular tunes. They called these plays *comédies-en-vaudevilles*. The genre remained important in the repertory of the French theatre through most of the nineteenth century.

By 1760 the Fair companies were concerned over the growing importance of the Boulevard du Temple as a fashionable rendez-vous for Parisians. Consequently some of the Fair troupes began to open theatres there, although they continued to perform at the Fairs as well. The new arrangement allowed the troupes to operate throughout the entire year. This move signals the gradual transformation of the Fair theatres into what came to be called the Boulevard theatres.

Of the troupes which opened theatres on the Boulevard du Temple, four were of primary importance: those of Audinot and of Nicolet, the Théâtre des Associés, and the *Variétés Amusantes*. Both Audinot and Nicolet featured pantomimes, which gradually assumed all of the characteristic traits of melodrama.[1] The plots showed innocence persecuted by villainy, and the eventual triumph of good over evil. Music underscored the emotional qualities of scenes and accompanied the numerous dances. Movement, ingenious stage devices, and spectacle played important rôles. By 1780, even dialogue had been introduced, and many of the offerings were billed as *pantomimes parlées et dialoguées*.

But these theatres did not restrict themselves to pantomime by any means, and during the 1770's they raised a new threat to the official theatres. The Comédie-Italienne, having found comic opera more and more profitable, in 1769 ceased altogether to offer non-musical plays in French. As a result, the French playwright was faced with the same situation which had existed during the years between 1698 and 1718: there was only one official theatre to which he might submit his plays. Since the repertory of the Comédie-Française was composed primarily of older plays, the market for new works was extremely limited. As in the time of Le Sage, then, there was no place to turn except to the Fair theatres.

It was during the 1770's, therefore, that the Fair companies began to present spoken drama. For example, all of Mercier's plays written prior to 1780 were produced at the Fairs. It is amazing, however, that the spoken plays achieved any success at all under the circumstances. Before the Fair troupes were allowed to produce a non-musical play, it could be censored by three groups: the police, the Comédie-Française, and the Comédie-Italienne. This meant that, even if a play were passed by the police, either of the official theatres had the right to retain the script for itself or to make whatever changes it wished. It was often asserted that the Comédie-Française mutilated any play it did not wish to present so as to insure its failure if produced elsewhere.

[1] For an extended treatment of the relationship of pantomime to melodrama see Alexis Pitou, 'Les Origines du mélodrame français à la fin du XVIIIe siècle', *Revue d'Histoire Litteraire de la France*, XVIII (1911), 256–96.

The Undermining of the Classical Ideal

The mutilation of plays was only one of the devices used by the Comédie-Française to restrict the audiences of the lesser theatres by driving away the middle and upper classes, from which its own patrons were almost entirely drawn. It did not wish to attract the lower classes and was willing for the Fair theatres to present programmes for them. Its contempt for the lower orders is demonstrated, however, in the kinds of plays it would allow the Fair troupes to produce.

The Comédie-Française made a further attempt to drive the upper and middle classes from the Fair theatres through the control of admission prices. It was able to get even the highest priced ticket (24 sous) at the Fairs placed within the means of the working class. (After 1753 the lowest admission fee at the Comédie-Française was 25 sous.) One reason behind this ruling was the belief that the upper and middle classes would cease to attend the Fair theatres rather than mingle with the lower classes.

None of these stratagems was effective, however, for the audiences of the Fair theatres continued to be made up of a cross-section of French society, from the court to the lowest class. All felt at home at the Fairs, but the lower classes were never welcomed by the Comédie-Française. It is not surprising, therefore, that by the time of the Revolution the official troupes were associated in the minds of the lower classes with the aristocrats.

The restricted market for plays after 1770 had still another effect. Considerable agitation developed for the establishment of a 'second Comédie-Française' and the Fair theatres became symbols of this threat. The movement in favour of another official troupe gained enough support that in 1780 the Comédie-Italienne, to forestall such a move, reintroduced French comedies and *drames* into its repertory.

By the early 1780's all of the official troupes were sufficiently disturbed by the popularity of the Fair theatres to attempt their destruction. They did not co-operate in this move, however, and had entirely different ideas as to procedure. The Opéra, without the knowledge of the others, petitioned for the right to exploit the Fair troupes. This petition was granted in 1784 and the Opéra was permitted to exact heavy fees from the minor troupes for the right to perform, or to close or take over those which refused to pay.

Nicolet immediately accepted the Opéra's terms and thereafter enjoyed great freedom in regard to his repertory. Audinot, thinking this another of the many storms which the Fair theatres had weathered, held out, only to be dispossessed. After two years of petitions and the help of many influential friends, he was reinstated in his theatre, but on the Opéra's terms. The Variétés Amusantes was taken over, leased to new managers, and the company moved to the theatre at the Palais-Royal. Other theatres were closed, but those which remained had achieved a semi-official position as subsidiaries of the Opéra. Consequently they were emboldened to trespass even further on the rights of the Comédie-Française and the Comédie-Italienne.

The advent of the Revolution prevented further significant developments, and in 1791 all monopolies were revoked. Freed from restrictions, the theatres deserted the Fairs and made the Boulevards their permanent homes. The Fairs were reduced to their original forms of entertainment: tightrope walking, acrobatics, freak shows and marionettes.

Although developments after the close of the Fair theatres are not of primary concern here, a brief look at subsequent events is necessary. One influence of the Fairs can be seen in the serious plays of the 1790's, the period of greatest freedom from critical strictures on dramatic form. Twenty-four different genre descriptions were applied to the 225 serious plays written or produced in these years. Furthermore, only about one-half of the serious plays were called tragedies (as almost all would have been in 1700), and three acts were used as often as five acts even in those plays called tragedies.[1]

Perhaps the most significant development, however, was the emergence of melodrama. About 1800, Pixérécourt's plays fixed the form of melodrama, which was to become the most popular

---

[1] For a complete list of the plays, see: Jean-Alexis Rivoire, *Le Patriotisme dans le théâtre sérieux de la Révolution (1789–1799)* (Paris, 1950).

dramatic type in the years between 1800 and 1830. These melo-dramas are direct descendants from the pantomimes produced at the theatres of Audinot and Nicolet prior to the Revolution. In turn, the work of Pixérécourt is the greatest single influence on the dramatic techniques of Dumas *père* and Hugo. Lacey, after extended study, concludes that Romantic drama differs from Pixérécourt's melodramas only in limited respects: the Romantic plays often use verse, are written in five acts, and avoid happy endings.[1] Charles Nodier, a noted critic of the period, stated that Romantic drama is merely melodrama elevated by the artificial pomp of verse.[2]

By 1830, therefore, plays with the same basic characteristics as *Hernani* had been enormously popular for over a quarter of a century. The issue in the controversy over *Hernani*, then, was not so much over a new form, as whether a form which had grown out of the secondary theatres would be given critical sanction through its acceptance at the Comédie-Française, the last fortress of neo-classicism. The triumph of Romanticism was also a victory for those forces which had been at work in the minor theatres since 1700.

Looking back over the struggles and experiments, what can be said of the Fair theatres and their achievement? First, the Fairs offered freedom from the strictures of neo-classicism under which tragedy and comedy had been placed. Not bound to the rules, the Fair theatres were free to experiment, to defy all accepted tenets of playwriting. In fact, they were forced to experiment in order to exist. Deviations from accepted genres were not taken seriously at first, but gradually the official troupes appropriated the new forms as they emerged. Furthermore, by the 1760's Parisian dramatic critics had begun to take notice of the new types. Many of the critics merely condemned the bad influence of the Fair theatres and blamed them for the corruption of taste in drama. Other critics defended the Fairs and their plays, and

---

[1] Alexander Lacey, *Pixerécourt and the French Romantic Drama* (Toronto, 1928).
[2] See Nodier's Introduction to: René Charles Guilbert de Pixérécourt, *Théâtre choisi* (4 vols.; Paris, 1841–3).

one of them, Nougaret, even attempted a poetics for the new genres. By 1810, the productions at the Boulevard theatres were regularly reviewed in the newspapers and magazines of the day. Although the plays were still considered to be of secondary importance, a measure of respect is indicated by the frequent references to Pixérécourt as 'the Corneille of the Boulevards' or as 'the Shakespeare of the Boulevards'.

Second, the Fair theatres set out deliberately to cater to the widest possible audience. They reached vast numbers of persons who would not have attended the official theatres, although their audiences were by no means restricted to such persons. The Fairs helped to shape those tastes which later encouraged melodrama and Romantic drama.

Third, a great number of new dramatic forms were tried, some of which remained relatively important. Of these the most significant are undoubtedly the comic opera, the *comédies-en-vaudeville*, and the pantomime. These were the only forms employed consistently enough to be perfected at the Fairs. Much of the experimentation was unpremeditated and almost unconscious. Forms were altered, combined and abandoned as the situation demanded.

Fourth, the Fair theatres established a tradition of experiment which continued to bear fruit in the Boulevard theatres. In them, melodrama developed and became a force in the rise of Romantic drama. The later secondary, or non-official, theatres of Paris all have their roots in the acting troupes of the Fairs, and it is these theatres which traditionally have brought innovations to French drama – innovations which the more conservative official theatres are slow to adopt.

In assessing the significance of the Fair theatres, then, it should be recognized that, while they contributed no great plays, their importance as catalysts in the development of dramatic forms cannot be overestimated. Furthermore, although they were not the only force at work, they must be assigned an important rôle in the decline of the classical ideal.

Oscar G. Brockett

LIST OF

SUBSCRIBERS

LIST OF SUBSCRIBERS

Jean Allan
Nicholas J. Alldridge
G. Cavendish Allen
M. J. Apthorp
P. J. Attenborough
R. G. Austin
Catherine M. Badger
Colin F. Ball
C. Barratt
R. M. Bate
G. M. Beese
Hilary S. Belden
J. D. Bennett
Rosa L. Blandford
P. J. Bloxam
Margaret M. Bompas
A. J. Bowen
Betty Bremner
L. F. E. Bridges
Phebe M. L. Brock
G. L. Brook
Arthur Brown
R. J. T. Brown
Herbert Byard
John Caldwell
James Carnegie
J. Channon
Luke Kai-Hsin Chin
J. T. Christie
Ian R. Clark
H. M. Cohen

Ruby Cohn
D. W. M. Coleman
N. E. Collinge
Eileen E. Cottis
G. A. Coupland
I. W. Craig
James Cross
M. L. Cunningham
Janet E. Dale
Francis Davey
W. H. Davies
Janet Barrell Davis
J. A. Davison
Esther Dean
F. B. K. Dennis
Lucette Desvignes
Constantine Diamantopoulos
H. D. Dickinson
R. J. Dickinson
Valerie Dickman
A. E. Douglas
David Douglas
Helen M. Eborall
Mark W. Edwards
Victor Ehrenberg
D. E. Eichholz
K. C. Ellison
Gerald F. Else
A. N. Evans
Eileen M. Farringdon
D. C. F. Farrington

A. H. Fielding
M. Findley
M. D. Finnan
G. B. A. Fletcher
R. C. Fletcher
Elizabeth J. Fowler
David M. Gaunt
Cynthia Gee
Ruth Gilg-Ludwig
Margaret Goodbody
Willis Grant
Roger Lancelyn Green
D. B. Gregor
Robert E. Gregson
C. St. H. Griffith
I. S. F. Grindley
G. F. Gwilliam
T. J. Haarhoff
D. C. Harrison
June Harvest
W. H. Hewitt
Deirdre L. Heywood
F. M. Higman
Ursula Hodgson
Brian E. Holden
T. H. C. Hopkins
Margaret Hoskin
P. A. F. Houlder
E. Hudson
E. Frances Hunt
Frances Hurndall
Herbert H. Huxley
Mary M. Innes
K. Iversen
Edna M. Jenkinson
M. E. Jervis

Elizabeth Jones
Joy D. Keen
A. R. Kench
H. K. H. King
Richard Kissane
L. C. Knights
S. F. Knowles
Peggy Law
Carlos Leret
P. J. Levell
Elizabeth M. Lewis
Manuel López-Rey
R. G. Lunt
Peter Macdonell
D. M. MacDowell
Elizabeth Mackenzie
Chrystal Macmillan
E. I. McQueen
J. S. M. Maguinness
David A. Male
Norman Marrow
R. H. Martin
T. W. Melluish
S. Midgley
Norma P. Miller
N. H. de Montmorency
J. Moody
W. D. H. Moore
Estelle Morgan
P. J. O. Morley
Hilary F. S. Moule
Gordon C. Neal
I. S. Neal
Barbara Nickson
Cecil Norman
M. C. Paternoster

Janey Perry
W. E. Philip
G. M. Piller
E. des Places
Mary Powys-Lybbe
F. J. Tidd Pratt
M. W. Pye
D. O. Pym
Angela Quirk
S. Radcliffe
Ingvald Raknem
F. D. Revel
A. C. Reynell
J. R. C. Richards
R. C. Rider
Leighton Rollins
Lorna A. Ruff
Muriel O. Ryder
Roger G. Rymer
Gillian Sanders
E. F. Scott
E. A. Serpell
S. Sharp
Barry J. Sheppard
J. B. Skemp
H. Robin Slaughter
Cynthia M. Smart
Elys M. Smith
E. M. South
Hilda D. Spear
Geoffrey M. Stansfield

A. F. Stevens
P. T. Stevens
P. G. Stibbe
Julia Stobo
Maria Strzalkowa
Boleslaw Taborski
J. G. Talbot
R. F. Taylor
H. L. B. Thompson
J. P. Toomey
H. G. Tranchell
J. M. Travess
C. G. and L. Turner
C. N. Walker
Margaret I. Walker
S. A. Warman
Donald H. Watson
John L. West
J. Wharton
P. M. Wheeler
M. Whittaker
John Williams
Dorothy J. Wood
Jennie Woodford
E. J. M. Woodland
Katharine J. Worth
F. M. Wright
J. M. B. Wright of Auchinellan
Patricia Yates
B. W. Young
Douglas Young

INSTITUTIONS

Abingdon, Radley College Classical Library
Birmingham, City of Birmingham Training College
Birmingham, College of Commerce Library
Bolton, The Smithills Grammar School Library
Cambridge University, Christ's College Library
Cardiff, University of Wales, University College Library
Cashel, Rockwell College
Cheltenham, The Ladies College Library
Chigwell School Library
Clermont-Ferrand, Librarie du Musée
Dublin, University College Library
Dulwich College Library
Durham University Library
Eltham College
Ely, The King's School Library
Göttingen University, Romanisches Seminar für Romanische
 Philologie
Göttingen University, Seminar für Klassische Philologie
Harrogate, Convent of The Holy Child Jesus Library
Harrogate, Queen Ethelburga's School Library
Leeds University, The Brotherton Library
Lille, Institut de Littérature Comparée, Faculté des Lettres
Lisbon, Biblioteca Central da Faculdade de Letras de Coimbra
Littlehampton, Maud Allan County Secondary School
Liverpool University Library
London, Department of Education and Science
London University, Bedford College Library
London University, Goldsmith's College Library
London University, King's College Library
London University, Royal Holloway College Library
London University, University College Library
Marburg/Lahn University, Englisches Seminar
München University, Englisches Seminar
Plymouth College Classical Library

List of Subscribers

Reading School Library
Rousdon, Allhallows School
St Andrews, Queen Mary's Library, St Leonards School
Sydenham High School Library
Taunton, Bishop Fox's Girls School Library
Vienna University, Institut für Romanische Philologie
Watford Grammar School
Weston-Super-Mare Grammar School for Girls
Würzburg University, Seminar für Klassische Philologie